W9-CLH-411

"[*Smalltime* is] a story of family dynamics. Of love and loss and betrayal. Of [Russell] Shorto's hometown. Of his own relationship with his father and his father's relationship with his father. . . . [O]nce Shorto's on the highway, steering us along with his usual humor and eye for quirky detail, settling an hour from his hometown for easy access, we are with him. All the way."

—Helene Stapinski, *New York Times Book Review*

"Shorto finally turns a key in the proverbial locked drawer of his family's chest, only to find a web of mob figures waiting to tell their story. . . . [T]he story of his family's hidden figures vividly unfolds."

—Juliana Rose Pignataro, *Newsweek*

"With *Smalltime*, Shorto traces his decision to learn the truth about his family's past, discover its long-buried secrets, and explore unforgotten slights and how decisions made decades and decades ago continue to leave their mark."

—Joe Heim, *Washington Post*

"Shorto presents a fascinating institutional history of small-town organized crime and a moving family saga with equal amounts of detail and heart. Mob history lovers will especially enjoy this colorful account."

—*Publishers Weekly*

"Shorto tells us the story of a small-town, smalltime mob, but, much more than that, the story of an American family over three generations. By turns tender, poignant, and unsparing."

—Kevin Baker, author of *The Big Crowd*

"Russell Shorto is a magnificent writer and *Smalltime* is a delicious story. A world so vividly rendered, you will find it hard to leave."

—Adriana Trigiani, author of *Tony's Wife*

"*Smalltime* is a big pleasure—an emotionally astute, deeply personal work of family and cultural history."

—Tom Perrotta, author of *The Leftovers* and *Mrs. Fletcher*

"Russell Shorto, one of our most celebrated narrative historians, is expert at mining history for fascinating gems, but here it's as if he breaks through into his own heart."

—Francisco Goldman, author of *Say Her Name*

"A compelling memoir, one that reads with the forward momentum of a good novel. A splendid book in every way."

—Jay Parini, author of *Borges and Me*

"Written with a keen ear for the darkly humorous inflections of Italian American speech, Shorto's story of a small-town USA mobster, his grandfather, ought to change forever how we think about the mafia. La Cosa Nostra flourished not only in big cities but across the continent, wherever there were mines and factories, as much a part of the post–World War II industrial boom as smokestacks, union bosses, and big cars with fins. *Smalltime* is also a deeply personal and moving reflection on the bonds between Italian American grandfathers, fathers, and sons. Beautifully written, brilliantly researched, *Smalltime* establishes itself immediately as a classic of the Italian American experience."

—Robert A. Orsi, professor of religious studies and history, Northwestern University, and author of *The Madonna of 115th Street: Faith and Community in Italian Harlem, 1880–1950*

"This immersive, poignant memoir reminds us all to question the stories and myths we've grown up with. These pages are both gritty and elegiac, tense and tender, embodying the contradictions at the heart of all families. A deeply satisfying read."

—Christopher Castellani, author of *Leading Men*

"Part memoir, part narrative history rich in mesmerizing detail, at the heart of *Smalltime* is the abiding love the author clearly holds for his colorful and flawed Sicilian immigrant family, one which looks so very much like the American family. I could not put this book down, and you won't be able to either."   —Andre Dubus III

"*Smalltime* works because it travels on the twin rails of Shorto family history and a well-researched deep dive into the rise of the Mafia in small towns across the county. These competing points of view lend the narrative a balance that seems to fit the author's strong suit, as his well-received earlier books, *Amsterdam* and *Revolution Song*, also rely on historical research."   —Fred Shaw, *Pittsburgh Quarterly*

Smalltime

Also by Russell Shorto

Revolution Song

Amsterdam

Descartes' Bones

The Island at the Center of the World

Saints and Madmen

Gospel Truth

Smalltime

A STORY OF MY FAMILY AND THE MOB

Russell Shorto

W. W. NORTON & COMPANY

Independent Publishers Since 1923

Frontispiece: Russ and Mary at Club Harlem in Atlantic City.

Copyright © 2021 by Russell Shorto

All rights reserved
Printed in the United States of America
First published as a Norton paperback 2022

For information about permission to reproduce selections from this book, write to
Permissions, W. W. Norton & Company, Inc., 500 Fifth Avenue, New York, NY 10110

For information about special discounts for bulk purchases, please contact
W. W. Norton Special Sales at specialsales@wwnorton.com or 800-233-4830

Manufacturing by Lakeside Book Company
Production manager: Anna Oler

Library of Congress Cataloging-in-Publication Data

Names: Shorto, Russell, author. | Shorto, Russ (Russell), 1914–1981.
Title: Smalltime : a story of my family and the mob / Russell Shorto.
Description: First edition. | New York, NY : W. W. Norton & Company, [2021] |
Includes bibliographical references.
Identifiers: LCCN 2020032361 | ISBN 9780393245585 (hardcover) | ISBN 9780393245592 (epub)
Subjects: LCSH: Shorto, Russell—Family. | Organized crime—Pennsylvania—Johnstown—
History—20th century. | Criminals—Pennsylvania—Johnstown—History—20th century.
Classification: LCC HV6452.P39 S56 2021 | DDC 364.1092/274877—dc23
LC record available at https://lccn.loc.gov/2020032361

ISBN 978-1-324-02017-2 pbk.

W. W. Norton & Company, Inc.
500 Fifth Avenue, New York, N.Y. 10110
www.wwnorton.com

W. W. Norton & Company Ltd.
15 Carlisle Street, London W1D 3BS

1 2 3 4 5 6 7 8 9 0

This is for all the Shortos

Contents

Smalltime

1

The Setup

It STARTED ONE evening when I was home for the holidays. Picture a too-warm living room so crammed with relatives that people's limbs are overlapping. A day or two after Christmas, a cloudy gray night sky, snow starting to fall. I'm a writer of narrative history, by the way, someone who makes a living telling nonfiction stories about the past, so, in terms of subject matter, you might think this one would have been obvious to me long ago. It was not. Anyway, the TV is blaring from one corner of my parents' living room, the tree is stuffed into another, a tray of cookies is going around, and somebody mentions that Frankie is in town.

"Who's Frankie?"

"Your mother's cousin: Frankie Filia."

I'd met Frankie once or twice. I knew he was a jazz singer who had left town a lifetime ago for Las Vegas, that he had a long career there, playing gigs and tending bar in casinos. After five decades of fingering the thick strings of the stand-up bass, crooning for an endless succession of smoky rooms, he'd decided to retire and come home.

An hour later, a couple of carloads of us figure we'll head down to the lounge where Frankie now plays once a week in a local geriatric combo. Stepping from the snowy night into a dark room, confronted by the dank smell of all old bars, and there's Frank, luridly lit on the makeshift stage, a little guy in his late seventies, roundish body flanked by the shapely neck of the bass. He puts a hand over his eyes to peer at the doorway, smiles as he sees us—distant relations here to partake of what he's offering. We pile in, order drinks, stand there with our big coats on, ranged around like Easter Island statues. Frank's got a nice, foggy-breezy voice, the kind that invites you to take a ride with him. *Volare.* Fly me to the moon.

At a break in the set there are kisses, greetings. We're standing in a circle, and at some point Frank looks across at me and wags a finger. "Russell! I been wantin' to talk to you. You're a writer. What are we gonna do about the story?"

"What story?"

In the middle of asking, the answer is right there, fully formed in my mind.

I feel a need to declare here that I had a normal small-town America childhood. Meaning that it was weird or quaint in all the standard ways: going on Sunday drives as a family, playing strip poker with hushed friends in somebody's parents' basement, whatever. There was an element of Italian American self-awareness, but it was mostly limited to food and emotiveness. Long conversations about spaghetti sauce and aunts who kissed you on the lips: those were the ways we were Italian.

Frank shakes his head in exasperation. "What story?! Your grandfather! *The mob!*"

A silence settles on the little group of mostly older relatives. My aunt Josie is visiting from Detroit, where she and my uncle moved about six decades earlier, but everyone else still lives in town. And while some will on occasion tell a story or two about *back then*, the inclination has been to maintain a bit of a veil of silence over the topic.

I maintained it too. It's not like I didn't always know that my grandfather was a small-town mob honcho of some kind. As a little boy, that time my mother and I ran into him on the street downtown, the discomfort I felt toward the solemn almost-stranger in front of me, who I somehow knew had been ostracized from the family, was wrapped around that awareness. Even the gesture he made in that awkward and almost wordless sidewalk encounter—taking off his watch and giving it to me, draping it over my skinny wrist (I can still see it hanging there, with a weight to it that wanted to pull me down to the pavement)—felt ominous in its inappropriateness. It telegraphed that here was someone who was used to outsized acts, to ignoring the norms. But I had no idea what that meant—no idea who he was, really. I didn't want to learn more, and I never did.

No doubt partly because Frank had lived for so long out of town, outside the circle, he hadn't hugged the silence into himself. Strutting the streets of his hometown, a teenage bookie with a pocketful of money who'd just dropped out of high school and was proud to be in on the action: those were golden memories for him. It's also true that he was just an open kind of guy. Some people are natural excavators of the past, blessed or cursed with the conviction that if you haul memories up into the light of day they will glow like gems and be worth something.

Frank's about to go back up to the mic, but he presses me one more time, tossing out a few lurid details about back in the day, oblivious to the awkward suffering of the others.

I turn to my dad, the mobster's son, expecting to find a look of censure that will help me to end this. There's something in his eyes—but it's almost a glint, an eagerness. I find it embarrassing, like seeing a parent naked. Pondering for half a second, I realize I shouldn't be surprised. My father has always been more daring than me, willing to jump into things, to risk making a fool of himself.

I shake my head confidently at Frank. "Not my thing."

He gives me a look. "Whaddaya mean? You write history. This is American history! It's right in front of you!"

He's getting personal now—telling me how to do my job. And just for a second, the marketable outline of my grandfather's world spreads across the front of my brain like a banner ad, the kind of thing you could sell to your publisher: *Everybody knows the mob, but nobody knows the story of the small-town mob.* How it was as much a part of midcentury American life as the hot dog. How, just like the interstate highway system, it stitched together the Schenectadys and Scrantons, the Zanesvilles and Topekas, the Wichitas and Amarillos and Fresnos. You could make a case that this was the *real* mob story, maybe in a way the real *American* story of that era.

In the same instant I get a glimmer, too, of how our family fits into that broad picture. As Frank is waiting for me to say something I have in my head the image of the somber man in a baggy gray suit forcing his watch on me, along with a few other shavings that the magnet of my childhood brain pulled in. A secondhand image, borrowed from my dad's memory, of stacks of money arrayed across the surface of a bed. Men talking about "the boys," and me knowing they were not boys like me: "the boys downtown . . . the boys in Pittsburgh." In my grandmother's basement a large cage with dice in it, which had a handle for turning it, and me halfheartedly trying to play with it but knowing it wasn't a toy.

But no—I can't do this. I know, standing there, that at the center of this story is this dimly lit figure of my grandfather. Which means that it would involve my long-suffering grandmother, with whom I spent so many summer days in my early childhood, sympathetically studying her solitude and bitterness out of the corner of my eye, sitting skinny-legged on her sofa pretending to read comic books while she peered beyond at the soap operas on the TV, chain-smoking Pall Malls and reflexively pouring from a quart bottle of Schmidt's beer into a tiny glass. Such a story would gather her up into it; in all likelihood the research would lead me to the source of her pain. And the pain, like a stain, would spread.

I give Frank a patronizing smile and shake my head again. Not interested. Too much on my plate. And anyway, my subject area is further back—long ago, far away.

THE THINGS ARE spread out on my desk. A brisk cursive hand itemized them in blue pen on the outside of the yellowed envelope into which they were tucked, an envelope my aunt has kept for decades:

1 Wallet
1 Pen
1 Pill box
1 nail clippers
1 key ring and several keys
1 match book

The itemizer—"S. Shackelford R.N."—dated the envelope, which gives me ready access to the day my grandfather died: 5/28/81.

The wallet is cheap leather. You can tell it's of another era because it's got the insert of plastic sleeves into which you were supposed to slide snapshots of loved ones. There are two in the front slot: both children, who as far as I can tell have nothing to do with my family. And right there is a window creaking open: the man had another life. The insides are stuffed with business cards: attorneys, concrete companies, car dealers. One card, "Compliments of Cal and Dot's Inn," says on the front

Pick A Number
1 2 3 4

And on the back:

> . . . All Sex Maniacs Pick 3

There are membership cards: the Touchdown Club, the Elks. Little slips of paper that have carefully written lists of names and phone numbers. On a small sheet from a Jacquin's Liquor notepad ("Prestige Liquors Since 1884") there's a penciled series of important dates:

> Got sick Sat. June 29
> Entered Hospital July 3rd
> Discharged July 14

It's odd that Nurse Shackelford didn't note the race tickets. There is a whole handful of them, $1 to $20 bets—a few "exactas," but mostly he liked the trifecta: betting on each of the first three finishers. Because—and this feels like cheesy fiction but is the flat truth about the end of my grandfather's life—this lifelong gambler died, long after he'd gotten out of "the business" and after years of vacantly walking the streets he had once lorded over, at the racetrack, fist in the air, still chasing the dream.

He'd had a recurring problem with the ticker, had been seeing a heart specialist, whose card was right there in the wallet, ominously enough, right next to a card for Kitzmiller Memorials, Complete Cemetery Needs.

He'd just had his sixty-seventh birthday.

He wasn't the big boss. He was the number two man in town—Johnstown, Pennsylvania, in those days a rollicking steel town in the southwestern corner of the state—which made him a force, but he wasn't what they call a made man. I was told he was denied a formal position in the mob on account of his drinking, which makes the mafia sound like a police academy or something, but maybe it's true.

He was the one who knew everything, the one you talked to, the guy who got things done.

Charles Town Race Track, in the West Virginia hills, was a three-hour drive from Johnstown back then. The phone rang at my parents' house an hour or so later. My mother answered. The woman had a steely, professional tone. She said she was calling from a hospital in West Virginia.

Is this the family of Russell Shorto?

Did I mention that I was named after him?

I was in college in Washington, D.C., at the time of my grandfather's death—not so far from West Virginia. My mother said she felt a long moment go by during which the room began to spin. She stammered something about her son at college, which caused the voice on the other end to break its professional tone. *Oh no, I'm so sorry for any confusion. This is an old gentleman I'm calling about.* My father took the phone. After imparting the basic facts, the woman added, apparently intending to comfort loved ones, that the heart attack had been so massive that he died instantly—"before his head hit the ground," according to my dad's recollection of the call, though I doubt the hospital representative would have been so colorful.

Namesake. Archaic term. A person named for the sake of someone else. I guess that was what kept Frank's entreaty—his offer—alive in my mind. But for the next year or so after seeing him that night at the club, whenever I thought about my grandfather I pushed it away. I write history, not memoir. More to the point, I write nonfiction, and that requires sources. My grandfather and the small-town tough guys of his world were dead, and surely they hadn't left notebooks behind.

I was living far from my hometown at the time: in Amsterdam, to be precise. Eventually, the voice in my head became annoying enough that I decided to make an exploratory trip home. I would devote a week to putting the matter to rest—convincing myself that not enough sources of information existed on my grandfather and the world he had inhabited to bring it to life.

I phoned Frank when I got there. "Russell! I knew you were gonna call sooner or later!" He told me to meet him at his hangout, Panera Bread. I thought we were going to have a little one-on-one, but shortly after we sat down another old man walked up and greeted us. Then two more arrived. Later others trundled over. Frank had put out the word. My grandfather's cohort was dead and gone, but here were the youngsters who had latched onto those guys, looked up to them, did jobs for them, wanted to *be* them. They'd soaked it all in.

It turned into a four-hour chat. Before it was even over I realized that what they had given me—Butch, Donnie, George, Frank, and the others—was a skeleton, an outline. It was what I'd been sure didn't exist anymore. Of course, each of these old men, sitting there nursing his coffee, shooting knowing glances at one another, eyes momentarily lighting up, had his own story, his own collection of memories, which were, surely, of variable reliability. But memories can be checked against other sources. That's what you do as a writer of narrative history. They were giving me an inkling of a lost world, a different way of seeing a familiar time period: America in its brawny postwar prime. What I would be setting off on was a familiar kind of adventure. Basically this was history: third-person, past tense.

Of course I knew that was a lie I was telling myself. I glimpsed the truth beneath it in my father's expression—hurt? puzzled?—when I stopped in to see my parents on my way out of town after the Panera Bread chat session. Why hadn't I invited him along? He knew all those guys. He was Russ's eldest son. He was the most direct connection to my subject. He belonged there.

If, during the Panera Bread conversation, I let myself ignore what might be a more intimate layer to the story, the minute it was over I was steered right to it. For four hours, while Frank and the other boys had swapped stories, the oldest of the bunch, a guy named Joe

LaRocca, had sat in the back, silent, resting both hands on his cane, peering into the middle of the circle with something like a scowl on his face. I knew from things the others had said that he'd been pretty close to my grandfather. As we got up to leave I went over to him. His silence had felt heavy—I figured I would lighten it up with some small talk.

Before I could say anything, though, he spoke. "You know why I came here?" he asked, his eyes transfixing mine. I shook my head. He punched an index finger at my chest. "Because your name is Russell Shorto."

There it was. Namesake.

2

The Victim

I'M NOT SURE whether it's obligatory for a mob story to have a murder at its center, but I realized quite early in my research that this one has one. I became obsessed enough by it that the victim, the excellently named Pippy diFalco, whose murder has never been solved, became a presence in our house. "What are you working on?" my wife would ask. "Pippy," I'd say. Or "Pippy's autopsy." Or "Forensic speculation as to whether it's possible to determine for sure that it was actually an ice pick that Pippy was stabbed in the chest with or just some generic thin, pointed blade."

Or "Pippy's last day." One particular moment of which hovered in my mind. It hovers still.

It's February 6, 1960, about five in the afternoon. Darkness is falling. The Chevy Bel Airs and Ford Thunderbirds maneuvering their wide bodies off of Walnut Street onto Main are snapping on their headlights, making a sheen against the wet pavement. Saturday night is coming. Pippy diFalco is limping across Main Street. The weather is sleety, temperature in the high thirties.

Pippy is a small man wearing a big overcoat. He has an open face, puppyish eyes, shows lots of teeth when he smiles—kind of a goofy expression, which gives an impression of innocence. But that's misleading. People say there was always something else going on. "Nice guy," his onetime partner told me, "but not a nice guy."

Pippy was what you would call a creature of habit. He left his home in the morning—he lived with his wife and infant son in an apartment in Morrellville, one of the oldest sections of town, a neighborhood of steelworkers' houses and lots and lots of churches—and drove along the river. On his right rose a steep, wooded hill, at the top of which the town's rich families had their homes. On his left he passed one of the four steel-mill plants that powered the town's rise in the twentieth century. Today they are as silent as Greek ruins, but in Pippy's time they incessantly poured smoke out of their high, skinny stacks. Every day the smoke put a fresh red-gray coat of dust on all the cars in town, which nobody minded wiping off because if the mills were churning, so was the town.

Johnstown had just peaked as a small industrial powerhouse. The population of 53,000 was already on the decline (it hit its apex of 67,000 in 1920), but good blue-collar jobs were still plentiful, and there were lots of managerial and professional types as well. Today the city is largely hollowed out, with neighborhoods of boarded-up houses and a population less than a third of what it once was. In Pippy's time it rocked: shift workers crowding into the mill gates, the trolley cars full, housewives browsing the downtown storefronts.

He crossed the river and entered downtown. If he chose to follow Washington Street he would have driven past the public library and the big squat rectangular box of the Penn Traffic department store, its display windows showing lady mannequins stiff but elegant in sheath dresses. He found a place to park on Vine Street and limped down to the Acme supermarket on Market Street. He bought the same thing every day: a loaf of bread, a half pound of sliced bologna, a small pot of mustard. Then he headed up to Main Street, turned left, and came to

Johnstown in its heyday, with steel mills at full capacity.

a stop in front of the ticket booth of the Embassy Theater. Today the marquee said OPERATION PETTICOAT. The 11:45 a.m. show flickered into the mostly empty hall: Cary Grant and Tony Curtis, bright in Eastman Color, were officers on a navy sub who had to contend with "five nurses who just had to be squeezed in!" as the trailer screamed over a sexy flash from the horn section.

Sometime after the picture started, Pippy's stomach would have been rumbling. His routine was to pull out a pocketknife, use it to spread the mustard, peel off a few slices of bologna, and start eating his sandwich. He'd do the same thing later for an early dinner, watching shows in succession if it was a double bill, or, in this case, the same one over and over. Pippy wasn't a movie buff; he was just killing time. Sometimes he had to leave the theater and walk around outside a bit, to stretch his legs, fill his lungs with air. But doing that meant he had to pay again to get back in, so he didn't do it often; when it came to hoarding money, Pippy had great fortitude. Money was Pippy's elixir. In his pocket as he sat in the Embassy was a thick roll of bills. Nobody knows exactly how much he carried that day, but the man who many people think killed him later that night told me with cheerful certainty that Pippy had "two pocketfuls of hundreds" on him. Pippy was famous for his cash rolls. People say he typically toted $3,000 in cash as he made his rounds, a pretty fabulous sum in 1960.

He left the theater for good around 5 p.m., ready to start his real day.

So here he was now, making his way across Main Street. He had taken shrapnel in the war, and ever since, despite wearing a corrective shoe, he'd had the limp, which made work not so easy, given what he did, but he did it anyway because it was what he knew, and because he relished it.

He was called Pippy from childhood: a nickname for Giuseppe, the Italian form of Joseph.

The sign on the building across the street said CITY CIGAR. Its name was both descriptive and deceptive. Cigars were nominally on offer, but its location, two doors from city hall, a handsome structure of rough-cut sandstone blocks on the corner of Main and Market, was crucial to its purpose.

My research takes us this far, brings me right to the front door of City Cigar, the headquarters of the mob back when it flourished in my hometown. But while City Cigar was an important stop on Pippy's itinerary, I'm not entirely sure he went inside that night. Was he maybe avoiding the place just then?

If he did pull open that door, on his left would have been the shelves of cigars and cigarettes and a rack of newspapers: the *Racing Form* and the local daily, the *Tribune-Democrat* (the day's headlines: "U.S. Answers Soviet Threat"..."Not Running, Johnson Says"). On the right side was a little lunch counter, run by Anthony Bongiovanni—

Main Street in Johnstown in 1962. City Cigar was in the building beside the "Democrat Club."

Nino, everyone called him. Was Nino standing there, skinny guy with thick eyebrows and a shock of black hair, arms folded across his apron, looking him up and down? Nino wasn't so fond of Pippy. Nino was thirty-one: eager, methodical, loyal. He was a cook, which was all he ever wanted to be, and this was a good gig, and he didn't want anyone to mess it up. Pippy was forty-five, and he liked to be liked, but over the years he'd crossed a lot of people, including, lately, the two men who were both of their bosses.

One of those men might have been right there at the counter, where he liked to perch on a stool. His name was Joe Regino, but everyone called him Little Joe. You said it with respect. Little Joe ran the town. He was born fifty-three years earlier in southern Italy, emigrated with his parents, and grew up on the mean streets of Philadelphia. He got involved in the mafia before most Americans had heard the word. His first arrest, in 1928, was for armed robbery. Later he did time for counterfeiting. As the mob was expanding, he was offered control of Johnstown, with its population of hardworking, hardscrabble immigrants—German, Polish, Welsh, Irish, Italian. So he made his way across the state, married a local woman named Millie Shorto and befriended her brother, Russell or Russ, who became his closest ally. He made Johnstown his home and his world. He was a strikingly small, soft-spoken, unfailingly polite man who favored double-breasted suits and loyalty.

Little Joe was my great-uncle. I'm told I was around him somewhat when I was very young, but I don't remember. What I've learned about him comes mostly from cross-referencing FBI files—which list "highway robbery" among his achievements, a crime I had thought went out with the stagecoach—with family reflections: "He had the sweetest disposition.... He was very quiet.... Uncle Joe helped everybody."

So Joe Regino, the little guy who was the big guy in town. Who was on equally intimate terms with both the local Democratic Party boss and his Republican opposite. Who hobnobbed with judges, who had the governor over for dinner. He hung out at Nino's lunch counter, which occupied the space in front of City Cigar, because he liked to keep an eye on things. He could swivel from watching the street to checking on what was going on in the back room. There was a little slot in the wall behind him, which he could slide open.

Let's assume that Pippy diFalco, after leaving the movie theater, had some brief interaction with Little Joe out front and then went in back. We'll follow him, pushing open the swinging door. We're met by smoke: a light cloud of it hovering in the center of the long room. The furniture consists of ten pool tables, one billiard table, and several pinball machines. At this time of day you'd have maybe half the tables occupied: office workers, municipal employees from city hall, a few lawyers. All men, of course. Pool halls were as common as Laundromats in mid-twentieth-century America; Johnstown had half a dozen within a few blocks of City Cigar. But this one was a little different. The low rumble of the players' chatter was spiced not only by the bright clack of ivory balls but by the constant *chicka-chicka* of the ticker-tape machine. It sat out right in the open, at the end of the counter that ran along the left side of the room, chucking out sports scores.

And here, in his natural environment, overseeing the landscape of green felt and blue smoke, invariably dressed in suit and tie and with a Lucky Strike in the corner of his mouth, I locate the object of my search. He was of medium height, bearish in build, and had a handsome, wide face and squinting eyes. I've always thought he looked a bit like Babe Ruth. Russell Shorto went by Russ. "Hiya, Russ." "Russ, we got a problem." He was forty-six years old and at the height of his success—or rather, just past it. In fact, not long before, he had been cut out of the business by his brother-in-law. My grandfather was Little Joe's second-in-command; the two men had built the mob franchise in town together; they were close. But Russ had a drinking problem, which had gotten so bad that Little Joe decided he had to let him go. Later, though, Joe had relented, given him a second chance. So Russ was now on a kind of probation. He needed to steady himself. He needed to make sure things went smoothly.

From hundreds of hours of interviews with family and acquaintances, I've gleaned four distinguishing traits about Russ. The first, truly an ace-in-the-hole for a gambler and hustler, was math: people told me they watched him cast his eye down a column of three- and four-digit figures and matter-of-factly record the sum. Never mind that he was an eighth-grade dropout; running the odds on a horse or a starting pitcher apparently came with the same easy satisfaction as drawing a breath of air.

Two: he was very quiet. You asked him a question, you probably got a muttered syllable in reply. Some say they believe this was really a manifestation of pathological shyness, and that it was the effort to break this grip that led to his third distinguishing characteristic. He was an exemplar of a particular category of true drunk, who might go for months without touching a drop then launch into a bender that would last for days. The fifths of whiskey were medicine to thaw the emotions. "When he was sober he was like ice, but when he was drinking he would hug everybody," his niece, Minnie Bermosk, who did the bookkeeping for City Cigar, told me. "A few drinks, and suddenly he was a lover. And a crier! He got sad. He'd call me sobbing and say, 'Minnie, you've got to come here.' And I'd say, 'I know—you're drunk.'"

Drinking, because it opened him up, giving him access to his feelings, probably connected to a fourth defining trait: he was a serial philanderer. It was his affairs, more than the mob, more than the threat of prison or the FBI pounding on the door, that caused the greatest havoc in his family.

Despite these outsized flaws, he had a talent for organization. He basically ran the operation—that's what the old guys told me. When I asked one of Russ's disciples why Little Joe gave him so much latitude, he said, "Because Russ was smarter than Little Joe, and Little Joe knew it. Russ could take a fuckin' dead cow and make it give milk."

Russ was largely responsible for having capitalized on the little steel town's postwar boom by building an operation that generated what one knowledgeable person estimated at $40 million over the fifteen years since the war's end (about $370 million today), a portion of which was sent off weekly to "the boys" in Pittsburgh. From there another portion supposedly was sent on to New York.

Gambling was the heart of Russ and Little Joe's operation. Before there were legal, state-run lotteries, when even tossing a pair of dice against a wall and betting on the numbers that came up was considered immoral and a threat to public health, gambling was what the mob was all about. It was illegal—yet, in the glow and relative prosperity of the postwar era, people were crazy for the possibilities it offered, the giddy thrill of turning a bit of pocket money into sudden wealth. Gallup surveys in the 1950s showed that more than half the country's population gambled on a regular basis. The mob—Russ and Little Joe—provided a service; a public utility, as many saw it.

In Johnstown, City Cigar was the center of things. The place itself was a hive of legitimate commercial activity: eight-ball was in its heyday, and there was a regular ebb and flow from the lunchtime rush to late at night. Sometimes Russ booked special events, bringing in a nationally known sharpshooter, like the world billiards champ Willie Hoppe, to put on an exhibition. The tables generated income. But, as Minnie said to me, looking back sixty years, as if the realization was just then dawning on her, "I guess you could say City Cigar was a front." (Minnie worked in a little office just behind the pool tables, where she was in charge of paying the staff—"always cash, never checks.") Gambling was the real revenue stream. And just like state-run lotteries today, the mob offered customers a variety of ways to lose their money.

The centerpiece of the Johnstown operation was something Russ created not long after the war, a cleverly named entity called the G.I. Bank, which sounded like a bedrock institution, something that supported the returning troops, but was simply a numbers game that half the town played. It was a labor-intensive operation. Maybe a hundred people were employed by Russ and Little Joe in the G.I. Bank. There were people who booked on the side—bartenders, deli clerks, and waitresses—and people for whom the numbers was a living. Runners fanned out through the neighborhoods—Conemaugh, Moxham, Woodvale, the West End—and on the floors of the steel mills, collecting bets and betting slips, then bringing the take back. In the office above City Cigar people registered the numbers played and the money. A player won by hitting three numbers; you could play them straight or in combination. Like a lot of other local books around the country, the G.I. Bank took its winners from the closing numbers of the New York Stock Exchange. That made for a virtually tamper-proof system that encouraged bettors' trust.

There were other games. "Tip seals," a tear-off game much like today's scratch-off lotteries, brought in millions in revenue. There were organized card games and craps games throughout the city, some of which had pots that got into the thousands of dollars.

Then there were the legitimate, or semi-legitimate, enterprises. They owned, wholly or with partners, diners, restaurants, pool halls, and bars. Little Joe also owned two vending-machine companies. Keystone Sales supplied cigarette machines to bars, cafés, and diners around the city. P and C Amusements distributed pinball machines and jukeboxes. It's hard to appreciate how big a thing pinball was in mid-twentieth-century America, but here's one way to get at it: according to the Pacific Pinball Museum, from the late 1930s, when the first electric machines appeared, into the 1960s, Americans spent more money on pinball than on movies. The attraction came from the fact that while the machines were labeled FOR AMUSEMENT ONLY they were actually gambling devices, and especially after 1947, when the innovation of flippers gave the player a feeling of control, they were everywhere.

In fact, the story of pinball machines tracks the phenomenal rise and steady drop in fortune of the small-town mob. The machines' popularity through the 1940s and 1950s was related to the limitations of home entertainment. In 1950, only 9 percent of American families owned a television; people went out for a little fun, and the mob was on hand with its amusement services. By 1960, 90 percent of households had a TV, and the boys were already seeing a decline in people who wanted to spend their nickels on pinball.

I DON'T IMAGINE for a minute that the situation in Johnstown was unique. What Little Joe and Russ created in the period from the end of the Second World War to 1960 was mirrored in smallish cities across the country. New York and Chicago drew the attention of journalists and politicians, and therefore of the public, but the mob spread itself across the map like a corporation opening branch offices. In Pennsylvania, besides big operations in Pittsburgh and Philadelphia, there were Little Joes and Russes in Scranton, Reading, Braddock, New Kensington, Sharon, McKeesport, Penn Hills, Allentown, Wilkes-Barre, Greensburg, Monessen, Pittston, and Altoona. In 1957, when the FBI began to try to get a handle on the scope of things, it identified mob activity in such unlikely places as Anchorage, Alaska, and Butte, Montana. Bosses communicated, cooperated, and vied for power with one another in a continent-wide network.

It took me a while to appreciate that Little Joe and Russ did not run all the gambling activities in town themselves. Bookmakers were essentially self-employed. But they worked within a system that Little Joe and Russ oversaw. The bribes that the operators of City Cigar paid, to everyone from the district attorney to beat cops, formed a protective shield around all bookies in the area. Little Joe and Russ also provided the odds that sports books needed. And they functioned as a bank: an individual bookie could lay off large bets with them to avoid being hit with a win he couldn't cover. In exchange for all of these services, bookies paid a portion of their earnings to City Cigar.

Russ oversaw much of this activity, but his particular area of focus was the sports book. It's not like he was a dyed-in-the-wool fan (an old bookie set me straight on this: "Russ could give a fuck about sports"), but his way with numbers, his ability to set the odds, which required great precision, made him especially suited to sports-related gambling. He managed the bookies who took bets on baseball, football, basketball, horse-racing, and prizefights.

This is what brought Russ into regular contact with Pippy diFalco. Pippy booked sports. He had a regular route and regular customers, who knew where he would be at what time, and City Cigar was a part of that schedule. But lately Pippy had been light in his payments. Russ and Little Joe tolerated a certain amount of this. As Pippy's onetime partner told me, "They knew that in a business full of cheats you gotta give guys some leeway." They themselves were surely shortchanging the bosses in Pittsburgh, just as Pittsburgh was doing it to New York. Russ was something of a first-class cheat himself, especially with cards; he had probably gotten in his 10,000 hours of practice—false shuffles, second dealing, dealing from the bottom of the deck—before he was old enough to drive.

So: it took one to know one. Either Pippy had taken too much liberty this time or too many people had become aware of it. That's why I think it's possible that Pippy was avoiding City Cigar just then. Then again, if he had skipped his regular stop at the pool hall, wouldn't that have sent a pretty nervy signal? He was just a guy, just a sap with a game leg and a stupid grin and a wad of bills in his pocket; he was in no position to give the mob the finger. So maybe he came in to offer an explanation of his situation.

If they talked, what did Russ say? What kind of threat might he have made? People tell me Russ carried a gun at all times, but I have no indication that he ever used it, and there didn't seem to be a reason for anyone to fear for his life—not in Johnstown in 1960. "It was an innocent time," more than one guy told me. But he and Little Joe knew how to use muscle. "If a bookie ran out on Little Joe, he'd call me," one of their former enforcers told me from his nursing-home bed. "I'd go beat the guy up—get the money. Maybe I'd bring a .48 to scare him. Minor shit."

So maybe we can go out on a limb and assume that Russ threatened Pippy that if he didn't start making up for lost time, he would send somebody after him. One guy in particular they used for muscle—a guy called Rip, tall, lean and vicious, with blond hair and horn-rimmed glasses—would have been just the guy to put a healthy scare into Pippy. Once before, in a dispute over money, Rip had beat Pippy up, beat him real bad. Maybe, as that evening got under way, Pippy had the image of Rip in his mind.

Eventually, then, on this February evening in 1960, Pippy went off on his rounds. He probably headed east down Main Street, passing the one-square-block of Central Park on the left and Woolworth's on the right, turned left at Clinton Street, past Coney Island Lunch, "world famous" (locally) for its chili dogs, and made his way to the Clinton Street Pool Room. It, too, was controlled by Little Joe and Russ. The same activities went on here, but whereas City Cigar was a leisure center favored by city officials, lawyers, and other elites, Clinton Street was a working man's hangout. There was a counter where you placed bets, and spittoons at intervals. It was looser and louder than City Cigar, with clients like Johnny Atlantic, a flamboyant drunk who talked with exaggerated professorial diction: "Please re-frain from ex-pectorating in the re-ceptacle!" Everyone knew that Red Picklo, a slow-witted regular who acted as a bouncer, a man with a bulbous nose who looked like W. C. Fields, was a softhearted lunk, but fancied himself a gangster. He'd work himself into a rage over word that the boys from New Kensington were muscling in on the Johnstown rackets and bellow empty threats: "I'll get a machine gun and wipe out all them motherfuckers!" Red worked for the city sanitation department. He had a big Packard but didn't drive. Instead, somewhat madly, he had a chauffeur, a Black man named King Lemore, whose stock phrase was "Long live the King!" He would shout it from the doorway to whoever was inside, and someone would shout back, with a mixture of humor and scorn, "Fuck the King!" He waited outside because the color barrier was in effect; "coloreds" had their own gambling places.

Pippy presumably met clients that evening at the Clinton Street Pool Room. He passed a little time with Frank Filia, my mom's cousin, the one who got me into this project. By this time Frank had been working for the manager, Yank Croco, for nine years as a numbers runner and as counterman in the pool hall. Frank performed with the George Arcurio Orchestra on weekends and was building a name

in town as a crooner. He was also an artist: in his spare time behind
the betting counter he liked to make sketches of the regulars. When I
asked, during a follow-up to our first Panera Bread session, what some
of the people from his youth looked like, he picked up a stack of cock-
tail napkins and spontaneously re-created a few:

Frank told me he had been feeling a little uneasy around Pippy around this time. Everyone, it seemed, knew that Pippy was welching on the mob. Or maybe that's all hindsight.

Night came on. Nowadays if you venture to downtown Johnstown on a February evening you'll find yourself in a rustbelt ghost town, but in 1960 the streets got lively even in winter. People headed to Hilda's Tavern, where on this night the Harmony Tones were playing. The Gautier Club, a strip joint right above the Clinton Street Pool Room, was hosting its All-Star Floor Show and Orchestra, plus comedian Allen Drew. Back at City Cigar, the place filled up with men and smoke. It got rowdy; floor men stood ready to break up fights (one told me he had kept a broken cue stick on hand, and used it frequently). Even in bad weather, the opposite corner of the street outside, called Wolves' Corner, was alive. Guys hung out there and whistled at broads, hoping for something to happen.

Midnight came. The sleet stopped; the streets glistened. At two o'clock the bars emptied. Then it got quiet.

Two doors down from City Cigar, the top floor of a three-story building became an illegal after-hours joint on weekends called the Recreation Club. It wasn't much: a jukebox, two sofas, a little bar with its lineup of offerings: Kessler Whiskey, Walker's Gin, Mogen David wine. Tacked to the wall was a board listing football and basketball scores. You had to be known to get in. It was seedy, smelling of old carpet and cheap wine, but it could get packed.

Pippy showed up here sometime after two, with a woman nobody had seen before. He was a married man with a two-year-old son at home, but everyone—including his wife, Barbara—knew he had a weakness for ladies. He didn't have much going for him in terms of natural attractions, which was a likely explanation for the otherwise unnecessarily large wad of cash. People noted it that night, the flash of the bankroll, and the grin. Making an impression. Eventually he left, with the mystery woman on his arm.

3

The Comeback

So THERE I am, zeroing in on Russ and Little Joe, tracking Pippy diFalco's last day on Earth, doing the work of a writer of historical narrative—archives, police records, the county courthouse; researching, compiling timelines, gathering events and newspaper headlines and the behavioral tics of people of the past, trying to corral it all into a story—when I get the call from my mother. The ambulance had just left. I arrived at the hospital as the symptoms and diagnoses and prognoses were cascading. My father had had a long history of health problems, with the ruinous combination of heart disease and chronic obstructive pulmonary disease foremost among them. He hadn't been anything approaching hale and hearty in many years. We were apparently witnessing an "exacerbation," a sudden, precipitous downward slide that COPD patients can suffer. He basically couldn't breathe. The deterioration was very rapid.

I was surprised by the intensity of my reaction. We had a nice relationship, pretty much free of discord. I loved him. But I had told myself some years before that I would be ready for this.

Instead, I spent an entire night weeping—sobbing, really. I looked at myself and found I was overwhelmed by . . . regret.

About what? That I hadn't spent more time with him? Gone fishing or something?

It dawned on me during the course of that night that for a long, long time I had been holding my father at arm's length. Not just in the matter of my research into his father. Somewhere way back I had thrown up a wall between us. We communicated regularly, but I realized that our relationship had been a wee bit hollow. I didn't know why. But I felt—the way you feel that a dream was threatening even though you can't remember it—that the core of it lay *back there*. Which was maybe partly why I hadn't wanted to go there in the first place, and why I'd been holding back on involving my father in my research. At the same time, I'd been aware of how ridiculous that was. My dad—Anthony Shorto; Tony—was Russ's eldest son, and Little Joe's nephew. Most of what I had known about Russ before I started on this book had come from Tony. He had lived through much of the period I was researching. He saw things. Those things became part of him. Indeed, a defining feature of my childhood was my dad's anger toward his father. Even though my grandfather was never around our family, the very mention of him could set my dad off.

A memory surfaced, something I hadn't thought about for a long time. I don't know how I came to know it, but somewhere mid-childhood I became party to the news that shortly after my birth my grandfather had tried to take me from my parents. I have no recollection of how I absorbed this startling fact when it was disclosed to me, but it left a lasting impression: a fear of the man. That alone—fear, healthy and robust—could have been what caused me to balk when Frank Filia suggested I try to re-create my grandfather's world. If it was my mother who offered up the information in my childhood, the look on my face would presumably have caused her to follow it with some explanatory cover: *We were very young.* My parents had eloped as nineteen-year-olds once my mother realized she was pregnant with me. "We ran off to Virginia Beach and got married," she told me when I asked her to recount the tale of their elopement. "The next morning we went to the beach. Then we called home and told them what we'd done." The startled reaction from their parents rattled them enough that the newlyweds reverted to children who had been disobedient. They drove straight back home—"We were still in our bathing suits," my mom said, laughing at the memory of herself as that much of a crazy kid. Some months later she gave birth to me, and her father-in-law, having apparently decided that the two of them were too young for such responsibility, issued his decree concerning me: He would take it from there. I should note that this fit an established pattern. Like a medieval potentate, Russ had a history of moving small children around among those he had power over. Rearranging families to suit his sense of order.

But if this event was some kind of key to my relationship with my father, it surely wasn't a source of regret. If anything, I was proud of him for his response. Tony had stood up to Russ—on my behalf. *Like hell you will.* The skinny kid, confronting one of the town's biggest badasses, his father.

Tony stood up to Russ on another front too. Also somewhere in the depths of my childhood it was made known to me that when my dad had reached a certain age his father had decided it was time to bring him into the business—to groom him to run the town someday, I suppose—but he had refused. As an adult I tried, in the way you do, to pull these memories and stories apart and line them up in chronological order, to make sense of them. All of this was around the same time: Tony and Rita (my mother) run off and get married; have a son; the volatile father tries to take the grandson away from them and is rebuffed. And Tony has a decision to make: will he become his father's right-hand man, an underworld figure? Fate gave him one of those fork-in-the-road moments—and, in the way I saw it when it made its way into my juvenile brain, he chose for Good. He rejected

Russ and his world, said no to the boys. A primordial father-son struggle, ending with bitterness on both sides, and a severed relationship. Tony, I grew up feeling, had done this for us—my mom, me, and eventually my brother and two sisters.

Appearances reinforced the child's gloss I put on the situation. Where Russ was a quiet, brooding, muttering, heavy, shadowy presence, my dad was open, bright, gregarious. Russ wore a somber suit, tie, and fedora, like a character in black-and-white TV reruns. Tony and his slim young pals laughed a lot, wore blazers, loafers, and "white on white" shirts with cufflinks, breezed through the '60s listening to cool jazz. When I walked down the street with my father, everybody we passed said hi to him; it was indescribably thrilling to have your dad be such an easygoing public presence, to cruise along in the wake of his gregariousness. These two men who stood behind me in the biological chain—each of them, like me, the first son—were the white knight and the black knight.

The dark energy between the two of them extended throughout my childhood. It explained my grandfather's absence from our life. As Tony's family grew, and his father failed to play any part in it, never showed up for a grandchild's birthday or a Sunday dinner, my dad's feelings of hurt and rejection grew as well. Maybe Russ, too, felt hurt—that his son hadn't followed in his footsteps, had rejected *him*, saw the work he did as dirty. To me, my dad was precisely the kind of person that he himself admired, what he called a go-getter. Having staved off the mob, and with no help from his father, he scraped and scrapped and carved out a career as a small-town entrepreneur. He moved from high-school dropout to salesman to owner of his own bar to local real-estate mogul. His path was certainly wobbly. He had a quietly spectacular collapse in mid-career, essentially lost everything—including our family house—and had to file for bankruptcy. But when it was all said and done he had provided for his family in more or less the traditional manner.

And all the while his father had existed in an alternate universe. Year after year, Russ and Tony, father and son, ran their separate enterprises in the same small city, weaving around each other's lives, barely crossing paths, barely communicating. When someone mentioned his father, Tony, who had a pretty fierce temper, would seethe. Those moments—watching my dad's eyes tighten, listening to him erupt into cursing, feeling that my world might explode—were punctuation marks in my childhood, occasions for me to ponder that fork in the road, the other life that might have played out—for him, for me, for all of us.

Morning came. I had wept and puzzled myself into a corner. I could find nothing in my memory bank to make me want to hold my father at a distance. And now it was too late for answers, too late for everything. What a fucking idiot. Regret. It tasted like acid in my throat.

And then, a week later, somehow he's being released from the hospital. I go to visit—I had by this time moved from Europe to a town in Maryland an hour away from Johnstown, in part to work on this book—and find him shuffling around the house. Sitting there, looking shrunken, skin hanging in bags around his body and with a hoarse rasp, but conducting his old zesty dialogue with the lineup of MSNBC hosts. A couple of weeks after that and he's wobbling out the front door, levering himself into the car, motoring slowly to the supermarket. Being a man about town again. Telling the same jokey stories over and over. Cruising the aisles of Giant Eagle in the motorized shopping cart, saying hi to everyone in the Depends section. He's back in the world—at maybe 30 percent of what he once was, but he's back.

And me blinking in amazement at this, this return from the dead. I can't believe it, this opportunity I've been given.

So I initiated a little conversation, which went something like this:

ME: Dad, do you want to work on this book with me?
HIM: Work on it? I'm not a writer.

ME: You know what I mean.

    (Pause.)

HIM: OK, yeah. I do.

ME: Do you think you knew him, really? Your father?

    (Long pause.)

HIM: Maybe not. I know he loved us. But he couldn't show it.

ME: He was shy, right? People tell me he had this hard, scary shell. Aloofness. But that in fact he was shy as hell.

HIM: I don't know about that. He . . . he was filled with shame. And he did bad things. Most of all to us. To my mother and me, and my sister and brother. But I forgive him. I forgave him a long time ago.

ME: That's nice. But I think that's your years of AA talking. It's how you feel now. If you're going to do this with me, it would be good to unlearn the Twelve Step stuff. Can you do that?

    (Long, long pause.)

It wasn't going to be easy. It seemed to me that where it mattered most Tony had put up walls, surely out of self-defense. But he wanted to try. We would stumble forward together, two generations of Italian American firstborn sons, groping, in search of what came before. A father and son looking for a father.

RIGHT FROM THE start, I was amazed at how much Tony knew. He had been a kid during his father's heyday, but he knew names, knew all the bigshots from Pittsburgh and beyond; he imitated their mannerisms and ways of speaking, how some of the guys played up the mobster thing. Somebody was "a real Damon Runyan kind of guy." He had a sense of the scope of the operation. I couldn't believe how much he had soaked up. It just came tumbling out: "They always called it the outfit . . ." "Frank Palumbo, the big guy in Philadelphia—they admired the hell out of him." "They had the DA in their pocket." "The time the governor came to the house for dinner . . ."

We started a routine of going off on local trips, driving around town, passing empty storefronts and soot-stained warehouses that bore silent testimony to what the place had once been, pulling up in front of old haunts. The building where City Cigar had been was being renovated, in the process of being turned into a Christian school, which seemed mildly amusing. "They took bets up there, on the second floor." Sitting in the car looking at the facade fired up a memory in him, and we swung around the block and pulled up in front of a brick building on Market Street. It had a fresh coat of red paint but, like many others downtown, was empty. "People went in to bet on the horse races. It was packed in there! They had their own announcer on a microphone calling the races. Sometimes if they wanted to beat a guy they'd pull a con, give the result a minute later. Like *The Sting*."

As Tony got into the job of being my researcher he looked up people he hadn't talked to in decades, phoned them out of the blue. *You around this afternoon? How about if we come by?* Stories came tumbling out of unexpected places. The picture got more complicated. It wasn't just "the mob," whatever that even was. It was the town, a family, the intricate, mostly small, sometimes painful connections between people.

And yet, something was missing. We were filling in details, but I didn't feel like we were getting very far on Russ. Example: Russ brought big-time pool players to town, trick shooters, to put on performances. They would have a competition the week before, to pick the city's five best players, who would go up against the sharpshooter. It's easy to imagine the club packed to the walls, people craning over each other, cigarettes bent, peering into the smoke hovering over the green baize. But where was Russ in this?

Example: Tony told me about the boxing gym Russ had on the third floor above the Melodee Lounge. He sponsored prizefights.

"One time he brought in Billy Conn, the Pittsburgh Kid!" Conn had been the light heavyweight champ, famous for the time he had Joe Louis beat through twelve rounds then got cocky and ended up getting knocked out in the thirteenth. ("Why couldn't you let me hold the title for a year or so?" he asked Louis after. "You had the title for twelve rounds and you couldn't hold on to it," Louis shot back.) Having the Pittsburgh Kid in town was a big event, and Russ was the precipitator, but where was he in this story?

More harrowing example: The alcoholic and the womanizer. Tony told me—and his sister, my aunt Sis, gave me her version of it—about the time their dad came home from an affair, one that my grandmother Mary knew about. And she was ready for him. The fight was epic: dishes thrown and smashing against walls, clothing torn, buttons flying, the kids cowering, My grandmother shrieking like a woman in a Greek tragedy. Then as the tempest quiets down, Mary, leaning into a familiar pattern, digs out a bottle of Seagram's VO and a shot glass. Russ slumps onto the sofa and starts hitting it, filling one little glass after another. The fight picks up again, then subsides. Russ keeps going at the bottle, finishes it, pukes into a bucket. She gets him another bottle, brings him upstairs to bed. They're both in there, the door closed, the kids listening from downstairs, and things fall quiet. Eventually she comes downstairs, her lips pursed, eyes surveying a distant landscape. Much later, in fear of what he might find, Tony sneaks upstairs and creaks open the door. The room is ghostly dark and ice cold. It's wintertime, but the windows are wide open, snow drifting into the room. And there is his father, lying on the bed wearing only his underwear, arms folded over his chest. He's dead drunk, snoring. His breath is visible. She has surrounded him with lit candles and houseplants, created his funeral. "His lips were blue," my dad said. "I really thought he was dead. And when he woke up, he did too!" He laughed at the memory, the craziness; after seventy years there was nothing else to do with it.

This story tells you a lot—about Mary. But Russ doesn't *do* anything in it, only reacts. His actions, which set it all up, take place offstage. I began to feel that I was searching for a void. Everything people said about Russ was a negation. *He was very quiet.* The stories about him mostly weren't: instead they revolved around him, as if the events and characters were in orbit around a dark star at the center.

I went over my notes from talking to the old guys, where I asked them what Russ was like. *Not flashy,* somebody said. *You didn't see him in no limelight or nothing.*

The further we went, the more it felt to me like Russ was one of those people who hide themselves in plain sight. It was like dealing with a magician and being faked out at every turn: the more carefully you think you're looking, the more you're following his misdirection. It started to feel like one of his cons. What was I looking for anyway? *Namesake.* Why? Where was this going?

I think Tony felt it too as we went along. His father had hidden himself from his own family. For decades my dad had been content with that abortive presence, made his peace with it so that he could pursue his own dreams. He had locked the dark void of his father into a closet. And now I was dragging him along to join me in the hunt for this man. He wanted to do it, and he dutifully unearthed memories. "Jesus, I haven't thought about that for seventy years!" Here and there, he was a boy again, staring up at the towering colossus of the father. But I don't think he was finding much substance in the childhood vision.

Then I had an idea—which was a relief, really. Go back onto the other tack: Do what I do for a living. Set the personal baggage aside. Don't look for my grandfather. Look for a historical figure.

4

The Immigrant

RUSS'S FATHER'S NAME was Antonino Sciotto. When I visited his village, high in the mountains of eastern Sicily, and found the very house he was born in, the notion popped into my head that when he first opened his eyes, in the summer of 1876, it would have been onto a sky so blue and so near, so enveloping, it must have felt, as he grew, like his true home. Just as intimate and enveloping would have been the noises of the mountaintop enclave. Carts groaning against cobbles, bells on animal necks clanking musically, the shuffling of wild pigs at night followed in the morning by the brassy clarity of church bells.

The village, remote, pre-plumbing and pre-electric, hemmed by stands of cork, cypress, cedar, and hazelnut trees and far from any major trade route, was in some ways not much different in his time from when it was founded in the ninth century by Arabs, in one of the successive invasions of the island. The narrow, stacked houses stood huddled close to the central street. There was one well. You got water by leading a donkey up and down the steep and twisty paths, coming back with your sloshing jugs and buckets. You kept it for use in clay pots in your house. At night you lit candles or oil lamps.

The name the town eventually received—San Pier Niceto, or Victorious Saint Peter—was apparently a nod to the later Christian reconquering. From the highest spots you can see the metropolis of Messina down below, but from up here the port city seemed as remote as Rome. Even today seafood has no part in the local cuisine, as if the Tyrrhenian Sea glimmering down below was suspected of being an optical trick. The parade of invaders—Carthaginians, Greeks, Normans, Swabians, "Saracens"—had left a population comprising a veritable database of ethnic markers: dark to fair, straight to kinked, lithe to squat.

The boy—who would grow to exemplify the dark and squat end of the spectrum—wasn't special. Not in his first name—calls of "Antonino" rang out in every stony corner of San Pier Niceto—and as for his last name there were Sciottos scattered throughout northeastern Sicily. When I brought my family to the town, Mario Italiano, its unofficial historian, took us on a *passeggiata* through the streets and introduced us to residents. Probably half a dozen people we randomly encountered had my great-grandfather's last name. In the Middle Ages the Sciotto family apparently had some power; there's a Palazzo Lo Sciotto in the town of Pace del Mela, six miles away, a remnant of feudal grandeur. But there was no power in Antonino Sciotto's family—the whole town was poor, including his parents. The house where my great-grandfather was born was a bastion-like stone structure with a bricked arch over the door in the manner of the ancient Romans; Mario, my guide, said it dated to the late Middle Ages. It sat on the edge of town, a few steps from a cliff.

Antonino's parents, Santi and Petronilla, were farmers. Both had spent their whole lives in the village, as had their forebears going back at least into the early 1700s. The boy had no schooling—illiteracy was the norm in nineteenth-century Sicily. He went to work as soon as he was able, probably with olives and grapes, the two main pursuits of the townspeople. There were also shepherds, men and boys who picked their way along perilous tracks wearing leggings and jackets of shaggy goat hide, looking like they were in the process of merging with the animals they were tending. But paying work of any kind was hard to find. The region—the island—was in the midst of a harrowing depression that had begun before he was born.

At age twenty-one, Antonino was compelled to make a sudden change, "compelled" being the operative word. He didn't want to do it, but after months of what must have been bitter fighting between two of the village's oldest clans he finally showed up at the *municipio* with a sixteen-year-old girl named Francesca Spadaro, bringing two of his workmates along to serve as witnesses. The reason for the haste would have been perfectly evident to Placido Bruno, the man who registered the marriage, for in addition to being mayor he was also an obstetrician.

I was fortunate enough to find an assistant in my research into my great-grandfather, in the person of Giuseppe Ruggeri. Joe, as he goes by in English, was born and raised in San Pier Niceto, trained as an economist, spent his career in Canada, and, in his retirement, returns for a portion of each year to the Sicilian village we have in common. After doing some research in the local archives for me, he confirmed the situation between Antonino and Francesca in an email:

> The marriage was definitely forced and there must have been quite a lengthy negotiation because the banns were made very late. He was 21 and could marry of his own will, but she was a minor and needed approval from her parents. As long as she was a virgin when he impregnated her and he later married her, the family honor was preserved on both sides.

Since Francesca was seven months pregnant, I wonder whether the mothers of the bride and groom would have carried through with the traditional morning-after ceremony. They were supposed to make the newlyweds' bed and hang a bloodstained sheet out the window to certify the bride's virginity. At any rate, two months later, Dr. Bruno would likely have been the one to handle the delivery when Francesca gave birth to a son. They called the boy Santi, following the Sicilian tradition of naming the first male after the man's father. Two years later they named their daughter Petronilla.

He was a restless young man, this Antonino, with a roving kind of hunger in him—dangerous in a place where lethality was acceptable in protecting family honor. At some point while still a newlywed with a shotgun-marriage bride he was conducting a flirtation with another, even younger, girl in the village—a teenager from another family of ancient local origin. Both her parents had died, and her sister, her only sibling, had married and gone off to live with her husband. Maybe Antonino had preferred this girl from the start, and the inconvenient pregnancy of Francesca had changed things. Or maybe he found her tragically alluring in her orphaned state, a thing to be pitied and cosseted. Then again, she also possessed some tenacity, which could have attracted him. She had been resourceful enough to get the nuns at the convent in the center of town to give her a job working in their kitchen.

But such a relationship could only be doomed: in a small village, he wouldn't have dared to stir things up. Most of the time, presumably, he worked, or looked for work, and cared for his wife and growing family.

And he listened. In the public squares tucked around the village young men were talking about the outside world. They were talking, with scorn, about something called Italy. Three decades after the unification of the peninsula it was still a largely alien concept in Sicily. People in the village didn't speak Italian (Sicilian diverges enough from Italian to be considered a separate language, containing borrowings from Greek, Latin, Arabic, and Medieval French, its many dialects making it difficult at the time even for people from different parts of the island to communicate with one another) and didn't know Italians. And Italians—meaning those from the northern part of the Italian peninsula, who had led the push for nationhood—didn't know them. An emissary sent southward in 1860, as part of the initial effort to pull together the disparate, foreign-controlled duchies and principalities into one nation, informed his superiors with news-flash horror: "This is not Italy! This is Africa."

"Africa" was shorthand for alien, barbarian, lawless. Sicily's location, at the center of the Mediterranean Sea, coupled with its distance from the major powers around the perimeter, meant that its culture had taken shape in a constant crucible of invasion, in which one occupying power held sway for a time even as another was preparing to mount the next assault. Europeans, North Africans, and Near Easterners had been raping and plundering the island's landscape since long before the time of Christ. A visiting Englishwoman in the 1800s described the conditions she found as being utterly different from the rest of Europe: the cities "are in a state of indecency, almost inferior to that of the ancient tribes of Africa. The prisons and sites of detention are places where beasts can hardly be kept. There are no public fountains, no clocks, conditions not in the least fit for civilized quarters." Another result of the centuries of abuse by alien empires, for people in villages such as San Pier Niceto, was a complete distrust of authority.

Having endured so many centuries of multifarious oppression, Sicilians were suspicious and inward, beswarmed by superstitions. Their Catholicism was nominal, a surface under which a liturgy of incantations, spells, and rituals thrived—to get you through the day, to bring a healthy baby into the world, to make it rain, above all to ward off the *malocchio*, the evil eye. Like all other young men and women, Antonino Sciotto would have been taught to trust only family, and to trust family utterly. Reverence for parents and grandparents was on a level that is hard to fathom: for example, he probably addressed his humble, impoverished father as "Excellency."

Meanwhile, northern Italians—with forebears like Galileo and

Leonardo, not to mention Julius Caesar—considered themselves the creators of European civilization, the forgers of the modern world. What fueled men like Giuseppe Garibaldi, the leader of the revolution, was a desire to get back to the greatness that had been lost with the collapse of the Roman Empire. The fight for a united Italy—the Risorgimento, or Resurgence, an endless cycle of alliances, invasions, sieges, annihilations, raids, assassinations, and banishments—consumed most of the nineteenth century. It culminated, on September 20, 1870, with a three-hour cannon assault by an Italian army on the walls of Rome, the capital of the Papal States, the last major piece of the peninsula holding out against the idea of a unified Italy, and the eventual capitulation of the pope. Victory—independence—was announced in 1871, five years before Antonino's birth. Rome became the capital of the new nation. It had to be the capital, for were they not rebuilding the empire?

Unification turned out to be the last straw. The northern Italians who ran the new government accomplished, within the first two decades of Antonino's life, what the Carthaginians, Vandals, Goths, and other invaders of Sicily had not: they brought the island to a state of ruin and its people to starvation and despair. Northern leaders couldn't fathom the opaque structure of Sicilian society. They found it was controlled by two groups—large property owners and the Catholic Church—both of whom seemed to be manipulated by a little-understood organization called "mafia." The roots of this society went back at least into the previous century and perhaps much further. Even the term was a source of confusion. An Arabic word, *mu'afa*, which was taken up into Sicilian, meant "a place of refuge." It seemed to refer to a community formed to protect against outside threats, of which the people of the island had experienced many.

As far as the leaders of the new Italian government were concerned, such layers of cultural obfuscation did nothing but allow corruption and malfeasance to flourish. They had no choice, they felt, but to impose, as one wrote, "our superior intelligence and superior morality" directly on this alien people, so that "we can hope to govern and master them." Waves of new taxes were levied—at the same time that prices for locally produced goods were plummeting, and also while a virus was decimating the island's grapevines. Even in better times the diet was dead basic. Today we fetishize Italian cuisine; these people subsisted mostly on bread—the poorest on *balurda*, a type of cornbread—supplemented by field greens like dandelion. And now they were actually starving. Women went to extreme measures to feed their families, like scraping the outer layer of plaster off the walls of their homes and mixing the powder into their dough to make it go further.

Young Sicilians reacted to the crisis. In villages like San Pier Niceto they went to meetings of a new movement called Fasci Siciliani, Sicilian Workers Leagues, which called for social justice.

Others opted for a different response. Foreign enterprises—railroad companies, mines, governments—had come to see opportunity in the crisis in southern Italy and began actively recruiting workers. Suddenly there were posters in towns all over Sicily advertising high and secure wages for those willing to travel.

Some of the first Italians to leave in numbers headed for, of all places, the state of Louisiana. The upheaval in Sicily coincided with the end of the American Civil War, which freed slaves and left plantation owners desperate for cheap labor. An enterprising group of former slaveowners calling themselves the Louisiana Sugar Planters' Association established a regular steamship route between New Orleans and southern Italy. They advertised good working conditions, solid wages, and free passage.

More than 100,000 young Sicilian men went to Louisiana. They worked the sugarcane alongside Black sharecroppers, or took the places that former slaves had abandoned as they sought what they hoped would be a better life. If it wasn't technically slave labor, it was close, both in terms of it being backbreakingly difficult and in the way they were treated. They became objects of degradation and disdain to white Louisianians and far beyond. The eleven men who were hanged in the largest mass lynching in American history—in New Orleans in 1891—were not Black but Italian. The *New York Times* defended the extralegal executions, calling the victims "sneaking and cowardly Sicilians, the descendants of bandits and assassins."

And yet. Many of those who staked out a life in America found that it was better than what they had left behind. As it happens, we have a reliable observer who was able to compare the situation of peasants in Sicily with Blacks in the American South. Booker T. Washington, the Black educator and adviser to U.S. presidents, traveled through six European countries in 1910 and wrote a kind of antithesis to the travel guides that were popular at the time. He wrote *The Man Farthest Down* for those, like him, who were freed slaves, and for their children. How did their suffering and abuse under the Jim Crow system compare with living conditions elsewhere?

Washington toured salt mines in Poland and visited London slums. But he found the subject that best fit the title of his book when he got to Sicily. "I have frequently seen men who had done a hard day's work sit down to a meal which consisted of black bread and a bit of tomato or other raw vegetable. In the more remote regions these peasant people frequently live for days or months, I learned, on almost any sort of green thing they find in the fields, frequently eating it raw, just like the cattle." Peasants worked like animals for absentee landlords, being forced during harvest time to exist on two hours' sleep. Bare and bleak landscapes; old men dying in gutters—Washington found signs of "physical and mental deterioration" in both the land and its people.

Washington served up his wan summary of comparative hope for Blacks in America: "I have described at some length the condition of the farm labourers in Italy because it seems to me that it is important that those who are inclined to be discouraged about the Negro in the

South should know that his case is by no means as hopeless as that of some others. The Negro is not the man farthest down. The condition of the coloured farmer in the most backward parts of Southern States in America, even where he has the least education and the least encouragement, is incomparably better than the condition and opportunity of the agricultural population in Sicily."

This was what Antonino left, and why he decided to leave, in 1901. Other entities—U.S. states, shipping companies, mines, and factories in Argentina, Venezuela and Australia—had followed the lead of the Louisiana Sugar Planters' Association. When men like Antonino ventured down out of their medieval villages to the big city of Messina, a sprawling place on the cusp of the twentieth century, they found walls papered with posters. Recruiting agents—*padroni*—would stop you on the street and ask if you were ready for adventure. They would sign you up like it was for a stint in the military.

Many of those looking for a way out followed friends or family members. Antonino's wife's brother had gone to work in a coal mine near Punxsutawney, Pennsylvania. He doesn't seem to have stayed long, but he blazed a trail. Pennsylvania would become the second most popular destination for Sicilian émigrés, behind New York. Antonino was like the majority of those who went there, settling not in the big cities but in smaller towns. These were the locations of the mines and factories most in need of desperate, hardworking foreigners.

So he left everyone and everything, made the journey, first down the hill to Messina, and the port. I presume he waved tearfully; I presume Francesca saw him off, along with their two little ones, filled with whatever cauldron of emotions, waving to the figure of him up on the high deck. He had grown somewhat in the four years since they had married; he was thicker now, and sporting the brawny mustache that southern Italian men of his generation favored: "Moustache Petes" they would call them in America.

He would be back, of course. This was—for him, for most of the millions who formed this tide of which he was a part—migrant work, a source of cash. He had every intention to return to the world that mattered to him.

Eighteen days later came the arrival at Ellis Island, and the line of southern Italians—the ship had made calls at Naples, Messina, and Palermo—wending down the plank and into a great hall. The paper you were clutching as you waited your turn told the immigration officer what he needed to know. Then an agent from the coal company thrust a packet into your hands: your food for the journey. There was the brief, frightening or healing magic of beholding the New York City skyline, then the roaring train ride across Pennsylvania.

Walston was the name of the town, a community just north of Punxsutawney and eighty miles from Pittsburgh. It was named after Walston H. Brown, president of the Rochester & Pittsburgh Coal & Iron Company. Mr. Brown himself was back in New York; he worked in Manhattan, and lived with his wife—an energetic advocate of the women's suffrage movement—north of the city, in Dobbs Ferry. Their mansion, with its views across the Hudson River, was about as far removed from Walston, Pennsylvania, as could be.

The new life asserted itself. There were the rows of miners' houses: six families to a house, or an equivalent number of single men, partitions between rooms so thin that everyone could hear every single thing that everyone else said and did. Jobs were doled out: miner, coke-puller, coke-worker, scraper, hauler. Charging the coke ovens was the hottest work; people likened it to being in hell. As coal baked, the ovens gave off a cloud of blue smoke, which later turned yellow. Everyone in town could not only see it but taste it: "disagreeable" was the word that one local reporter found to describe it. The ovens stretched out like railroad cars, a train of beehive structures that went on for more than a mile and lit up the night sky. When the works first opened, an observer declared that "driving along the road at night, in full view of this serpentine-like line, the spectacle is simply grand."

The railroad tracks ran right up to the ovens so cars could be loaded. Sometimes hoboes emerged from the empty cars, heated up their cooking pots on the ovens, made friends with the workers for the short duration of their stay, then headed out. From them the cluster of foreign workers got news of exotic places: Omaha, Sacramento, Denver, Jersey City. America, whatever that was, out there somewhere.

A coal-industry journal said the workers in Walston were of "all known nationalities except Turks and Indians." You were living in a company town, and you tried to surround yourself with *paesani*, for security and for comfort. Life was primitive: eat, work, sleep. But you were paid well compared to what you'd left. No: better than that. A coke-puller got $2 per oven, and could make $5 a day. That wasn't good—it was breathtaking. When you had time, there were shops to go to, and you had money to buy things. On Sundays there was beer. When you clanked tankards with Irishmen and Poles—*Sláinte! Na zdrowie!*—you were celebrating freedom, the giddy falling-away of cultural mores. In that absence there was suddenly a wee bit of room to contemplate something that essentially hadn't existed before: yourself, as an individual.

Antonino settled in. He made a decision—far crazier than the one to come here, which had really been a matter of necessity. This was something else: a lunge, a shout from a mountaintop into an echoing valley, the bellowing call of an ego demanding to be fed. It was a tradition-defying act of selfishness. He must have been shaking inside as he dictated the letter to a Sicilian coworker who could write. The message was simple: *Come*. It's good here. Or good enough. Better, anyway.

The letter made its measured way across the ocean. Somehow, it wound through the Byzantine postal system at Messina. It got loaded onto an animal's back for the steep climb up into the cypress-scented hills. But it wasn't his wife, Francesca, who opened it. It was addressed to Annamaria Previte, the orphan girl.

5

The Cheat

I assume Annamaria's was a somewhat different journey from San Pier Niceto to the port at Messina. The transport would have been the same as when Antonino went, mule having been the standard means well into the 1950s. But I'm imagining that my great-grandmother made the trip alone, rounding the steep bends and trundling down toward the cobalt, salt-scented coast with some mixture of anxiety, panic, and excitement at the mad step she was taking. She had no family, after all. She must have had a confidante, for just as Antonino needed someone else to write his letters she needed someone to decipher them, but otherwise it was only the two of them in this scheme. Her ticket was paid for, by Antonino. He had sent her money for the voyage: $10. And he knew the drill at customs, so he must have instructed her on what to say to the American officials. She dutifully listed him as her contact in the United States, referred to him as her "cousin," and gave his address, 244 Findley Street, Punxsutawney, Pennsylvania, as her destination and new home. This was a carefully orchestrated coup, on his part a clear act of betrayal, on hers a lunge at a future.

A year later their first child was born. They called her Anna. They hadn't married and never would—not surprising, considering that he already had a wife and they were both Catholic. But they began presenting themselves as husband and wife shortly after her arrival, and my family always assumed they were.

The next part of this sustained act of subterfuge came a few years later, when they left town. The coal mine had lifted both of them from poverty, but it was ruinous work. In Antonino's first full year on the job, 2,232 miners died from mining accidents in the United States, which was only a fraction of the true toll. For untold thousands, work in the mines led to the black-lung cough; the sufferer filled handkerchiefs with what one writer dubbed "inky expectoration," then weakened rapidly until "in the course of a few years, he sinks under the disease."

The little family traveled sixty miles south to Johnstown. Where Punxsutawney had been all about coal, Johnstown was a steel town. And it was growing furiously. Two decades before they arrived, a visitor described it as "new, rough, and busy, with the rush of huge mills and factories and the throb of perpetually passing trains." Just then it was having another growth spurt.

The town had come into being a century before as a hardscrabble coal and iron center, with mostly German and Welsh immigrants working small mines and foundries tucked into its wooded gullies.* A man named Daniel Morrell gave it trajectory when he arrived from Philadelphia to run the Cambria Iron Company in the 1850s. He was one of the first people in the world to take advantage of a new, dramatically more efficient, process for turning iron into steel, and by the end

---

* Actually, there had been two earlier iterations. A group of Delaware Indians called the Conemack had had a village at the confluence of the two rivers that would form the northern tip of downtown. The first European settlement came when an Amish farmer named Schantz arrived in the valley with his family and set up a farm, betting on establishing a town that would become the county seat. When it was passed over, he upped stakes. Nevertheless, his name, Anglicized, would become the town's.

of the Civil War he had turned Johnstown into the steel-producing capital of the United States. Morrell was a benevolent dictator, who abhorred unions but believed in taking care of his workers as a father would his children. He gave the city its first hospital and library, and ran the town government, the department store, and the local bank. Despite Morrell's anti-union policy there seems to have been little outward expression of grievance from workers, who under him had a better standard of living than they had ever known.

In the 1870s, while Antonino Sciotto was taking his first steps in the cobbled lanes of San Pier Niceto, a new generation of industrialists in Pittsburgh, seventy miles to the west, made a run at Morrell's empire. Morrell dismissed the upstarts—who included Andrew Carnegie, Andrew Mellon, and Henry Clay Frick—as mere financiers rather than real steel men, but within a short time they made Johnstown subordinate to Pittsburgh. They also ushered in a newly confrontational relationship between factory owners and workers. And, almost as if they had wanted to fashion a symbol of their relationship to lowly workers, the Pittsburgh titans conceived of a fairy-tale recreation area for themselves and their families in the hills above Johnstown. They formed a social club, erected a seventy-two-foot-high dam near the town of South Fork, and diverted water to create a gravity-defying mountaintop lake. Each member of the club built a palatial "cottage" around the lake, where their families could spend summers away from the heat of the city. Visitors described it as like something out of a dream, with women twirling parasols while servants worked oars and sails, fancifully sailing boats on top of a mountain.

As this paradise was nearing completion the people of Johnstown became alarmed: the South Fork Dam stood just east of the city, and 450 feet above it. Everybody feared the spring floods, which roared with biblical ferocity down the steep slopes. Morrell sent his chief engineer to inspect the dam; he reported "serious elements of danger." The lords of the South Fork Fishing and Hunting Club ignored complaints. In 1889 the dam burst, the water cascaded into the valley, and 2,209 people in Johnstown were killed, most within ten minutes.

The Johnstown Flood was the greatest natural disaster in U.S. history to that time. It focused national attention on the concept of disaster relief (Clara Barton spent five months in the city, with a team of fifty Red Cross doctors and nurses). And the flood washed away the idea of an industrial overlord as a benevolent father figure. Newspapers across the country delivered a unanimous verdict on its cause: "The Club Is Guilty"..."An Engineering Crime." Rebuilding took years. U.S. Steel and Bethlehem Steel moved into town in the aftermath. The mills expanded and modernized, and the town grew, but so did the class divide and the mistrust.

The steel mills became the focus of everything. Johnstown was roaring like a beast—as were the other little cities encircling it: Altoona and Youngstown, Morgantown and Wheeling. As Antonino and Annamaria arrived the mills downtown were clanging and booming and grinding out their girders and sheets. There was hope here, and not just in income but quality of life: the mills were easier on the body than the mines were.

In making his decision to move, however, Antonino apparently hadn't factored in discrimination. To the town's original German and Welsh inhabitants, the newcomers who had been flooding in for the past several years were all "Huns" or "Hunkies," whether they came from Hungary, Poland, or Italy. The caste system in early twentieth-century America put Italians' status roughly on par with that of Blacks. At around the time of the family's move, a native-born white man earned $14 a week, while the average Black man earned $10 per week. For southern Italian immigrants in the United States, the figure was closer to $9. Decent jobs in the mill weren't generally open to Italians.

But maybe the couple zeroed in on Johnstown precisely for this reason. There was a strike on at the Bethlehem Steel plant around the time they arrived. Striking workers complained that the company had brought "a couple of car loads of Negroes and Italians into the plant." Antonino was apparently one of these scabs. He worked in the mill's car shop, painting railroad cars. Eventually, though, the strike ended, and he wound up back in a coal mine.

So no, the move did not bring about a better work life. Instead, the significance of relocating to Johnstown turned out to be in the evolution of identities. From now on their names would appear differently on official documents. In Johnstown, Antonino Sciotto and Annamaria Previte became Tony and Mary Shorto.* The change wasn't just due to vague notions of Americanness, of making pronunciation easier, and of fitting in. It was also a way to distance themselves from the past, from the village in the hills of eastern Sicily, and Antonino's wife.

Soon Annamaria—Mary—was pregnant again and Antonino—Tony—was making the first of several trips back to San Pier Niceto. His mother was still alive: I'm told by family members that he traveled back in part to see her. And since his original plan to seek work in America had been to help support his wife and their children, he would have to see Francesca on his return trips. Did he stay with her when he visited, as man and wife? Was he able to dupe them all into thinking that he was on his own in Pennsylvania?

It doesn't seem likely. His Sicilian village was truly a village. Everyone had to know what he and the orphan girl had done, were doing. What kind of homecoming did he have? How did Francesca receive him? Shortly after he first left for America, in 1901, their second child, their daughter, had died, at the age of two. Did father and mother console each other on his return? Or did she refuse to see him?

I think not. One of his trips back was in 1908. In 1909, Francesca

---

* The actual change of the last name probably came compliments of a census taker or town clerk or some other official. If an illiterate, non-English-speaking Italian pronounces "Sciotto," an American ear would hear it as something very like "Shorto."

gave birth to a third child, and Tony Shorto—or rather, Antonino Sciotto—is listed on the birth certificate as the father. (In Pennsylvania, at the same time, Mary, his American "wife," was pregnant with *their* third child.) If the married couple were on intimate terms seven or more years after he had first left for America, that suggests to me that he kept his ties to his wife in other ways. Surely he was helping her financially throughout this period. I'm not entirely sure why this mattered to me—maybe I was trying to find his internal logic, what he told himself about what he was doing, how he justified this complex life he had fashioned. This seems to me so much a part of the work in doing family history—or for that matter any narrative digging into the past: trying to suss out what was going on in heads that are long dead. Maybe this is one's own ulterior motive. Consciousness, even one's own, is such a tenuous and unfathomable thing; maybe we try to look into our predecessors' to shore it up in ourselves.

But no sooner had I reached this conclusion about my great-grandfather—that he must have been taking care of families on both sides of the Atlantic—than I received a surprising email from Joe Ruggeri, my informant in the village:

Hi Russell,

This morning I went to the dentist and I met someone I knew as a child (he is a few years older). He knew Francesca Spadaro, the wife of your great grandfather. He did not provide child support. She supported herself and her two children by washing the clothes of the wealthier families in SPN. This involved getting up early in the morning a few days a week, collecting the dirty clothes, walking down one mile to the river with the clothes and a tin container and soap, washing the clothes on the canal that carried the water from one grist mill to another, and then carrying the partly wet (and heavier) clothes back up the hill. Have a nice weekend. Joe

If this is true, then the story—and my great-grandfather's self-justification—becomes even more complicated. How could Antonino have returned to Sicily repeatedly, lived with his wife while there, fathered another child with her, yet not have supported her?

I can try to game out different scenarios, but at the bottom one has to resort to the truism that human beings are complex creatures, buffeted by circumstances, sometimes of their own devising, whose motivations can shift on a dime, then later shift again, and then again. I'm left to conclude nothing more than what the evidence suggests: that Tony Shorto returned to his ancestral village repeatedly to visit his mother and others close to him; that on at least one occasion he was intimate with the wife whom he was actively betraying; that, despite this fact, as of a certain point—perhaps later—he stopped sending her money; and that the center of his life, these trips aside, was in Johnstown, Pennsylvania.

There, he and Mary had three more children in the next four years—all girls, making for a total of five girls.

Then, in 1914, came their first son. They called him Rosario, after Mary's father, but it quickly became Americanized to Russell, or Russ.*

The family's first home in Johnstown was on a street filled with Hungarians. Neither Tony nor Mary ever learned much English, let alone Hungarian. They moved to another neighborhood near one of

---

* Regarding Sicilian naming patterns: tradition dictated—and still dictates—that a couple name their first boy after the father's father and their first girl after the father's mother. I knew this long ago, and thought it strange that Antonino's first son, my grandfather, was not named after the paternal grandfather, Santi. This was my first hint that the whispered story in my family—that Antonino had another family in Sicily—might be true. In fact, Antonino's first son was the child he had with his wife, Francesca, in Sicily, whom they did indeed name Santi. Again following the Sicilian naming practice, the second son would have been named after the mother's father. This relative was named Rosario. Hence, my grandfather was named Rosario, which became Americanized to Russell. I likewise was named after him. Russ, meanwhile, named his first son after Antonino.

the entrances of the mill, rented the house, and took in boarders: four Italian men, all of them working in the coal mines. Besides a couple of Irish families, they were now surrounded by Italians.

And this is how the next generation grew up: Anna, Perina, Angeline, Sarah, Carmella (who went by Millie), and their little brother, Rosario, or Russell. Later there would be three more: Anthony, Catherine, and Nancy. Nine Sicilian American children raised in a Sicilian-speaking household in a rough coal-and-steel ghetto, surrounded by the thick wilds of the Pennsylvania mountains, by the plumes of smoke and dust from the mills, and by the matter-of-fact prejudice of Americans, who were threatened by this sudden rush of southern Europeans, who felt themselves whiter, more entitled to the available jobs. For the children, there wasn't an issue of this being unfair. It was the way the world worked; it was reality—not the American dream but American waking life.

Then their lives changed. In 1920, Tony got word that his mother was dying. He left Mary and the children at the train station in Johnstown (seven-year-old Millie, who was old enough to appreciate the gulf of time he would be gone, was crying her eyes out on the platform as he waved goodbye), made the familiar trip east across the state, boarded the ship, traversed the imponderable ocean, rode the mule shuttle back up the hill, and so came again into the twisty, medieval streets of San Pier Niceto. The story my dad's aunts used to tell was that by the time he got there the crisis had passed: his mother had recovered her health.

I don't know how long he stayed, but there was an air of celebration at his departure. It had been a number of years since his last visit, and much had changed. I gather he was feeling richer. He took some family members to Messina with him the evening before he was to leave. There was a nice dinner at a proper restaurant, something unheard-of among the generationally impoverished villagers. Tony Shorto, the American, who these days was known to sport a three-piece suit, starched collar, tie, and cuff links, wanted to dazzle the hill people he'd been born among—wanted, I guess, to show how much he had distanced himself from them.

The story of what happened next came to me from Cindy Shorto, my father's cousin's wife, who got it from my father's aunts: "He was leaving, so he took everybody out to dinner. When it was time to pay, these two guys saw his money belt, how thick it was. Later they got hold of him and kicked and stabbed him. He lived for three weeks and then he died." He was killed for his newfound wealth.

For all his American inclinations, then, Antonino Sciotto's story would end in Sicily, violently and abruptly, at the age of forty-four. He left two families on two continents. A little irony to end this anecdote: his mother, whose impending death had precipitated his visit, lived on for years after.

Antonino Sciotto.

I imagine news of this magnitude would have been sent by cable, but that supposes that someone in the village knew that the orphan girl Annamaria Previte was living in Pennsylvania as Antonino's wife and the mother of his children. So maybe not. Maybe it came slowly, haphazardly, eventually reaching her in her home on Church Avenue in Johnstown, Pennsylvania, a whisper or a letter conveying the information that a brief act of violence on an island in the middle of the Mediterranean Ocean had transformed her world. There's an odd story that has survived in my family, which holds that two men showed up at her home in Pennsylvania one day, presenting themselves as relatives of the person or persons who had killed her husband. The story goes that they had come to apologize. It's strange enough that it might be true. Maybe they were the ones who broke the news to her that her husband was dead.

What could she do now? She was an unskilled mother of nine, alone in America, whose English was restricted to a few phrases (example: my father remembers her anger coming out in a homemade locution of "summon-a-bitch!"). She had her boarders, who provided a little income. She had her children, the oldest of whom, Anna and Perina, were fourteen and thirteen, respectively, and could work, probably already were working. She had also brought her Sicilian hill-country survival strategies with her. She had the children set traps around the yard for sparrows and robins, which she would fry up; she gathered dandelions and wild mushrooms from the woods.

Russ was six when his father died. His childhood would come to be governed by his mother's peasant wisdom. If a cut became infected, she packed it with cow manure. Come down with intestinal pain and you received the bonus unpleasantness of an egg-white enema. The smallest of the children were sent off along the railroad tracks to gather chunks of coal that flew off the trains. When they got meat they ate the whole animal—brains, lungs. Mary herself hardened and toughened as time went by. She was known to open a bottle with her teeth.

The house was pretty rough too. Grandchildren who eventually came along remember it being infested with rats and cockroaches; she kept chickens in the backyard, a pig kept under the porch (which eventually grew so big they had to dismantle the porch to get it out) and a goat for milk in the basement. The goat surfaces in one of the family stories about the period, which people point to as an early indication of Russ's resourcefulness. One of the girls was struck by appendicitis, which forced Mary to rush her to the hospital, leaving the other children alone. Soon the baby started crying in hunger. In her panic, Mary hadn't thought of this. It was Russ who had the answer. He and his sisters descended to the basement, he held the goat's hind legs, one of the girls introduced the baby to the teat, and the problem was solved.

DESPITE A WORLD of hardships, Mary had a sliver of luck in the timing of Antonino's death, for it coincided with the start of Prohibition. The thumbnail understanding of Prohibition—the way I saw it until I began researching—holds that it was a movement in which militant church ladies pushed for a ban on alcohol in order to improve the morals of their menfolk. That notion turns out to be so simplistic as to be almost a lie.

Take a step back. What was America like in the 1920s? It was roaring, right? There was a party going on. Jazz, flappers, Hollywood: it was all new, all being invented, furious and delirious and sequined. Theaters, whose sculpted grandeur had been meant to evoke ancient Greece, were suddenly being repurposed, Vaudevillians shouldered aside by the jaw-dropping high tech of the moving picture. Babe Ruth was revolutionizing baseball, and *there he was*, ghostily inhabiting your local venue, the Sultan of Swat swinging for the fences in newsreel footage. People were going out and doing something crazy-new and liberating: buying themselves a car. Then thundering off under their own steam like lunatics across the landscape, racing and weaving and crashing and bursting into flames. And if they survived, doing it all over again. Radio, too, was relatively new—the eerie magic of being connected to a mass culture only really became a thing in the 1920s. I can imagine Russ and his siblings bending over a box to hear the reedy, hissy sounds of the world out there. And to those first listeners the buzzings and cracklings weren't just interference but part of the experience, part of the deep interconnectedness, for you were swimming in the world of physics, surfing the electromagnetic waves along with the rest of humanity, all together in this act of discovery.

But while you are imagining America in the 1920s as this mass hoopla, you also have to picture the place seething with a hundred hatreds. Because this jazz party was being foisted onto a country that until a minute before had thought of itself as overwhelmingly and decisively comprised of white Christian farm folk. Think of the couple in "American Gothic" suddenly finding their pious little house on the prairie invaded by cocktail-swizzling Charleston enthusiasts. Great swarms of immigrants were pouring into the country's ports; new fashions, technologies, and innovations were changing life at the speed of light. For many, it was too much. Someone had to pay.

In fact, researching Prohibition is like reading the backstory to recent history. Yes, per capita alcohol consumption in the early twentieth century was considerably higher than today: the nation had a drinking problem, and targeting it was a motivation for temperance leaders. But the ban was also in a very real sense an effort to preserve "American values" by lashing out at people who were seen as threatening. The targeted groups were basically two: urban elites and recent immigrants. White Americans throughout the country's heartland were alarmed at the sudden influx of millions of immigrants, who were widely believed to be of a lower order of humanity, who were thought incapable of self-control and prone to violence and rape. That alcohol, which weakened morals, was important to their cultures—the Germans had their beer halls, the Italians their wine, the Irish their whiskey—was proof that the newcomers constituted an anti-American invasion. From the perspective of Prohibition leaders like Carrie Nation, who became famous for barging into saloons swinging a hatchet, America's cities were filled with nightclubs where elites developed perversions like homosexuality, and with hordes of immigrants who got sozzled in beer halls then rampaged through the streets. Beneath Prohibition's Christian morality flowed a current of racism. It wasn't coincidental that one of the forces behind it was the Ku Klux Klan, or that the Klan—a post–Civil War phenomenon that had long since faded—reemerged as an element in American life right at the time Prohibition went into effect.

In Johnstown, Prohibition was presaged by a weeklong revival led by one of the nation's leading temperance champions, a former baseball star for the Chicago White Stockings known as Billy Sunday. He had made a second career out of railing religiously against every human manifestation of wickedness: drinking, dancing, gambling, theatre, the teaching of evolution. (Baseball, however, was OK.) Groups like the Anti-Saloon League hadn't yet made much of an impact in the town, perhaps due to its sizable immigrant population, but Mr. Sunday's event (which began and ended on a Sunday) changed that. The newspaper reported that 24,500 people showed up on the first day alone. People must have come from miles around to take in the show, for total attendance for the week supposedly topped half a million, in a town whose population was less than 60,000. And it was an all-out spectacle. Sunday's performance was built around his athleticism. He writhed and flung himself across the stage, executing a kind of three-act battle with Satan for his own soul and the eternal salvation of those watching in stunned attention.

After Sunday wrapped things up with a parade down Main Street, the newspaper chronicled the change: "One week of Billy Sunday and the old town has been turned topsy-turvy." Prohibition became wildly popular among the city's white Protestant majority. Many of the leading citizens—the mayor, city councilmen, the heads of the Cambria Steel Company—jumped on the bandwagon.

Italians and other minorities pushed back. Western Pennsylvania had become known as "the wettest spot in the United States," in part because of the concentration of minorities whose cultures involved alcohol—and this in turn probably led a couple of decades later to the particularly strong small-town mob presence in the same part of the country. The tension between them and the white Protestants increased. Many of the town's able-bodied white men had been shipped overseas to fight in the World War, and Cambria Steel began recruiting Black replacements from the South. As had happened ten years earlier, when Tony and Mary Shorto arrived during a strike and Tony got work for a time in the mill, white workers railed against Blacks and, as they said, other "undesirables" taking their jobs.

Anger led to action. By January 1922 "a large class of prominent men in town" had joined the Ku Klux Klan, according to the newspaper. Soon after, the Klan staged a series of publicity stunts around town. After giving advance notice so as to gather a crowd, a group of men in white robes with hoods would file into a public building, such as the YWCA on Somerset Street, as if for a business meeting. They handed the clerk behind the desk literature describing their aims, as well as an envelope containing cash, in an effort to build goodwill.

The Klan in Johnstown seems to have had about 1,700 members at its height—a large number for a small city, surely because of the presence of industry and thus the threatening influx of immigrants and Blacks. The Klan was anti-Black, of course, but more to the point Klansmen considered themselves "pro-American," meaning in favor of a white Protestant vision of America. According to KKK logic, only

that slice of the racio-religio-ethnic pie could be considered as comprising the true descendants of the pioneers who had wobbled across
the continent in their Conestoga wagons. Some of Johnstown's leading citizens fell in with Klan teaching, believing that they and their
fellow white-robed ones were pure stock, "the vanishing Americans,"
being drowned in a sea of newcomers. Immigration was making the
country, in the stirring words of William Joseph Simmons, the Grand
Wizard who had resurrected the Klan in 1915, "a garbage can."

Italians in town felt the rush of WASP purity like a slap and
wanted to slap back. One of my elderly informants, relying on his
father's recollections, described the mood and the bitter logic in the
Italian community: "Back then the people who ran the town would
say, 'My ancestors were on the *Mayflower* with the Pilgrims.' And
my dad would say, 'Oh yeah? Well, who the fuck were the Pilgrims?
Thieves, jailbreakers, and whores. And England put them on a boat
and shipped them here. So the fuck what?'"

The nativist wave reached a haunting crest in Johnstown in August
1923. Newspapers as far away as Indianapolis reported on a lurid spectacle in the little steel town in western Pennsylvania. The ethnic mix
of working-class folk whose homes were nestled in the town's valleys
gazed up in silent wonder one warm evening as, in the words of the
mayor, Joseph Cauffiel, "No less than a dozen flaming crosses were
burned on the hilltops around the city." White-robed men with their
faces hooded flanked the crosses like sentries. The mayor was horri-
fied at the spectacle and the violence that erupted in the following
days, in which two policemen were killed, and acted promptly. He did
not, however, take the step of seeking out the identities of the hooded
intimidators, but rather ordered a mass removal of "all negroes who
have resided in that city for less than seven years," which he said was
for their own protection.

Blacks weren't the only targets. The building resentment toward
Italian immigrants was sharpened in 1920, just as Prohibition went

into force, when two Italians, Nicola Sacco and Bartolomeo Vanzetti, were accused of murdering two security guards in a botched robbery in Massachusetts. The story riveted the nation, and the trial of Sacco and Vanzetti became a fault line separating two Americas: one that feared the changes that had swept in, the other that wanted to find ways to make immigrants into Americans and help the country to adapt to the modern world.

Those in the first camp saw Sacco and Vanzetti as representatives of their "race": murderous, addicted to alcohol, unable to control themselves, and above all vehicles by which the dreaded Catholic Church was infiltrating the body politic. Klan leader Hiram Evans characterized the view with language that was almost contractual. Catholics had to be opposed because the Church was "fundamentally and irredeemably, in its leadership, in politics, in thought, and largely in membership, actually and actively alien, un-American, and usually anti-American."

You don't read much about the KKK in accounts of how the mob got its start during Prohibition. I think that may be because most such accounts focus on the big cities, and the Klan had the greatest impact in smaller places like Johnstown. But its fury was bound up with, and became part of the force behind, the passage of the Volstead Act, which outlawed intoxicating beverages. The law went into effect in January 1920. Johnstown had six very active breweries. Like others all over the country, they halted production.

Has there ever been another law that generated such a tidal wave of unintended consequences? The Volstead Act created a nation of lawbreakers. Speakeasies sprang up in cities around the country. Doctors essentially became bartenders, prescribing whiskey to treat medical conditions. Most consequentially, Prohibition ushered in the era of organized crime. It gave Italian immigrants in particular— who had been marginalized by native-born white Americans, pushed into the lowest and most dangerous jobs, humiliated—a new role, one of power and respect.

Somehow I had gotten through life without ever reading a textbook on "organized crime," which turns out to be a surprisingly loaded concept. Digging into my grandfather's story meant trying to understand what the mafia was. The obvious path to studying the mafia—the one I traveled down first—involves looking into its beginnings in Sicily, how it was tied into the island's twisted history, and how it made the jump to America. But the less obvious line of research takes you to places you never thought to associate directly with the likes of Lucky Luciano.

The standard textbook on the subject, *Organized Crime*, by Howard Abadinsky, begins its historical analysis with, of all things, a section devoted to the careers of John Jacob Astor, Cornelius Vanderbilt, and John D. Rockefeller. What could the legendary founders of modern American capitalism have to do with the mob? Those men have been dubbed robber barons for a reason. With their "rampant—that is, uncontrolled—capitalism," Abadinsky explains, which involved violence, fraud, bribery, and intimidation on a national and sometimes global scale, these men not only built empires so colossal they became too big to fail, they provided striving newcomers models for success American-style.

Vanderbilt manipulated entire Central American nations, the U.S. State Department, and the Marine Corps to get his way in shipping. Astor built his fur empire by systematically swindling native Americans, and got rich as well as by smuggling opium. And they were not imprisoned for crimes but lionized as the great visionary leaders of their day. They defined American success. As Abadinsky says, "While contemporary organized crime has its roots in Prohibition, unscrupulous American business entrepreneurs, such as Astor, Carnegie, Vanderbilt, Drew, Gould, Sage, Rockefeller, Stanford and

Morgan, provided role models and created a climate conducive to its growth."*

Imagine yourself one of the turn-of-the-century immigrants who arrived in vast numbers while these titans of industry were having their way with the continent, its natural resources, the American people, and the nation's laws. You sweated in your lowly job and came home after twelve or fifteen hours of work to your family huddled in a cheap cold-water flat while the great men built castles for themselves. But you didn't begrudge them—you admired them. They were showing the way things were done. In the land of opportunity, you saw, the idea was to take what you could get. Those striving newcomers kept their eyes open for a rung, a way up.

Prohibition provided it. Suddenly there was a runaway consumer demand—on every block of every street in every town—waiting to be filled. The illegality of the product must have seemed charming to recent immigrants. It was like declaring it against the law to breathe oxygen. Everyone knew that people were going to continue to drink. But astoundingly, the Volstead Act hamstrung the entire industry involved in the production and sale of alcohol, leaving the field wide open.

The term "organized crime," I learned, came into being in part as a way to use ethnicity as a dividing line. The Irish, Jewish, and Italian mobs that grew up around the business of providing alcohol during Prohibition, and the American mafia that was weaned to maturity on it, were not so different in their tactics from Astor and Vanderbilt. But the label put them in a different category. There's a suggestion, among scholars of the field, that, as with the impetus behind Prohibition, the

* While some of the more ruthless features of nineteenth-century capitalism were later blunted by laws, Michael Woodiwiss, another author on the history of organized crime, asserts that the business culture these men established continues in America's largest corporations to this day, giving them the power to defraud the public in everything from drug policy to environmental regulations, to the point where "much of [the nation's] business activity can be defined as simple racketeering."

concept itself was a kind of official complement to the uncouth work of the KKK—it was invented as a way to separate "real" Americans from the ethnic gangs of newcomers.

So THEN, RUSS SHORTO, my grandfather, enters the scene here, in the same way that thousands of others did. "This is where they lived. Uncle Tribby, my parents. All those families packed into one house. Animals in the backyard. The pig under the porch." I'm sitting with my parents in the car outside a row of houses on a steep hill in the Conemaugh Borough section of Johnstown. My dad is riffling through memories, his own colliding with things his parents told him about life here before he was born; it's a four-generation pileup of ruminations. "Baba had a still down there. That's how she supported the family."

I'd heard before how Russ's mother—my dad's grandmother—operated a still in the basement. Mary, recently widowed, grieving and in need of money to support her brood—would fill empty Coke bottles with booze, stopper them with corks, and send the older kids out to the mill entrance to sell them.

Russ was six when Prohibition began, and nineteen when it ended. He was the oldest boy, the man of the house. He dropped out of school in the eighth grade. His real education, his chance at success, at a life different from what his father had been able to achieve in America, came thanks to the country's alcohol ban, which was rooted in the seemingly eternal battle over American identity.

I don't think my great-grandmother's basement still was her own idea and execution. For one thing, her situation matches closely with what was going on elsewhere in the country. Bootlegging gangs sprang up everywhere. The commonest way for gang leaders to get product was to pay people to set up stills in their homes, and a goodly number of the operators were women, typically single mothers desperate for income. In a study of female bootleggers during Prohibition in New Orleans, for instance, Tanya Marie Sanchez found that

> most alleged bootleggers were between the ages of thirty and forty. Most were widowed, divorced, or separated from their husbands, who were usually stevedores, laborers, or grocers. Female bootleggers were almost always mothers, who were often burdened with numerous children. A surname analysis of alleged bootleggers indicates that most of the women were of immigrant stock, usually of Irish, Italian, Spanish, or Jewish ancestry, and most resided downtown, in working-class neighborhoods.

All of this fits Mary Shorto to a tee. So do the rationales that Sanchez identifies:

> For working-class mothers, bootlegging was both a convenient and lucrative method of supplementing meager family incomes. The production of alcoholic beverages was easily done in the home, for food and beverage preparation were traditional female domestic activities. Bootlegging also allowed mothers to earn money while remaining near their children. Although their activities put their children in proximity to alcohol, this posed no great moral dilemma for most female bootleggers, who appear to have been immigrants or children of immigrants whose cultures embraced a positive view of alcohol. For many white ethnic mothers, the making and selling of alcohol was both culturally acceptable and economically necessary.

The reason I don't think Mary was alone in operating her still is that it was precisely around this sort of activity that Italian men of a certain stripe, in cities large and small, formed the groups that would evolve into the American mafia. And one such man appears on the scene at this time in Johnstown. His name was Philip Verone. When I say he appeared on the scene I don't mean that he was a romantic interest of Mary's. She had already taken care of that. Not too long after Antonino's death she had done the practical thing and gotten herself remarried, to one of her Italian boarders, a man named Anthony Tucci, whom everyone called Tork.

Or rather, my family had always assumed they married. I was mildly perplexed that I couldn't find marriage license on file for them when I began my family research. Later, however, a genealogist named Julie Pitrone Williamson, who had assisted me with earlier puzzles, emailed me out of the blue with information she had found proving that, just like my great-grandfather, Anthony Tucci had had a wife and child in Italy whom he had left behind when he emigrated to work in America. Mary's luck, it seems, was to be the second "wife" of not one but two two-timers. Which makes me wonder how prevalent this sort of thing was among those Italian immigrant men.

This second husband, Tork, was even rougher than she was. "He was like a wild man," said Eugene Trio, one of his step-grandchildren, "built like a boar, with thick fingernails. He could carry a hundred-pound sack like it was nothing. He didn't wash too often." The wildness doesn't seem to have bothered Mary unduly; her last child, Nancy, was with Tork. And there are reflections among Mary's grandchildren that suggest that Tork and Mary settled into a comfortable companionship—people recall them sitting on porch of an evening, Tork wearing a straw hat, passing a jug of wine back and forth, no fussing with glasses for them.

But there aren't many indications that Tork provided what you would call a father figure for Russ, who would have sorely needed one. This is where Philip Verone came in. "The same guy who taught me taught your grandfather," one of my oldest informants told me early in my research. "His name was Verone. And he was a black-hander."

"Black Hand" is a kind of catch-all term that has been used to refer to the pre-mafia in the United States. The first appearance of it in print was in 1903, when the *New York Herald* published the story of a wealthy Italian contractor who had received a letter threatening to dynamite his house if he didn't pay $10,000. It was signed *Mano Nera*. Shortly after, the *New York Times* was reporting on the "Black Hand Society" as a loose gang of blackmailers, which preyed mostly on other Italian immigrants.

The old boys in Johnstown had a slightly different take on the term. To them "black-handers" were certain men of the generation that came of age in the first two or three decades of the twentieth century. Some extorted other Italians, but others were seen as protectors of the community, who led the way through the ethnic thicket of a gritty and growing small city. The local leader was a man named Siciliano. His number two was Philip Verone.

As to what these men did, you might say that, with Italians squeezed into narrow economic corners, the black-handers looked for opportunities. Prohibition, and the instantaneous and exuberant demand for alcohol that came with it, was the chance of a lifetime. The network of stills cooking home-brewed spirits blossomed seemingly overnight—"Fumes of boiling mash filled the air," went one description. Ten months after Prohibition went into effect, the *Johnstown Tribune* reported that "'runners' for various 'big fellows' are peddling the stuff openly." I read that and see Russ and his sisters in Conemaugh Borough, literally between Coal Street and Steel Street, peddling their Coke bottles full of fire water, working for Mr. Verone.

The threat of being caught appears to have been modest. The mayor, Joseph Cauffiel, worked to block the sale of alcohol, but he had such an uphill struggle the accounts read like comedy. It wasn't unheard-of for him to hire a "special policeman" to inspect bars and cafés then later, as head of police court, find the same man brought before him following his inspection rounds, charged with drunkenness.

Yet there were crackdowns. In Mary Shorto's house, the kids were trained to roll the barrels out of sight if someone thought a cop was coming to the door. Once, they weren't in time; she was caught, convicted, and sent to the Cambria County Jail for six months. "Aunt Millie told me the kids were by themselves that whole time and they were so scared," Cindy Shorto said.

Russ therefore grew up under the cope of Prohibition justice. As a boy he learned what many never do their whole lives: that while the system appears rigid it is actually a highly fungible thing; that it's possible for a tough-enough guy to leverage guts and power and recast it according to his will. The most resonant struggle in the town during those years was between Mayor Cauffiel and a burly tavern owner named Dan Shields. Shields kept his bar open despite the ban on selling alcohol, ostensibly restricting himself to coffee and sarsaparilla, but in fact he was a flagrant flouter of the Prohibition law, and Cauffiel had him in his sights. The mayor gathered evidence that Shields was selling alcohol and charged him, following the lingo of the local ordinance, with operating a "tippling house." At first Shields failed to show up in court. When he was forced to, he gave as his defense that he didn't know the meaning of the verb "to tipple." The two met several times in court, each more heated. On one occasion Shields challenged the mayor to "meet me out in the woods."

The feud widened. Shields had not only broad shoulders but wide-ranging aspirations—in real estate and politics. One of his properties had been a brewery; he had sold it, but Cauffiel apparently discovered that it was still producing beer—29,000 gallons of it since Prohibition had taken effect. Shields was held to be still involved in the business and was charged with violating the Volstead Act as well as with bribery for paying off the police and sending money and gifts (chocolates and flowers) to a female federal officer. He was found guilty, appealed, and the case eventually went to the U.S. Supreme Court, where William Howard Taft, the chief justice (and former president of the United States) dismissed the ruling on a technicality. On retrial Shields was found guilty again and ordered to serve two years in prison. But he called on connections in Washington and managed to have President Herbert Hoover commute his sentence. He served no jail time, continued his confrontational relationship with the city government, and rose to greater heights, unveiling an innovative new building in downtown Johnstown: an office and entertainment complex called the Capitol Building, with a splashy automobile showroom on the ground floor.

Shields's fiery relationship continued with the next mayor, Eddie McCloskey, Shields once accused him of lying at a city council meeting. "Nobody calls me a liar and gets away with it!" McCloskey replied. The two men fell on each other, and Shields landed several punches on the mayor's head before the police pulled him off. Despite collaring Shields, they had to be impressed by his pugilism: McCloskey was a former prizefighter.

Shields's battles with the city government carried on over the whole of the 1920s and into the 1930s, culminating with him becoming mayor in 1936, and provided a local counterpoint to the robber-baron activities of previous decades—provided a model, that is, to Johnstown's Italian bootleggers of how to work the system. You make connections. You bribe. You use guile. And if need be, you knock heads.

HERE, MAYBE, I begin to make some headway with Russ. At some point in his teens he caught the eye of the black-hander Mr. Verone. This Verone was a very short man, and a tough one, the kind who sees himself as a neighborhood protector. Maybe Russ showed some smarts to Mr. Verone in calculating what his family had taken in over a given week on bootlegged booze and what the gang owed them. Maybe Verone also singled him out because of his status as the oldest male in his family: he knew the kid would need a leg up in the world. Or maybe Russ took the initiative: feeling the lack of a strong father figure, desperate to get ahead, he offered himself to Verone. However it happened, the boy went into training.

Gambling was going to be the next big venture. It was already booming. Gambling was like alcohol under Prohibition. It was illegal but everybody did it. There was an endless market for it. And as the gang moved from booze to gambling, it took on an increasingly ethnic character. There was an unspoken subtext to the training: Italians couldn't expect much in the way of respect or opportunities in WASP-ruled America, so they had to carve their own path. I don't have a recording of those training sessions, but I have the memory of someone else who, several years later, was also trained by Verone. This man—I'll introduce him shortly—would become Russ's protégé.

Verone taught Russ cards. How to gamble, what the odds were on getting a flush or two pair, when to fold. But not just that. Getting ahead in an unfair world meant you had to improve the odds. Tony remembers being a boy watching his father at the dining-room table practice for hours at dealing the second card without the sleight-of-hand being noticed. Like an athlete, he had a regular warm-up routine before a big game.

Verone also taught Russ a new word: "skeech." Maybe it was of Italian origin—*schiacciare*, to squeeze. It meant to cheat at dice. Not by loading them. You had to be able to do it with normal, unadulterated dice. Here's how Russ's protégé characterized the teaching:

"Philip Verone was the best dice man I ever met in my life. He had me practice and practice and practice. I could get a pair of dice and I could skeech 'em. I could roll a two—two aces—when I wanted. I could throw anything I wanted. After I was taught that, he says, 'Now I'm gonna give you the hard part.' He had a banking board, like they have in Vegas. Now he says, you gotta learn to do exactly what you been doing, but with that banking board. And man did I fuck up. But he taught me. You do this and you do that and you do this. But you don't do that! He taught me right from wrong when it came to dice. That was his specialty."

In December 1933, Pennsylvania became one of the last three states to ratify the Twenty-First Amendment to the Constitution, which repealed the Eighteenth Amendment and allowed the whiskey to start flowing again. Three years before, a movie called *Chasing Rainbows* had hit theaters—smarmy and lackluster, but with two memorable features. One was a sequence in color, which made audiences gasp. The other was the song that ended the film: "Happy Days Are Here Again." It had been a hit then; now, three years later, it became a kind of national anthem. In Johnstown as elsewhere, the party spilled into the streets; people cheered passing beer trucks as if they were carrying President Roosevelt himself (who had been elected in part for championing repeal).

But the darkness that had precipitated the ending of Prohibition— the Great Depression—didn't go away. A major impetus behind repeal, besides the demand for alcohol, had been the jolt to the economy that would come with reopened distilleries and breweries: half a million new jobs, millions in revenue for the depleted Treasury. Four years on, with unemployment hovering around 25 percent, the Depression was as devastating in Johnstown as other places. Yet it was a boon to the new industry that Russ had hitched himself to. When you're down and out, do you not crave all the more the thrill of hope that gambling brings?

So Russ's character was formed by Prohibition. And by the time he was nineteen he felt he was ready. Verone had taught him well. And not just in the technical and mechanical stuff, the use of the wrist and fingers to control the dice. He had given him something else, or helped tease it out of him.

And here I do feel that I've got my finger on something elemental about my subject. A philosophy. It was distilled from the hard life in the Sicilian mountains, a life of which Russ himself had no direct experience but whose lessons had been pressed into him by the ghostly presence of his father and further kneaded by his omnipresent mother. It was buffed by the flinty prejudice that ruled America's towns, large and small. And it flourished in the encouraging climate of early twentieth-century American business, of capitalism in the raw. You figured out what people wanted and you gave it to them—or better yet you pretended to. You perfected a craft: of *seeming* to fulfill their need. It was a wisdom that characterized a profession that spans every nation, era, and background but became something of a hallmark of this period of American history. *The cheat.* That defines my subject, as well as any pat term could. Russ was a cheat.

6

The Made Man

THE AMERICAN MOB came into being in the '30s and early '40s. That's my own reckoning: others date it to the 1920s. Either way, that's a long time period for the "coming into being" phase, and it's a big country. In other words, there are good reasons for the multiplicity of theories and narratives regarding its founding.

As far as I can tell from stitching together archival and book research with my more intimate interview-based inquiries, two things were happening simultaneously in the formative era, one of which was represented by Russ and the other by his partner and brother-in-law, Joe. One: the old way was persisting. Gangs, which had previously used Prohibition as a moneymaker, had switched to gambling after the passage of the Twenty-First Amendment and in the midst of the Great Depression. They were operating small outfits to take advantage of all those dreaming of a strike. Often the scales were tipped in these games: in other words, the con was on. This was what Russ was up to in his late teens and twenties. Shooting craps and using his skeeching skills to get the dice to fall his way. Motoring up and down the hills of Johnstown, running a traveling gambling enterprise out of the spacious trunk of his Packard. A freelancer, working with a couple of pals, offering a service, and if circumstances were right shaking down a customer.

The mob, meanwhile, came to town in the person of Little Joe, my great-uncle. He was born in Reggio di Calabria, just across the strait from Antonino Sciotto's hometown—the province forms the toe of the boot that is giving Sicily a kick. His infant lungs filled with sea air as his parents made their passage in 1910. The family stayed long enough in their first American home, Philadelphia, to become comfortable with it, so that they would later choose to return. But not too long after their arrival Little Joe's father, Mario Regino, or sometimes the last name appears as Regina, got work in a coal mine a few miles north of Johnstown and lugged everyone across the state and into the wooded hills.

I don't know which of the companies in the area lured Senore Regino, but there were four: the Conemaugh Smokeless Coal Company, the Cramer Coal, Coke & Stone Company, Lackawanna Coal & Coke, and Baker Furnace. Each was located in a company town, with names like Boltz, Claghorn, and Smokeless. All were small operations, employing between twenty and fifty men, so these were tiny fiefdoms in the wilderness, in which every aspect of immigrant life was controlled by the company. The sensory impressions that defined the boy's life and his notion of the world as he grew included: flimsy worker housing; marching to the company store for your household needs; soot-flecked air; the low surrounding mountains bristling with forest; the glow of the charcoal pits; the high totem-like stack of the furnace. Italian and Polish men, with baggy clothes and hard-set faces, working their eternal, grinding shifts, then returning to the four cheap walls within which each family strived to maintain its Old World ways. And all the while the gossip from nearby mines forming an incessant stream: of accidents, deaths, explosions, lies, cover-ups, abuse. Worker grievances building to occasional defiant strikes.

Mounted police thundering in to keep peace. Power manifesting itself in guns and horses. A crack of gunfire or a whip. Then back to work.

As Joe grew and internalized the truth of power, he eventually discovered he wasn't going to do too much of it—growing, that is. He stayed short, and it contributed to his toughening. Johnstown, the big city, was twelve or so twisty miles from the company towns. He shows up in 1928, aged twenty-one, getting the hell out of the hellish setting in which his parents had raised him.

The town must have seemed like Philly in miniature. It had a wealthy class of men—company vice presidents, department-store general managers, office managers, doctors and lawyers—lording through the streets in herringbone suits and homburgs. And the women at their sides looked even classier than them. They would have shone like diamonds, these couples. Marks, targets. But even the working-class people here had money compared to the mining towns. Joe quickly got busy distancing himself from the mole-like existence his father had been forced into. He set himself up on a career path, shoving a gun in people's faces and getting them to cough up their dough.

Then before you know it he's busted, charged with "pointing firearms, stick-up, and assault and battery."

For whatever reason, maybe to get out of the mines, maybe to try to extricate their oldest son from his bad influences, his parents pulled up stakes soon after this and returned to Philadelphia. And there they all are in the 1930 census, living in a tidy-enough little shack, at 1003 McKean Street: Mario and Virginia, their son Joe, who has gotten a job as a truck driver, and Joe's four younger siblings.

But if his parents thought they were keeping him out of trouble, in reality they transferred their boy from the bush leagues to the majors. The neighborhood they had moved into—logically, because it was packed with Italian immigrants—was the home of the nascent South Philadelphia mob. Passyunk Avenue, ten blocks from the Regino residence, formed the central thoroughfare in the territory of John "Nozzone" (Big Nose) Avena, who molded the city's Prohibition-era bootlegging gangs into a professional gambling operation centered around the numbers—that is, into the Philly mob.

Avena (whose nose wasn't so big) cut a figure: posing for a mug shot in a three-piece suit, striped tie, and straw-boater, he would have been a natural role model for a toughened kid—certainly a more manly one than Joe's father, who went from digging in a hole underground to selling flowers on the street. I don't know what Joe's relationship was to Avena, whether he became an acolyte or right-hand man, whether he hung around him or admired him from a distance, but considering how faithfully he would later copy the features of Avena's organization, transplanting Philadelphia's mob template to Johnstown, he got close enough for it to matter.

As soon as the kid hit the streets he was embedded in Avena's operation. The family moved to Philly in 1930, or maybe in 1929; by 1932 he had been arrested for "suspicion of highway robbery" as well as "larceny of auto" and "larceny by trick and fraud." The latter is such a resonant phrase to someone not versed in criminology that I had to dwell on it, and spent a few hours' worth of pleasant googling. The more familiar part of the phrase, "larceny," is (in the words of *A First-Year Course in Criminal Law* by Daniel Yeager) "non-forcible" theft: in other words, stealing without a struggle. It involves acquiring property from its rightful owner without resistance but also "non-permissively." Pickpocketing is an example. The trick-and-fraud part translates as "by false pretenses." "By trick and fraud" lifts the theft in question onto a higher plane. You're working creatively, fabricating an illusion, scamming. Young Joe was learning how to con.

Not long after, Joe returned to Johnstown for a visit. I don't know what his motivation was, but I have a feeling it had to do with a place called the Dew Drop Inn on Main Street. It was a funny little makeshift building with a corrugated roof at the corner of Central Park;

you bought popcorn and candy there then sat on a bench and fed the pigeons. I think Joe had met the girl behind the counter before he went to Philly and couldn't get her out of his head. Carmella Shorto—she went by Millie—was a raven-haired seventeen-year-old who had the self-possession of a woman in her twenties. Joe fell into a routine: he would wander into the Dew Drop, linger, buy a drink from her, wrack his brain for some small talk, then come back in a while and do it again. "I never had so many sodas in my life," he would tell her later, in their married years. She was below the age of consent in Pennsylvania, so they ran off to Cumberland, Maryland, just across the state line, where they found a preacher willing to marry them.

Then he brought her back to Philly. She didn't like it there—too big, too noisy and dirty—but she had hitched herself to him and Philly was where his business lay. There were some bumps in the road. In 1933 he was arrested for "conspiracy" and "narcotics—suspicious person" as well as for "maintaining a gambling house." But that came with the territory. He was getting the hang of things. He started using an alias, and took a liking to WASPish-sounding alter-egos. He was a great admirer of America's rapacious style of capitalism, and everyone knew that *Forbes* magazine was its bible. Joseph Forbes had a very nice ring to it. Sometimes he altered it to Joseph Ford. Nothing said American business more than Ford.

Joe and Millie conducted their courtship in the early days of the Great Depression. By now half the banks in Philadelphia had closed their doors. Some of the boys apparently saw this as an opportunity akin to Prohibition. They set up a counterfeiting ring, of which Joe was a part. The FBI had reorganized in its modern guise only a year before; agents were alert for just such activity. In November 1936 they busted the ring. Joe was hit hard: an eighteen-month prison sentence.

He refused to name his principal accomplice in court, and he held his silence in prison. When he got out he was rewarded for his trustworthiness in a manner that tracked broader changes that were taking place. In the aftermath of Prohibition, the mob was reorganizing on a national scale. According to some accounts, the leaders of crime syndicates in big cities like New York and Chicago were enamored of U.S. corporations, with their efficiency, their ability to game the system and their naked lunges for money. They had the idea to copy the mechanisms by which corporations spread. Throughout the 1930s the heads of the top crime organizations held a series of meetings in Chicago, Kansas City, and New York at which they divided the country into regional territories. Each then began sending out branch managers to set up regional offices.

The man Regino had shielded was a rising force named John LaRocca, who was at that moment becoming a power in Pittsburgh. I'm imagining a meeting in which LaRocca, appreciative of the younger man's *coglioni*, wanted to express his gratitude. They had a lot in common. Both had been born in Italy and spent their youth in western Pennsylvania, where LaRocca had worked in the mines starting at age fourteen. LaRocca had a string of convictions—assault, larceny, receiving stolen property, running a lottery—that closely matched Regino's.

But he was developing a sense of savvy that set him apart from the previous generation. As in other cities, Prohibition-era Pittsburgh had been a free-for-all of mob violence. The first acknowledged boss of the city was shot and killed in 1929; the next, Giuseppe Siragusa, aka "the yeast baron of Allegheny County" (he supplied the ingredients for illegal brewers) was gunned down after only two years on top, but his was the reign during which nationwide consolidation began, when, in New York, Salvatore Maranzano created the Five Families and declared himself "boss of all bosses." Siragusa started sending tribute payments to Maranzano, a system that outlived the two men (who were both killed in 1931). The next man to take control in Pittsburgh, John Bazzano, lasted only a year. But John LaRocca in Pittsburgh and Little Joe Regino in Johnstown would bring in a new, quieter, more businesslike era. The two men would stay on top in their respective territories into the 1980s.

Maybe in those meetings in the late 1930s Regino talked up Johnstown and the money the steel mills were producing there. Johnstown, and Cambria County, was within the orbit that LaRocca was in the process of dominating. The two men liked each other, trusted each other. They could work together.

So, after dutifully waiting out her husband's prison term, Millie got her way—she got to go back home.

Russ was waiting for them. Joe had met Russ, Millie's brother, a few years before, not long after Joe began hanging around the Dew Drop Inn. While Joe and Millie were in Philadelphia, and as Joe was detouring to experience the federal penitentiary at Lewisburg, Russ had been building a home and a business. One day in 1937 he went to the Central Cafe, the swankiest restaurant in town, the kind of place that featured lobsters on ice in the front window. Mary was working as hostess. People say he was wowed by her, just knocked off his feet. She was attractive, but in addition she had something that, given his limited experience of the world, he'd never encountered before. She had *it*. She was poised, sophisticated, worldly. She knew how to handle herself.

The *it* was very hard-won. My grandmother's was one of those grindingly painful early lives that so many first-generation Americans of the era endured. She was the eldest of eleven children who grew up packed with their parents into a small company house—no electricity, heat, or running water—in a little coal-mining community called Newtown in the hills above Johnstown. Her mother, Angeline, had emigrated from Poland, and not long after arriving had a child with a Croatian coal miner named Greganof. That child was Mary, my grandmother. Later her mother married a Serbian named Marco Yasika and they proceeded to have a slew of children. Marco worked in the mine; Angeline farmed the vacant lot next to their house and took care of the children. Mary was the anomaly: she was the oldest of the brood and the only one with a different father. When my sister Gina interviewed the youngest of her half-siblings, my great-aunt Vera—this was long after Mary's death—Vera broke down in tears as she struggled with her memories of her sister's life. Jeddo, as they all referred to her father and Mary's stepfather, routinely abused Mary, beating her with a belt, treating her like a servant over whom he had absolute power.

When she turned sixteen Mary got the hell out, bought a one-way train ticket to New York City. She got a job waitressing at a Childs Restaurant in Manhattan (one of America's first chain restaurants), and for the next ten years she wired money home. As some of her siblings got old enough she sent for them, got them jobs. When she moved back to Johnstown, circa 1936, she was an utterly different kind of woman from the miners' wives and daughters. She draped her tall frame in fashionable dresses and favored feathered hats and fur collars. She talked fast and with assurance. Her body language served notice: nobody was going to fuck with her ever again.

And what did Russ have to offer? He was a man on the make. He had opened a billiards room in the borough of Franklin. It was a couple of miles out of town, but only a few steps from the big metal gate that gave entrance to the mill where Bethlehem Steel fashioned railroad cars. When Russ brought her to his pool hall she must have been impressed by his upwardly mobile ambition and his smarts in choosing the location: workers came off their shifts and made straight for the tables. Plus, he was a bad boy, and that had its charm.

It was unusual in those days of ethnic enclaves for a Sicilian to court a non-Italian, but they fell for each other hard. He became a fixture at her mother's dinner table, got used to haluski and halupki, and to the smell of cooked cabbage penetrating his clothes. He'd toss out a Sicilian expression or two and make her brothers and sisters laugh.

Russ and Mary were married by the time Joe was out of prison

Russ as a young mobster.

and he and Millie returned to Johnstown. They were brothers-in-law now, family, and Joe was coming back to Johnstown with a plan, an imprimatur: to start a gambling franchise. Russ knew the town from precisely that angle. They joined forces. The outfit had come to town.

AND THE PLACE was dripping with potential. The Great Depression had lifted. Joe and Russ formed their alliance right about the time Germany invaded Poland. War was on in Europe, and within a short while the steel plants in town were hiring everyone they could. The Franklin plant, outside the door of Russ's pool hall, took a single order for 2,800 railcars. All of a sudden all the sidewalks in downtown Johnstown were packed. No, the people weren't rich, but that was just it. All these recent immigrants, or children of, these Azars and Babyaks, Espositos and Furnaris, Gomulkas and Haselrigs and Kohuths and Vitales and Vitkos and Yankos and Yarinas and Zapolas and Zarubas and Zieglers were working their hearts out, tramping day after day into the mills and the factories spread all over town. They were longing for the bigtime, or at least for something a little bigger and better than what they had.

And how did you get that? The mob had an answer for you. With 50-to-1 odds on a bet, somebody had to be the 1, right? It only cost a dime. Or you could shoot for something riskier—600-to-1, say—and if you hit, you were rich. There were so many ways you could win. *Winning.* America, as everybody knew, was for winners; that was practically written into the Constitution. Think of how much of a winner you were already just by being here. Your parents had come from some shithole in Latvia or Kilkenny, from hardship and disease and turmoil, getting pissed on by higher-ups, their faces streaked with dirt, their infants clotted with feces, sweating blood and nothing to show for it; oh the stories they told. Then there were all the stories that were too ugly for them to tell but that were written on their faces, that glowed deep within their eyes: the pogroms, the incest, the beatings, the children who bled, the heated prayers to the blessed Virgin for deliverance. And now what were you? A man with a house and a wife he had a full right to come home to, proffering a bag of knobby pork sparkling with fat and a big ripe onion for her to cook up; but wait, there's the mattress, let's get busy, let's do what this instant of joy in our veins impels us to do. You were truly a king of your castle, proud of your home and hearth. Your wife had babies who were born with expectations—which *you* have given them. You glowed with pride at this. All you needed to do was give them a little bit more. Running water, say.

That's what I imagine Russ and Joe talking about as they schemed to provide a comprehensive service package for the town. They were in the business of dreams. That plus shaking down the honchos when they got a chance, the men who ran the coal mines and the U.S. Steel and Bethlehem Steel plants, and the Griffith-Custer Steel Company and the Albright Equipment Company and the National Radiator

Company, bigshots in their monstrous houses up on the hill in West-mont, who deserved to have their pockets picked.

The start was modest. Joe joined Russ at the Franklin Billiards Parlor. Besides the tables, they were running a few games: craps, some cards, and Joe, working with the boys in Pittsburgh, might have intro-duced tip seals. Then, on October 13, 1939—Friday the thirteenth, wouldn't you know—the cops showed up. As the mills had revived with the economy—employment at Bethlehem Steel alone soared to 12,000 this same month—gambling enterprises had sprung up all over town, like a sudden infestation of weeds, and the same local leaders who had ardently backed Prohibition, and were annoyed at its repeal, wanted the authorities to do something about it. So, a crack-down; Joe was busted and locked up. The subpoena shows he already had his nickname: *Commonwealth of Pennsylvania v. John Doe—"Lit-tle Joe"—Joseph Regino.* Russ had to put up $1,000 bail, a large sum for such an offense. It was meant as a serious warning.

They took the hint and shut down the gambling operation, but only to regroup. An odd little drama then played out, which maybe defined this transitional era. Russ went back to what he had been doing before, running games out of the trunk of his car. And a Cam-bria County detective, a tall, heavyset, black-haired, blue-eyed fellow named John Carroll, was waiting for him. Carroll was fifty-three. He was a native of Johnstown who, after briefly working as a motorman on a streetcar in his youth, joined the police force, and had been at it now for more than twenty years. He took his job seriously. He was used to punks, who vanished once you taught them a lesson, and that was the logic he employed now. On February 5, 1941, a Wednesday night, he spied a group of men gathered around the back of Russ's car and moved in. He arrested Russ for "having in his possession, main-taining and setting up a Gaming and Gambling Device," which prob-ably meant a portable craps table. Officer Carroll took him in, booked him, filled out the paperwork. As with Joe a couple of years earlier, the $1,000 bail was meant as a serious warning, an amount that was intended to stop the kinds of hooligans Officer Carroll had dealt with in the past. Russ pleaded guilty and called a friend named Antonio Pantana, who showed up a little while later with the thousand bucks. Carroll released him.

But the following Monday the selfsame scenario played out: Detective Carroll, sensing something suspicious, tailed Russ, spotted him running a craps game out of his car, collared him, hauled him in, and sat him down on a long wooden bench while he laboriously pounded out the arrest report on a typewriter. Once again Russ pleaded guilty on the spot and blithely called another friend, Michael Graziano, who arrived with the $1,000 bail.

Was Detective Carroll beginning to think that something new was afoot? Was Russ intending to signal something—thumbing his nose at the cops? Or did he just figure that this was the price of doing business? I'd love to know what words they exchanged, but all I have are the pieces of paper that my dad and I requested one afternoon at the county courthouse in Ebensburg. I instantly understood Tony's reaction as the woman behind the counter handed over the thick stack of his father's arrests and indictments: "Well, I'll be a son of a bitch!" Here was cold documentary corroboration of so much of what he'd observed during his childhood. The stack reinforced his memories in complicated ways, reduced them to the humdrum level of bureaucracy but also elevated them, put an official stamp on them. We looked at each other, father and son, over the pile of our forebear's deeds, and silently exchanged a raft of feelings that are hard to put into words. Maybe we were thinking: *Somehow, this is who we are.*

Then, that Friday night, Russ upped the ante, so to speak. He put out the word that he was hosting a major poker event at his pool hall. Detective Carroll heard about it—surely Russ knew he would—and got a search warrant. He marched into the poolroom, past the tables, straight to the room in back where they were gathered, and busted him for the third time in nine days. Yet another colleague of Russ's, a guy named Nunzio Ziancola, arrived with the thousand bucks. Now it was clear: it was a little power struggle my dad and I were witnessing as we pored over the documents on my parents' dining-room table later that day, while my mom heated up leftover spaghetti and meatballs.* The detective was endeavoring to maintain the status quo. Russ was pushing toward something new.

Whatever Joe and Russ were building toward, the news that came over the local radio station, WJAC, on December 7, of the Japanese attack on Pearl Harbor, interrupted it. Over the next week a thousand local men signed up for the armed services. The draft had been in effect for the past year; both Joe and Russ had registered. Russ took a job working at the Franklin plant, which, because it was directly supporting the war effort, got him out of military service. Joe was drafted and prepared to head off to Camp Livingston, Louisiana.

They sketched out a plan for the future before he left town. Joe had brought with him to Johnstown a kind of playbook. Over the next few years he would painstakingly, item by item, put in place the features of the organization that John Avena, the boss of the Philadelphia mob (who had been gunned down on the street in 1936), had developed. There would be a numbers racket and a sports book: in other words, mass-marketing your product. And Joe would offer as well something for his elite customers, in the form of a couple of high-stakes gambling games at regular locations. He also adopted the same manner

---

* This is my family's elemental dish, the food equivalent of DNA. My mother learned it from Mary, my grandmother, who in turn got it from Russ's sisters. My aunts make it; so do I. In one pan, brown country pork ribs and chicken pieces. In another, brown chopped onions and celery in olive oil; add garlic. Add tomato sauce, tomato puree, tomato paste, basil, oregano, parsley, salt and pepper to the meat. Add the vegetables to the meat. Add a green pepper and let stew. Remove the pepper. The meatballs: ground pork, ground beef, ground veal, stale bread, Romano cheese, chopped onion, celery, parsley, raw egg, salt and pepper. Fry the meatballs, add some to the sauce and keep some separate.

of dealing with problems: handling them himself rather than passing them on. "I like to settle these things myself" was a motto of Avena's. For the old boys in Johnstown, Joe's most defining trait was his silent assumption of authority.

Most important, there would be a new strategy for dealing with the authorities. No longer would Russ and Joe hide out in a little borough on the outskirts, working out of a car and ducking the cops like neighborhood scamps. That was Prohibition-era behavior. It was the 1940s now; this was the modern world. They were grown men and they would comport themselves the same way outfits in bigger cities had been doing for some time. Rather than run from the system, they would become part of it.

7

The Organization

Russ and Mary's first child, born three days after Christmas in 1938, was a boy. Russ might have considered himself fully American, but that didn't mean he couldn't also honor Sicilian tradition and his own (distant) memory of his father—Antonino, the immigrant, who had died when he was six—by naming the boy after him. Tony's earliest memories were of life during wartime. The little family was living in Franklin Borough, two miles from downtown Johnstown and one steep block up the hill from the Franklin mill gate. My dad and I sat there idling in the car one afternoon about seventy-five years after the fact as he recounted what might have been his earliest memory: walking down the precipitously sloping street in winter, his mother holding his hand in one of hers and carrying a black metal lunch pail in the other. They were on their daily mission, to deliver Russ his lunch. Where all the other mill workers brought sandwiches with them at the start of their shift, Mary delivered Russ a hot meal. "She'd pile spaghetti in one side, and there'd be something like a breaded pork chop, and a salad," another family member told me. "The other workers couldn't get over it."

Tony remembered this particular day because of what happened: Mary slipped on the ice and they both went careering down the hill. They slid all the way to where the guard was stationed, by the gate. (The fact that the town's steel plants had armed guards spoke to their importance. Fiorello La Guardia, New York's mayor, who served during the war as director of civil defense, said as much to a reporter when he was in town in 1942: "The Germans are pretty aware of Johnstown and its steel mills. It would probably be one of the central targets in an attack.")

The war years were a bad time to start a new venture. Everyone had a job, but there wasn't much to buy. Everything from meat to sugar to gasoline to alcohol was being rationed. No new cars were being produced; if you drove your car for anything but work or medical reasons, you got fined. All new construction was halted.

But Joe and Russ had ideas. Before Joe headed off for basic training in Louisiana they made an investment in the future. As I say, I believe Joe modeled the small-town mob setup they eventually created on that of John Avena's Philadelphia operation. Most of those features were part of the general mob template, but Joe copied something else that was particular to Avena. Avena was big on having a legitimate business as a front, and his, at the intersection of Twelfth and Webster Streets in Philadelphia, was a cigar store. Just before Joe headed for Louisiana, he and Russ opened a business on Main Street in Johnstown, two doors from city hall. They called it City Cigar. It was right there in the open, right in the middle of town, and it was going to be the center of everything.

They brought in a partner on City Cigar. John Strank was Czech, not Italian, but he was a good friend and he came with advantages. He was a neighbor of Russ and Mary's in Franklin. In his youth he had been imprisoned for robbery; it's possible either Russ or Joe did time with him in the Pennsylvania Industrial Reformatory in Huntingdon. Both men knew him well and trusted him. And there was something more. In the years following his youthful indiscretion Strank had joined the police force, and rose to become chief of police of the little borough of Franklin. As such, he knew everyone on the Johnstown police force. That would be useful.

They rode out the war in this fashion. Joe was away in the service for a couple of years (at the military base down South—he never saw action), then back just as the war ended. Russ stayed employed at the mill and worked part-time at the cigar store, which really was a cigar store at first, to which they slowly added nine pool tables in the vast room in the rear, with one billiards table front and center. Strank, a tall, lumbering man with a kindly face, oversaw the place.

A lot of their friends were overseas, fighting in Europe or the Pacific. One day the hard news came in that John Strank's nephew Michael, who was five years younger than Russ and had grown up with him in Franklin, had been killed in action on a little island in the Pacific called Iwo Jima. At about the same time a photo appeared in the paper showing six Marines raising an American flag on a mountaintop on the island. It was Mike's company in the picture—that was him in the middle of the group, hands gripping the flagpole. He'd been the sergeant tasked with planting the flag, the leader of the squadron, and now he was part of this new symbol of American pride. He died a week later on the island. The guys at City Cigar were sad and at the same time proud as hell: would-be mobsters with a hero in the family. For the rest of their lives, as that photo went around and around the world and became perhaps the most iconic image of the whole war, they would talk reverently about Mike's achievement.

Less than three months later the *Johnstown Tribune* ran the largest, inkiest headline of its history: V-E DAY PROCLAIMED. People were happy that fighting was over in Europe, but the mood was oddly subdued—after all, local boys were still dying in the Pacific. By contrast, on August 13, V-J Day, when victory over Japan became official, downtown erupted in a madhouse of confetti and honking horns.

Picture red-white-and-blue bunting, streamers shimmering down from rooftops. Picture Russ standing outside City Cigar, cigarette dangling from his lips and hands in his pockets, as thousands of people lined the sidewalk on Main Street, men in their baggy pants, jacketless in the heat, women in summer dresses, standing in the bright sunlight cheering at the marching bands and horse-drawn wagons separated by boxy DeSotos, Packards, and Pontiacs.

Tony was there, too, a few blocks away, age six, holding his mother's hand, gawping. Afterward, a big treat, they walked to the restaurant where Mary worked and he was allowed to order an open-faced sandwich.

I feel like these were pretty good times in that family of three. Russ, just past thirty, was feeling strong, like he was getting a foothold. He was still behaving himself at this point, as far as I can tell. He and Mary loved each other in the way that results when there's a strong physical attraction combined with genuine admiration of the other person's most prominent traits. She had squinty eyes; he called her Chinky. He meant it affectionately. She may not have told Russ yet as she sat watching Tony eat his celebratory meal, but Chinky was nearly two months pregnant with their second child.

Other elements in Russ's world were growing too. He began the gambling operation out of City Cigar almost immediately after President Truman announced the end of fighting in Europe, even before Joe got back to town. And as was happening in other small cities around the country, he started making payoffs to local officials around the same time. Russ and Joe were lucky in that they began their enterprise at a time when the municipal government was weakening. In the earlier part of the century Johnstown's mayor and council had been activists, laying out and then putting into effect large civic-improvement projects: building an airport, new schools, and a sports stadium. Since the Depression, local leaders had shifted into a laissez-faire mode of governing, doing little more than collecting taxes and providing basic services. Without a proactive system of oversight, officials had latitude to define their jobs, and to profit from them, as they saw fit.

The first mayor elected in the postwar period was from an old Johnstown family and had been educated at no less a place than the Wharton School before coming back home to enter politics. He was affable, cultured, smart, but he had his predilections. Ned Rose—people called him Red Nose because of his taste for strong spirits—became a regular at City Cigar, walking the thirty or forty paces from his office at city hall for a chat or a game of cards, and presumably left with an envelope in his pocket.

Despite a general feeling of relief that the war was over, it was a hectic and confused time in Johnstown, as in the country as a whole. No one knew what to expect in the near future, for nobody had been through anything like the circumstances of the past several years. Troops were streaming back home even as other men were signing up and leaving town for military stints. Some factories went out of business. The Sylvania plant, in which 850 workers made radar equipment and components for antiaircraft shells for the army, closed down the minute the war ended.

But after a period of adjustment Johnstown, along with other manufacturing centers in the region, from Cumberland, Maryland, to Wheeling, West Virginia, shifted onto an upward trajectory. Cambria County was a place where people made things, hard things, and that output—bricks, ceramics, radiators, sheet metal—was in greater demand than ever before. A year after the war's end Bethlehem Steel, now the biggest employer in town, poured more than $100 million into modernizing its Johnstown facility.

Russ and Joe were investing in their business as well. But there were kinks to be worked out. On June 2, 1945, three weeks after VE Day, with downtown still glowing in the expectation that all fighting would soon be over and as City Cigar was alive with the clack of balls, crowded with bettors and pool players, a familiar, hulking form darkened the doorway. Detective Carroll strutted in, holding aloft a search warrant in which he had earlier asserted to the presiding alderman that he had "reasonable cause to believe and he verily does believe that gambling equipment is illegally possessed and used and gambling is permitted at the City Cigar Store at 411 Main St, in the City of Johnstown, Cambria County, Pennsylvania, all of which is contrary to the Act of Assembly, and all of which your affiant expects to be able to prove." He inspected the premises, saw what he expected to see, collared Russ, and brought him in.

Russ hadn't perfected the payoff system, apparently. Detective Carroll surely knew what was afoot, but he was determined that the rule of law would prevail. He busted Russ five times at City Cigar between June 1945 and September 1946.

Then something changed in the two-man power struggle. Someone above him either explained things to Detective Carroll or had him transferred. Russ was never arrested again. The organization was in place.

LATE 1945. RUSS is walking down the street in Conemaugh Borough when he passes a group of guys shooting craps against the side of a building. Something about the kid with the dice makes him stop. Russ had a wry little twist of a smile he would whip out when something interested him. He looks down at the kid. *I know who taught you.* They start talking. The kid acknowledges that, yes, Philip Verone, the same diminutive black-hander who taught Russ how to skeech, was his mentor.

What's your name?

Mike Gulino.

Russ's eyebrows shoot up. *The coal kid?*

Everybody in town knew the coal story. The backdrop to it was a massive strike in 1937 involving coal miners, workers on the rail lines that supplied coal to the steel mills, and the mill workers. As such groups of workers nationally came to realize they were allies in a struggle against rapacious industrialists, and began to unionize, the mill and mine owners in Cambria County resisted forcefully. There were confrontations in front of the mill gate that summer, and a near riot downtown that included cars overturned, organized brick attacks, and a young scab being stripped naked by the strikers and paraded through the streets. A rumor went around that forty thousand coal miners from all around western Pennsylvania were going to invade Johnstown. Governor George Earle declared martial law and sent in the state police; on top of which three hundred and fifty "special deputies" were appointed, each receiving a helmet and a stick. With industry leaders calling the strikers things like "racketeers" and "Communists," it was a serious-enough instance of class warfare to make the *New York Times*.

Eventually the strike ended, but the situation remained tense over the next couple of years. The big newspapers proclaimed that the Depression was over, but nobody in neighborhoods like Woodvale and Conemaugh noticed. People were still struggling in the most basic ways—with hunger and cold. And every afternoon, at about four o'clock, a big old train loaded with coal trundled right past people's houses and came to a stop inside the Bethlehem Steel plant. Sure, they needed it to make steel, but what about basic human existence? The animosity, the class tension between hordes of impoverished locals and the men who ran the big steel and coal companies, had hardened. One winter day a gang of men—Italian, Black, Mexican—doused the railroad ties with gasoline and ignited it as the train was approaching. As it came screeching to a halt they rushed out, opened the hoppers, and half the neighborhood emerged from the alley behind Maple Avenue with buckets, tubs, anything that would hold coal to warm their homes.

The next day there was a knock on the door of the house of Mr. and Mrs. Gulino in Conemaugh. Mr. Esposito, who acted as the neighborhood MD despite his lack of formal medical training, asked to see their son, Mike. *Jack Ragno wants to talk to you.* Jack Ragno was the top black-hander in the area—in other words, the community leader. Mike was scared—lighting a fire on the tracks had been his idea—but he went to see him. Ragno was an old man who only spoke Sicilian, but Mike had grown up with the language. *I like what you did.* Mike shook his head: *I didn't do nothin'.* Ragno grinned. *Listen, the railroad cops are lookin' for you. They don't know it's a kid that was behind the business with the coal. But I put the word out: nobody talks.* Then the old man changed the subject: *I understand you like gambling.*

Jack Ragno figured he'd help the kid, give him a leg up. He sent him to Philip Verone, the same man who, eight years before, had taught Russ. Verone taught him to skeech dice. Once Mike was able to throw a seven or a pair of sixes at will, Verone introduced a banking board, complicating the throw, and they started all over again. Then Ragno sent him to study cards with a guy in Hornerstown. He was still in his teens, but he was already a pro.

Russ took an immediate liking to the kid. Russ was building something; he could use an assistant. Plus, while he knew half the town, all his friends were adults. He must have figured it would be handy to have somebody in touch with the younger crowd. In a short time, he formed a strong bond with Mike Gulino, stronger than he ever had with any of his three children.

The recurring theme of my early research into Russ and his world, the thing that stumped me, was the imponderability of my subject. All the early stories I'd culled featured him prominently but as an opaque center. I couldn't get a fix on him. Taking a historical approach, backing up to his parents and their migration to America, filling in the background, had yielded some fruit. I was developing a bit of . . . sympathy for the guy. But I couldn't say I felt I knew who he was—or that anyone I'd talked to who had known him knew who he was.

I was still meeting regularly with Frank Filia, my mother's cousin, who had pushed me onto this path. Sometimes we'd get together at Panera Bread, other times I'd go see him play the Thursday lunch set at the Holiday Inn downtown. John Pencola on piano and Frank on bass and vocals, making small talk with the customers enjoying the all-you-can-eat pasta buffet, then launching into "My Funny Valentine." When Frank took a break he'd come and sit with me. Often several of the guys from the old days would be there too. I had mentioned three or four times now how frustrated I was in trying to pierce the mystery of Russ. Before, Frank had shrugged, said something about how Russ was a quiet guy. Once he said, "Your dad once told me, 'Frank,' he said, 'I hardly knew my father.'" This time when I started to complain to Frank about Russ, he was nodding. "I know what you said, I get it. Listen, I been talkin' to somebody. He wasn't sure at first. But he's ready now. And believe me, nobody knew Russ like Mike."

I had never even heard Mike Gulino's name before. Somehow he was going to be the key to unlock the safe? Frank pulled out his flip phone and called him—"Remember who I told you wanted to talk to you?"—and we got an instant audience. "You won't believe this," he kept saying to me as the car swept past the concrete-reinforced banks of the river and wound up the hill.

Johnstown is such a small place, it turned out Mike lived less than half a mile from my parents. We pulled up next to an old frame house covered in brown shingles sitting next to a gravel-strewn lot. His wife, Eleanor, opened the door and ushered us in. "I know your parents . . . I knew your grandparents . . ." We walked through a living room covered in wall-to-wall beige shag carpet, with brown, 1970s-era furniture. Mike, the old man who'd once been the kid attracting Russ's notice with his dice play, was in the kitchen. He wasn't exactly a large man, but he had the presence of a giant. He was in his mid-eighties, needed a chair-lift to get up the stairs, was hooked up to oxygen, and was half-blind. His glasses made his eyes bulge. But sitting there at the kitchen table, with a Formica backdrop and an antipasto platter that Eleanor had laid out in the foreground, he seemed like some kind of king. Maybe he was hard of hearing; anyway, his voice thundered. And these were the first words he boomed at me:

"Everything you heard about your grandfather, just put it in the ashcan! Because I know you heard a lot of negative things, see? Nobody knew Russ! Not like I knew him!"

Mike had had a storied career. The first part of it was as Russ's right-hand man: "Everything I learned, I learned from Russ!" Later on, he had an operation that stretched from Florida to Las Vegas. He'd known Lucky Luciano, the man who invented the American mafia, and he once had Dean Martin sitting on his lap in a Vegas casino, crying over the death of his son. He was a powerful bookmaker in his time, active up and down the East Coast. But as he told me in a later interview—I ended up sitting down with Mike eleven times in all, not to mention spending a great deal of time corroborating his information—he didn't see himself as a bookie or a mobster: "I'm a con man. That's all I am." But he went on to say that he had lived by a personal code, which had formed in the rough old days of class and ethnic warfare. "I fucked a lot of people in my life," he told me. "But I only fucked people with money, greedy people, people that wanted to be fucked. I never fucked the workingman. I beat banks. I beat corporations. Fuckin' bastards deserved it."

An hour or so into our first meeting, Mike gave me what he believed was Russ's philosophy. He unspooled it carefully, in a way that made me think it was memorized. "You gotta understand that Russ was my mentor. I soaked up everything he said. And Russ once told me, 'Mike,' he says, 'there's two different kinds of people. With the first, you throw a handful of shit in a guy's face and he knows it's shit. You forget about that guy—you can't make money off him. But with the other kind, you tell him the shit you're feeding him is ice cream ... and he'll believe it. You let him think that—you get him to love the taste of it. *And then you take every fuckin' dime he's got.*'"

We were silent then in the kitchen, Mike, me, Frank, I not knowing quite how he expected me to react. It felt almost like he thought of himself as a spiritual leader to whom I had come for wisdom, and he had given it to me, but in the form of a riddle, and he was testing, waiting to see how I responded. I think eventually I nodded. Then he leaned in, breathing salami and with his big, bulbous, rheumy eyes up close, and he said, very seriously, "That's one of the most important things Russ ever told me."

At the end of our first interview Mike said something I didn't quite get. "I also knew your father very well when we were young. Maybe, because of Russ, some things were tough for your father." I didn't really know where to go with this. I was already standing, ready to leave. He waved it off. "But I'm glad we're having this conversation," he said. "I've had this on my mind for years and years."

So: THE LATE '40s. Clark Gable and Rita Hayworth. Pontiac Chieftains and Plymouth Club Coupes. The suburbs rising. Big bands starting to seem a bit stale and flabby while the arresting drama of the solo voice—Bing! Frank!—is suddenly and utterly vital to quelling the existential angst and swelling the passions of the returning troops and their ardent lovers. And then, of course, came all the booming that made the baby boom. Guys I interviewed who came of age in that era could get pretty worked up thinking back on it. "We're talkin' pre-Elvis, pre–sexual revolution. There was no porn. Everything was hush-hush and mysterious. The first time I took a girl to a motel, Jesus, I can't describe how exciting. Of course, I lasted about a minute."

Johnstown's mills and plants were at full production by 1947—

people were calling the place Little Chicago—and a textile industry took off as well, with a focus on bras and dresses. Workers had a little spare change, even after buying the wife a new Speed Queen washer. Russ wasn't swaggering around town—he wasn't like that. But he was on the move. He and Joe assembled the pieces of their empire deliberately and fairly rapidly.

A big part of the business plan involved the numbers. The numbers racket had originated in Harlem in the 1920s (an outgrowth of a nineteenth-century game called "policy"). Then, post-Prohibition, proto-mobster Dutch Schultz forced his way in by making the Black bankers who ran the game in their various neighborhoods "partners," and eventually squeezed them out. It was a sweet, simple game: pick three numbers and depending on the combination you could win up to six hundred times the amount you bet. It quickly spread around the country as a mafia staple, eventually to be replaced by state-run lotteries.

There'd been a numbers racket in Johnstown for a while now. It was run by Charlie Catillo. Charlie was an old friend of Russ's. But Joe told Russ they were going to do to him what Dutch Schultz and Lucky Luciano had done to onetime legendary Harlem bankers like Alex Pompez and Stephanie Saint-Clair (aka Madame Queen): give him a percentage in exchange for handing over his business. Joe was calling the shots on this, maybe under LaRocca's guidance. *We're takin' that business over. You tell Charlie we're gonna take care of him. But we're takin' that business.*

Russ told Charlie. And within a year Charlie was working for them, and the G.I. Bank was born. Russ built it into a citywide bank, and gave it the spiffy postwar rebranding, a name that blended the patriotic energy of the returning troops with the solidity of a financial institution. The numbers may have originated in Harlem, but everything about the game suggested a different neighborhood of New York City, one to which the rising Italian immigrants aspired: Wall

Street. Wall Street was, of course, the money establishment. It was largely closed to Italians, just as other arenas of the American establishment were. An Italian had about as much chance of becoming a stockbroker as of being elected president. So, piece by piece, they created their own version of the establishment world. And since, given the illegal nature of it, they couldn't rely on the authorities to settle disputes between various parties, they had to do it themselves. That's one way of looking at the American mob.

What Russ and Joe were building in Johnstown—what Joe had taken part in in Philly, what guys like Lucky Luciano and Frank Costello and Salvatore Maranzano had created in New York—was a mirror of American capitalism. They took to the ruthlessness of that system, its rapaciousness, but also maintained the awareness that you couldn't just take without giving something back. You were selling a product. Booze was the first product. Then, after Prohibition, in prudish mid-twentieth-century America, the vehemence with which gambling was denounced and criminalized precisely angled it for these men as the next income generator. The general public's deep longing for it (there were an estimated 50 million American gamblers in the early '50s), combined with the puritanical forces that outlawed it, made for a sellers' market.

The numbers was different from other forms of gambling in a way that made it particularly appealing. Its very language mimicked Wall Street. In the lingo of the numbers, men like Russ and Joe were "bankers." Early players in Harlem talked not about placing bets but "making an investment." The authors of *Playing the Numbers: Gambling in Harlem Between the Wars* suggest that Black New Yorkers turned to the numbers in the 1920s in part because they were shut out from most banking activities. Sure, banks were happy to take their money and let them open savings accounts, but "borrowing money to open or expand a business, or indeed for any purpose, was almost an impossibility for African Americans." There was no such thing as a Black person getting a mortgage to buy a house, for instance. Blacks couldn't even work as bank tellers. Thinking of the nickels and dimes you gave to your bookie as an investment, therefore, gave you a feeling of legitimacy, of buying a stake in your future. Many looked at it as being as certain an investment as any other. By playing the same number every day, you were putting money into a kind of account; you believed that one day your number would hit and you would get back your original stake, plus interest.

The Italian men of Russ's generation, who wanted to be players in the American game as much as their WASP counterparts did, saw bookmaking as akin to running an investment firm. You were providing a financial service. Yes, you stood to make a fairly staggering profit—around 40 percent on every bet—but so did the titans of the legit financial industry. Joe knew the essential thing was to establish a system that had the regularity and convenience of a bank. His goal was to create something his customers trusted. He wanted it to be a bedrock institution in the community. I don't know if he achieved that, but everyone over a certain age I talked with in Johnstown saw the G.I. Bank as a kind of service, one that offered an attractive product and that was reliable. Trust began with the fact that you could look up the winning numbers yourself, Monday through Friday, in the black and white of the *Tribune*. They were the closing numbers of the New York Stock Exchange.

And for Joe and Russ, it was self-evident that you linked to the community by being *in* the community. You wanted to be as much a part of residents' lives as the post office was. So you made your product available wherever people gathered. At barber shops, like Angelo's in the Johnstown Bank & Trust Building, Harry's on Fourth Avenue, or Coppola's in Conemaugh. Your bookies stopped in at the bowling alleys, at the American-Slovak Social Club and the Polish National Alliance Club. They took customers' loose change over the counter at candy stores, like Kels Konfectionary Korner, and at novelty shops, hardware stores, and even in law offices. When people stopped in for a bowl of chili or a couple of hot dogs for lunch—at the Corner Inn, Franklin Lunch, Coney Island Hot Dogs, or in the Glosser Brothers Department Store cafeteria—the G.I. Bank was there. When you moseyed up to the bar for a beer after work, at the Hill Top Tavern, Jim Dandy's, the Essex House, the Four Leaf Clover, the Steel Bar, or the Terminal Café; at Lill's, Marie's, Mike's, Steve's, Angie's, Bertha's, Tony's, or Zip's, there was someone—maybe the bartender, maybe your wife's kid brother—able to take your ten cents or your four bits and record your favorite numbers. By many estimates, more than half the town played the G.I. Bank at its height.

Money poured into the office above City Cigar. Once a week Joe would call LaRocca, make an appointment, and get a driver to take him to Pittsburgh. In the trunk (I assume it was in the trunk: nobody I talked to could answer this question) was LaRocca's cut. As for the rest, Russ and Joe needed to launder it. I don't think, ultimately, they were in the business of crime per se. It was business *qua* business that they were after; criminal activity happened to be the ignition. So they surveyed the town for further opportunities. Joe and Millie weren't big on making the scene, but Russ and Mary liked to dress up and live a little, which gave them a perspective. They went to fancy supper clubs in Pittsburgh, and occasionally in Atlantic City. (I have a photograph of the two of them, smiling and looking sharp, Mary's neck and ears adorned with pearls, enjoying the show at Club Harlem, Atlantic City's world-renowned Black nightclub, which hosted the likes of Ella Fitzgerald and Cab Calloway.) With wartime restrictions at an end and locals having so much more spending money, wasn't it about time Johnstown had a high-class entertainment option?

I don't know what deal Joe and Russ struck with Chris Contakos, the owner of the building on Franklin Street that housed the Central Cafe, where Mary had worked and where she and Russ met, but they took it over one floor at a time. The top floor became a boxing gym;

the one below it they turned into Capitol Bowling Lanes, where Tony remembers working as a pin setter when he was a kid. But their pride and joy was the Melodee Lounge, on the second floor, above Central Cafe. They threw a mort of cash into creating a lavish interior that made you feel like you weren't in the middle of some western Pennsylvania steel town but rather on East Sixtieth Street in New York, at the Copacabana. They hired a chef for the place who could do a two-inch steak that sizzled as it was laid before you and a bar manager who understood the importance of pushing not just top-shelf liquors but colorful drinks to appeal to the ladies: Grasshoppers, "Punch Romaine," and the Millionaire. They hired a booking agent out of Pittsburgh who started lining up rising stars like Sammy Davis Jr. and the Will Mastin Trio. Russ understood that white Americans were drawn to Black entertainers—their shows were hipper, and the integrated atmosphere gave the place an edgy, urban vibe—so he made that a specialty. "Now presenting the finest sepia attraction in the entertainment business" went one of his ads. Among the first groups he booked was the Four Blues, who'd just had a hit with "It Takes a Long Tall Brownskin Gal (to Make a Preacher Lay His Bible Down)." But while things were changing fast in the postwar era, with Italians now being accepted as "white," the wall was still in place with regard to Blacks. Black performers couldn't sit in the audience after their set but had to retire to their dressing room.

Not long after, Joe and Russ opened a second club two blocks down the street. Just as Russ had done with his Franklin Pool Room, which he positioned right outside the mill gate in that borough, they placed the Gautier Club across from the main gate to the Gautier Division of the Bethlehem Steel plant. It was the mirror opposite of the Melodee Lounge in terms of demographics of both the clientele and the acts. Gautier was essentially a strip club for mill workers, a place where after eight hours as steel pourer or stove tender guys could let loose and down a few boilermakers while roaring at ladies like Christie Doll, who was billed as a "top-notch terpsichorean artist," and "lovely dancer Mignon." There was an ex-vaudevillian who emceed the shows, and an old lady accompanying the acts on piano. The club was on the second floor. Right below it they opened the Clinton Street Pool Room, which was likewise a proletariat version of City Cigar.

Russ's friends, guys he'd grown up with, run card games with, been busted alongside—guys like Sam Polina, Johnny diFalco, Pete Pagano, Tommy Croco, Charlie Torcia, Buster Tanase, Joe Picklo, Joe Bruno—all assumed roles in the rapidly expanding operation. So did Russ's brother Tony, and some of his sisters' husbands. Writing numbers. Taking phone bets. Running craps games. Managing the pool hall or the bowling alley. Keeping the customers off the ladies working the stage at the Gautier Club.

Others became part of things soon after. Either Russ or Joe hired Johnny diFalco's brother, Pippy, to write numbers. He was an odd sort—kind of sneaky, smarmy—but he'd been wounded in the war. Maybe they took him on out of a spirit of patriotism. Soon, though, he went out on his own, running a sports book. Which was OK, provided he turned in a percentage. Rip Slomanson came aboard, too, as an enforcer. He was young and crazy, tall, trim, all muscle and ready to fight anybody. LaRocca had suggested to Little Joe that they might use him—he'd done work for him recently. It wasn't long before the two newcomers clashed. Nobody knows what sparked it—whether Joe used Rip to send Pippy a little message about keeping up his payments or what—but Rip beat the hell out of Pippy one night, left him half-dead on the sidewalk. He bloodied him enough that later, when Pippy went missing, people's thoughts immediately went to Rip.

But that was years later. One day not long after they opened for business Joe had a talk with Russ. *The boys in Philly told me to always keep sports separate from other business. I want you on sports because of your head for numbers.* From then on, Russ had nothing to do with the

G.I. Bank. This was in 1946, the first postwar baseball season. Major League Baseball had continued through the war, but many of the top players had been fighting overseas. Now, for the first time in years, everyone would be back. With the talent, the stars—Stan Musial, Ted Williams, the imminent pivot of Jackie Robinson from the Negro Leagues—anticipation was high. And baseball was the biggest sport for betting action.

But just as the season was getting under way a problem arose. Running a sports book was all about "the line." The house had to weigh the two teams' likelihood of winning and add points to the underdog so as to balance things out. If you didn't have a razor-sharp oddsmaker, gamblers would eat you alive. The line came from the boys in Pittsburgh—they had the top bookmakers—but that spring, at the very start of the season, Joe got some bad news. Apparently due to a power struggle between some of LaRocca's guys and Little Joe's, there was a break in the information flow. "Little Joe says to Russ, 'We can't get the line.'" This is Mike Gulino telling me how it unfolded—and at the same time telling me the story of how he and Russ cemented their relationship. I'm back in his kitchen; Eleanor has laid a platter before us, made a pot of coffee, and gone out. This time I'd brought her some flowers. "Russ says, 'That's no problem, Joe. There's a young kid around here. You put him and me upstairs above the Melodee Lounge.' Now, Chris Contakos owned the building, see? Chris Contakos was the bum of all bums, by the way. But that don't matter. Upstairs he had a couple a rooms where guys could go with their broads—Chris did everything to make a buck. So Russ calls for me and he says, 'Listen, kid, I want you to go home and get some clothes. You and I's gonna move in up above Melodee Lounge.' And that's what we did—we set ourselves up there. Johnny Oswald was the only guy allowed up. He'd bring us all the papers every morning, and Russ got to work."

Russ did the math, mostly based on starting pitcher stats, and Mike assisted. They had a lot of numbers to crunch: 16 teams, 154 games, plus a best-of-three National League pennant series between St. Louis and the Brooklyn Dodgers and the World Series, between the Cardinals and the Boston Red Sox, which went to seven games (the Cardinals won). They basically lived together during that season, Russ and Mike. They ate together. They slept there so they were ready when the papers were delivered early each morning with fresh stats and they could have the line ready for the bookies.

"By the end of that season, me and Russ, we were like this." Mike wrapped two thick fingers around each other. And suddenly he wasn't talking about oddsmaking anymore but about my family. "All the work I did after that, over the next ten, fifteen years, it wasn't for the mafia. It was for Russ. You see what I'm saying here? Russ come off to everybody like a tough guy, a wiseguy. But deep down in his heart, he was a piece of cake. He was kind of an older brother to me. But in a way it was something more, like he was the father I didn't have. I had a father, don't get me wrong. But he didn't understand—he wasn't in the business. And I was a little bit like the son Russ didn't have, even though he had his two sons. But with me it was different."

It made me a little bit queasy hearing Mike talk like this. Suddenly, just sitting there, I felt like I was betraying my father by listening to him explain how he had placed himself in between my dad and my grandfather—or how Russ had given him that position. I thought back to the couple of times I'd asked Tony if he wanted to come down to Mike's house with me for one of my interview sessions. Why wouldn't he? They'd known each other all their lives. It was a two-minute drive down the hill. But he shook his head. Nah. Mike must have gotten himself thinking along a similar track, because he then said, referring to the bar my dad owned in later years, "I used to go down to your dad's place once in a while. I knew he used to drink a bit. I tried to get him to stop. He liked me, I think. But it was different with your grandfather."

I was feeling physically warm sitting there in Mike's kitchen, like the oven was on or something. I'd come for an interview about the mob, we'd been talking about oddsmaking and the 1946 baseball season. This was suddenly something else. But I pushed on. "What do you mean?"

This instantly irked him. "What do you *mean* what do I mean?"

"You say it was different with you and my grandfather. How?"

All at once he erupted: "The fuck you want me to say?! He loved me, OK? And I loved him. I don't know how else to explain our situation."

I was conscious of a lot of things. The tile flooring in Mike's kitchen. The smell of the coffee Eleanor had made us before she left— she always went out when I came to chat. Mike's eyes magnified by his glasses, the sheen of sweat on his face, the slight tremor in him as he gazed at me, as he came down from this emotional outburst. I was aware of how jarring the emotion must have been for him. And of how, as he'd told me before, he'd had this on his mind for years and years. And here I came, basically begging him to talk about it, even though I'd had no idea what it was. And he realizing that this was the obvious time for him to talk about it, and I was the very person. Namesake.

I was still being daft, though. I shook my head. "I don't get it. You say Russ saw you as his protégé. But why would he need you when he was grooming my dad for that?"

"Grooming your dad for what?"

"My dad told me Russ wanted him to follow in his footsteps, but he refused."

Mike was looking at me more closely than he had before. "I'm sorry, Russell, but it wasn't like that." It wasn't like that. What was it like? I knew by this point, but I asked anyway and he told me. "Tony was—what?—six years younger than me. See? This is a little later, now. Maybe 1953, 1954, somewhere in there. And your dad wanted to be a mobster in the worst way. I was working at City Cigar at this point, running the floor, so I saw everything that went on. Tony would show up, trying to hang around and be a tough guy. If Russ caught him he would beat the shit out of him. It was painful to watch. He didn't want his boy within a hundred miles of the place."

I nodded. I knew perfectly well that Russ had pressured Tony to be part of the organization, and that Tony had rejected him, for our sake, his family's sake. That story underlay my childhood. But now I also knew that what I knew was wrong.

"And . . . why?"

He was exasperated again. "What's so hard to understand? This was a criminal life. Russ wasn't going to do that to his son."

"But he did it to you."

"Because I was already in that world. We were two of a kind."

I DROVE BACK up the hill to my parents' house after my visit with Mike. They asked how it went. I told them Mike was a real character. We talked a little bit about his entanglements with the law. They debated how much time he'd spent in prison as a result of his final caper, in the 1990s, a pretty glorious little con that went on for several years, in which he scammed doctors and CEOs all over the mid-Atlantic region—*I fucked people that wanted to be fucked*—before he got caught. I said nothing about what Mike had just told me.

I did start going around to other sources, checking on all the information Mike was giving me, both to corroborate the particulars and to test his general veracity. Some of what he told me was fairly outlandish, but pretty much everything I could track down checked out.

AFTER SPENDING MUCH of the 1946 baseball season locked together in a room above the Melodee Lounge, Russ and Mike were a team. As the operation in Johnstown flowered, Mike became a sidekick, running around town and doing things for Russ.

Russ brought him into City Cigar, where he eventually took over the Harrigan table. The Harrigan game was very popular among gamblers. It made a lot of money for the house, and the house needed to have someone running it, like a referee. Russ's brother-in-law, Angelo Trigona, had been doing it. Simple work: you shook out the "pills," which were dice with only one number on each, and distributed two to each player. The first pill was the order in which you shot, the second was the number of the ball you had to sink. First guy to sink his ball wins. Simple: game over. But Mike complicated it. Mike practiced in the mornings to prepare himself for the job, transferring the skills Mr. Verone had taught him to another use. He got so he could manipulate the pills, holding a high number in one hand and a low one in the other. That way he could manage the games, keeping them short and brisk, which pleased Russ and Joe because the house made money on each game. He could also keep a hotshot from winning too many games in a row, which might discourage other players. "When Mike took over from Angelo, the Harrigan table became the hot table," one of the old boys told me.

THE NEXT TIME I was in town doing research, I asked my dad if he wanted to come down to the Holiday Inn with me to see Frank and hang out with the old guys who would be there. Most of the guys I'd first met at Panera Bread, and a few others, congregated around Frank's Thursday lunchtime set. He said OK. This was something new. As with Mike, he'd known them all his life, but for decades he had kept himself apart.

As soon as Frank sees my dad come hobbling into the dining room he barks into the mic: "Ladies and gentlemen, Tony Shorto!

Whaddaya know!" He leans down to confer with John, the piano player, then says, pointing a finger as my dad is maneuvering himself into a seat, "This one's for you, Tony." And launches into a languid rendering of "Dindi," an almost embarrassingly romantic bossa nova standard the Sinatra version of which was my dad's favorite tune back in the day.

Frank joined us after the set; we were already talking about the old days—me with my recorder going. Eventually somebody mentioned Mike Gulino.

"Sure, Mike helped," my dad said suddenly, utterly randomly. "He used to help my dad a little bit, setting the odds."

Beat.

"Mike helped a *lot*," Frank said.

"I remember him coming to the house," Tony went on, warming a little to the topic. "In a zoot suit and wide-brimmed hat. They used to call those hats bammers. With the three-inch brim. He was chomping on a cigar. He cut a figure, I'll tell you."

And just like that I had a picture, not only of Mike back in the day but of my dad as a boy in his teens, and a sense of what he felt way down inside, seeing this older kid coming in, at *his* dad's side, looking like the movies' idea of a mafia swell. While his dad refused to let him be part of that. Him staring at that older kid with awe, but with something else stabbing at him too.

8

The Con

RUSS AND JOE were successful men now. Through the war, both, together with their wives, had continued to live in the immigrant way, with extended family in narrow houses in the old part of town, near the mills and mines, one cramped bedroom to each nuclear family, each day a multigenerational hullabaloo of groans and sighs and smells and squabbles. After the war, both men bought houses in newer neighborhoods, Joe near the river in Dale and Russ on Rambo Street in Roxbury, the kind of neighborhoods with neat, modest streets filled with middle-class families, with Packards parked out front and Schwinns leaning against fences.

By now Russ and Mary had three children, what would be their complete family. Millie and Joe struggled in that department; they apparently tried to have a child, but something was wrong with one or the other of them. Finally, they adopted a baby girl.

There were wild amounts of money flying around now. One of Tony's early memories: "I walked into the bedroom one day, and my dad had more cash than you ever saw stacked all across the bed, must have been fifty grand. I realize now he was making the banks for different bookies." But you didn't act like you were swimming in cash. Joe and Russ wore nice suits, but sober, and never tailored. They drove Buicks; there was a no-Cadillacs rule in effect.

Joe also bought a big house in Pompano Beach, Florida, at this time, next to LaRocca's vacation house, and both Joe's and Russ's family began making regular winter trips there.

Maybe the money got to Russ. He stayed quiet and reserved, because that's what you did. But forces inside him were stewing.

The two families shared a housekeeper. Isabel was her name. She came from Altoona—forty-five miles away. It was Russ who found her—or, rather, she found him. He was in Altoona one night for a big card game, which was at the house of a guy Russ knew named Don Schmittel, who worked for LaRocca there. Don introduced them. *Russ, I'd like you to meet my sister. Isabel, this is Russ.* Isabel mentioned that she needed a job. She was tall, lanky, with lazy eyes. Russ said he could find something for her. She started doing the cleaning at his and Mary's house in late 1948.

Russ's drinking—his serious, medicinal drinking—began around this time too. Maybe it came on with the first rushes of cash, the cascades of ones and fives and tens and twenties, the gnarled bankrolls from the pockets of the bookies dumped onto the desktop. Maybe when he got his first handgun. Maybe when they had to start threatening people who tried to welch on bets. Maybe, when things got a little bit rough, he needed to fortify himself.

At home, the fights had begun. Mary could deal with drunkenness. Drunk husbands were everywhere. Johnstown's police records of the time seemed to use "staggering" as a synonym for drunkenness. "Staggering on sidewalk." "Slumped over." Can I give you a hand, buddy? All the old guys talk about how the whiskey flowed. "In those days whiskey was more powerful," one of them assured me. "So when people were drunk they were *really* drunk. They would piss their pants, they would bounce off the wall and fall dead asleep on the pavement." And it was always whiskey, always hard liquor. You sat down to shoot the breeze and somebody poured you a shot. Buy you a shot? Shot-and-a-beer? Mary didn't mind the drinking. In fact, she was known to abet it, hand him a bottle to help him pass out—better that than him running around on her.

Mary found out about one woman, a waitress named Tess, who worked next door to City Cigar, at the Mission Inn, who was bold enough to phone the house and ask for him. She went ballistic: screaming, firing dishes and glasses at Russ. Then she heard about another, name of Tootsie, and that was enough. Mary and Russ had just had their second child. Mary carried the baby to Russell's sister Perina, who was living in Franklin. Perina had become the matriarch of Russ's family—they called her "the General." Perina was the only person, besides Little Joe, with any authority over Russ. Mary thrust the baby at her: "Here, you can raise him." Eventually Perina got her to calm down by telling her she would talk to Russ.

But Mary didn't see what was right under her nose. When did the snuggling with Isabel start? It could have been one day while Mary was out for lunch with a group of lady friends, or over at her sister Vera's house: Vera had an abusive husband and needed her older sister just then. Maybe Isabel was changing the sheets on the marital bed and he came up from behind; he couldn't resist, she didn't say no.

But my dad's cousin Minnie—who was Russ's niece, knew him well, worked for him at City Cigar, considered him a good man, *loved* him—thinks it started before Isabel entered his employ. She told me Isabel made a play for Russ the night they met at her brother's house. "Russ was a good-looking Italian guy, and everyone knew he had money, he was on the rise." That, of course, is a darker scenario. It would mean that he knowingly planted a psychological landmine in his family home. If that were the case, I would have to back up, rethink his entire relationship with Mary, restart my whole study of this man and what formed him. Which I can't do: he hid things too well. One time Tony said to me, speaking of his father, "He never stepped out of character."

Lots of guys back then had mistresses. But what kind of person would bring his mistress into his household? And not just that. Tony tells me Isabel was a constant presence. She lived with the family for a time. They took her on vacations with them. These weren't little weekend getaways either. The modesty rule applied in town, but once you were out of town you could let loose with your wealth. An extended network of friends and family members packed off together for a month every summer in Atlantic City, staying at Haddon Hall, the classiest place in town, in a suite of rooms overlooking the ocean, with room service and their own reserved corner of the dining room. The place was so posh, the bathroom sinks had three faucets: hot, cold, and ice-cold. ("The kids drank so much ice water they would go to the bathroom constantly!" my dad's older cousin Marcia said.) Everyone dressed for dinner. In the evenings they regularly went to the 500 Club, the legendary place—it was onstage at "The Five" that Dean Martin and Jerry Lewis took off as a comedy duo—whose mobster owner, Skinny D'Amato, was a friend of Joe's.

At Haddon Hall the family had all the servants they could want. So why bring their housekeeper with them? As a babysitter, one might proffer. But they also brought Marcia expressly to watch the little ones. (She told me with amazement that Russ handed her a $100 bill every day to amuse the kids on the boardwalk, and gave another hundred to Tony, who was older and was allowed to go off on his own. In the early '50s, needless to say, a C-note bought a lot of taffy.)

So what was Isabel's role? What did Mary think?

Late in that first year, Isabel had to leave for a while; she went back to Altoona. Sometime later Joe and Millie made a little announcement. They were adopting another child, a son. Wonderful—let's have a toast. And now that they had two children, Millie would need some help around the house. Everybody decided that Isabel, when she came back, would work for them too.

And that's what they did, Joe and Russ. For years and years it went on like that. As the gambling empire waxed, as numbers were played and payoffs were made, as they took over more and more legit local businesses, as Russ began to slide downhill, going from slightly unstable to dangerously unreliable. As Russ and Mary fought about other women. As Tony and his siblings grew up.

"Isabel's mother wanted to take the baby and raise him," Minnie told me. "But Isabel didn't want that. She thought she was going to get Russell to marry her." But he wasn't going to do that. Instead, he and Joe decided the way things would be.

And yet, Joe didn't play an active role in this decision. Because as time went by a regular routine evolved at Joe's house. Isabel would clean the house, then get out: she and Millie made sure she left before Joe got home, because he wasn't comfortable with her being around. He seems to have agreed to the arrangement at the outset because Russ wanted it, but over time the psychodynamics became too messy for him.

Naturally Russ, Joe, and Millie knew about the con from the outset—and Isabel was in on it, of course, though against her will. Of the adults involved, only Mary was out of the loop. She would, as the years passed, feel self-conscious, aware of others—Millie's relatives, friends of Joe—giving her pitying looks, whispering, but not knowing the cause. The kids didn't know. And Joe and Millie's little boy—another Joe, whom they called Joey to avoid confusion—had no idea that Millie wasn't his mother, that the guy he called dad, who was the big boss in town, wasn't his dad, but that the one he called Uncle Russell was.

As Russ saw it, it was an arrangement that worked out for everyone. This way, see, Isabel could keep near her son. Making his bed, picking up after him. Why, it was almost like she was his mother.

The con became part of everyone's life. It worked its way into Russ and Mary's household. My aunt Sis was aware of it on some level. She was eight years younger than Tony, but remembers being a little girl watching her father lying on the couch moaning in a drunken stupor and observing the odd behavior of the housekeeper stroking his head and soothing him with words whispered into his ear.

Did Tony see any of this in the early days? He was the eldest, seven years older than the next sibling, which meant he was probably the only one old enough to truly be aware, to be formed by the nexus of his dad's business dealings, affairs, and drinking. What did he see?

He saw a lot. It's 1949; he's eleven. Cars are pulling up in front of the house, men in their baggy suits stepping out, the loud report of leather heels on the porch floor, deep laughter filling the living room. Important men. Sam Di Francesco was recognizable from the papers: the newly minted district attorney, whose rags-to-riches life the *Tribune* had just declared "outdoes heroes of Horatio Alger." A local hero! They pulled him in. He was a *paesan*, after all. He put some skin in the game, too, became a participant in their latest venture. Russ and Joe had taken over the lease on the Heidelberg, the old German-American Club, which had been shut down during the war. They were going to call the new place Shangri-La. It would be a big supper club in the woods, out toward Ligonier, on the way to Pittsburgh. It was gonna be posh as hell. They needed Sam to do some work for it. "The problem was the place was just over the town line, where you couldn't have a liquor license," my dad said. "With Sam's help, they actually got the line moved, so they would pay city taxes, and that way they could sell liquor." I had heard this story before, but this time, as Tony retold it, I was aware of something in his voice—pride, I think.

LaRocca, the Pittsburgh boss, came to the house, too, around this time. He was going to be a partner in Shangri-La. Even at his age Tony knew who he was. Everybody knew who he was. He had a serious edge about him. You treated him with respect.

There were other things the boy took note of. Maybe it wasn't especially odd that Tony's mother had new things all the time, but she got them in a way that none of his friends' mothers did. The big card games were going on now in the back room at the bowling alley, and when Russ had roped in a whale—Joe Marks, say, of Marks Apparel, across Main Street from City Cigar—he would sometimes agree to take his winnings in goods. He'd come home and give Chinky an order: *Go down to Marks and do some shopping. Take as much as you can carry.* The manager would watch as she browsed, assist her as she tried on dresses and coats, package everything up nicely. Instead of paying, she would sign a piece of paper, deducting the amount from the gambling debt.

Or, out of the blue, a brand-new RCA television set arrives from Glosser Brothers Department Store, unasked-for but, as far as Tony was concerned, wildly welcome. And just like that the household is transformed by the ten-inch screen, which broadcasts snow all day long but then flickers into extraordinary life from 7 to 10:30 p.m.: *Ed Sullivan. The Morey Amsterdam Show. Kukla, Fran and Ollie. Texaco Star Theatre.*

Sometimes a case of cleaning supplies would arrive on the front porch: "20 Mule Team Borax." Or chewing gum. Or candy bars.

To a kid, this was all like a pirate's booty. Because it was. It was also normal, for his family. Tony knew perfectly well what was behind it. He knew all about the G.I. Bank and the tip seals. Mostly he picked things up from overhearing conversations. But once his dad gave him something like a formal introduction to the business. Russ had a good pal named George Bondy, who owned the Mission Inn next door to City Cigar and was involved in the organization. One time Russ and George took Tony to Atlantic City with them. Even the drive down was memorable. George had a Cadillac; he told Tony to stick his arm out his window while he did the same on his side. "Now flap your arm! We're taking off!" Most of their working vacation was spent at the racetrack. The energy in a roaring crowd of gamblers was thrilling. Russ gave Tony some money, talked to him about horses, and Tony listened as if his future depended on it. Pedigree and handicapping; how to bet, how to work with odds; the difference between an exacta and a quinella. "I won fifty bucks!" my dad told me. "I was on top of the world!" Russ sat back and watched as his boy clutched his tickets and cheered.

They went to an illegal casino while they were there and Russ gave his son a direct insight into what he did. "I was mesmerized by the slot machines," Tony said. "He gave me a real stern look. 'Listen. They want you to be dazzled by all the lights so that they can take your money. Its designed to beat you. You can't win. You get it?' And I did get it. I never became a gambler."

These moments, I was beginning to realize, gave Tony an expectation, a feeling that he was being groomed for something.

But Isabel. Did Tony see anything there? A quick caress or a swap of glances, the kind of thing that, though barely glimpsed, might send a juvenile psyche into free fall? If so, he buried it. There was no trace of it in the memory of the old man who was my fellow researcher. But as a child he certainly experienced the fall-out from his father's affairs. He was aware at least in a subliminal way of a dagger being slowly plunged into the heart of his family unit; the energy from it zinged through him like electricity. Yet just when he was sensing his father's perfidy, and was ready to sympathize with his mother, she quashed it by letting him know that he and his siblings were to blame for her predicament. She only stuck around, she told him, "because of you kids." And well into her own self-medicating with alcohol, she would put an even finer point on it: "You're the reason I suffer."

As Russ's carrying-on continued, Mary's feelings of being trapped became overwhelming. "What really stands out is the time my mother cut up all the furniture," Tony said. "It was new, expensive stuff. She took a knife and slashed the couch and all the chairs, stabbed the cushions, the stuffing was flying." Tony took charge that time, got his little brother and sister out of the house. He wasn't old enough to drive but he got them in the car anyway and took off.

"Where did you go?"

"I don't remember. I just remember I didn't want the kids to see that."

As things spiraled downward, and feeling he had nowhere else to turn, Tony sought out the parish priest, a certain Father Francis. He didn't express his predicament directly to Father Francis. He didn't say, "I'm afraid at home." He tried to translate his dilemma into the kind of lingo he figured a man of God would go for. "What," he asked, "is the most important thing in the Bible?"

You might expect Father Francis to come back with "forgiveness," or "love," or "mercy," or "Jesus died for our sins." Or maybe to turn things around, ask the boy some questions about his situation, try to figure out what kind of answer would help him.

But no. He replied: " 'I am that I am.' " That, he informed the boy, was the most important thing in the Bible. One of the broadest, most obscure lines in the Old Testament. A dereliction of priestly duty, if you ask me; a failed opportunity to help a desperate young member of his congregation. Moses, in Exodus, is tending a flock when he comes upon the burning bush. God speaks to him from within the bush, instructs him to tell the Israelites that he has been ordered to lead them out of bondage. It's when Moses asks what name he should attach to the deity issuing the command that he gets the mind-tripping response. "I am everything" might have been one attempt at translating its meaning. Or the priest might have helped by pointing out that in the same passage the Lord also says, "I am the God of your father." Or at least he could have talked about the various interpretations of the Hebrew verb "to be." But the priest didn't clarify. He left the boy alone with a verse whose meaning has been debated by centuries of theologians.

And yet, somehow, the elliptical scripture inflicted on the eleven-year-old worked. It turns out the kid had a spiritual bent; he was a lover of koans and parables, things that upset the neat, rational template we try to impose on reality. He chewed on the linguistic twistiness of what the priest had said.

And he kept chewing. Zip forward a generation, and there *I* am, as a kid, about the same age as my dad was, having a theological conversation with him, sparked by what I don't recall. And my father defined God for me with the same formulation. I don't know how Father Francis intoned it to him, but Tony was an exuberant dad when I was young, who would get fully into character when he was telling a story, and he declaimed the verse in a theatrical baritone, as if he were doing voiceover for a Cecil B. DeMille movie, as if he had become Elohim, the God of the Israelites:

"I am . . . that I am!"

When—no-nonsense child that I apparently was—I asked prosaically what it meant, he just repeated the phrase, this time with such resonance I heard the echo of his voice upstairs in the hall that led to our bedrooms.

9

The Establishment

EARLY ON, RUSS made a point of befriending a man named John Torquato. Whenever his name came up in conversation with the old boys I interviewed, they spoke of him with something like reverence. If Italians were making headway in American society in the '40s and '50s, Torquato was pretty much single-handedly responsible for that in Cambria County. He was eight years older than Russ, had grown up in Windber, ten miles from Johnstown, and, rare for Italians of his generation, had gone to college. There, he found he was drawn not so much to any particular subject as he was to student government. He was forceful, friendly to everyone, and fascinated by how people organized themselves and allowed themselves to be organized by others. It was pretty clear what direction he would go in. "All John ever thought about was politics," a cousin of his would say. "He lived politics all the time, every day."

No one with an Italian background had ever had a political job in the county. The same was true for Irish, Polish, and Hungarian immigrants, but there was a particular animus toward Italians. The KKK in western Pennsylvania had targeted them; the steel mills only employed them in the lowest and most dangerous jobs. Back in 1911 the mayor of Johnstown made it a campaign promise that no one of Italian descent would work in his administration, not even as a street cleaner. Italians were the second largest immigrant group in the county, and for many people that was precisely the problem.

Torquato ingratiated himself with Democratic Party officials, got the lowest-level job in 1928, and worked his way up through a series of local, state, and federal positions until, in 1942, he was named chairman of the Democratic Committee in the county. He set about creating a classic political machine. If you voted Democratic and gave money to the party, he could help you out, and he did. Working with FDR's administration and Pennsylvania's Democratic governor he managed to shift the county from Republican-leaning to solidly Democratic. Along the way, he was on a mission to reverse discrimination against his fellow Italians. He appointed as many as possible to political jobs—provided they were Democrats.

It was natural for Torquato to form an alliance with Little Joe and Russ, and for them to want to join forces with him. But they didn't follow strict party lines. Tony remembers Andrew Gleason—a local lawyer who was the head of the Republican Party in the county—being as regular a presence in the family living room as Torquato. For that matter, Gleason and Torquato were friends too.

In 1947, Little Joe Regino and John Torquato met on a topic of interest to both men: the idea of running the young, up-and-coming lawyer Sam Di Francesco for district attorney. An Italian had never held such a high post in the area. They approached Di Francesco; he was raring to go. Once he became a candidate, a group calling themselves the County Christian League fought hard against his election, warning all Protestants they had to get out and vote to prevent a "Pope-serving Catholic" from becoming the top legal officer in the county. But Di Francesco was a great candidate, ambitious and affable. He'd fought in the war. He believed communism was a threat but thought Joe McCarthy's anti-Communist crusade was dangerous. When he won, the long-suffering Italian community in town suddenly had a power base. Joe and Russ, John Torquato, Sam Di Francesco: they didn't call all the shots, but together they called a lot of them. When the newly elected president of the United States came to town, John Torquato was at Harry Truman's side, introducing him, waving to crowds, leaning in to whisper in his ear.

The alliance didn't last long—at least, not in that form. In 1952 Russ went to Sam Di Francesco and asked a favor—precisely the kind of thing they had in mind when they worked to get him installed as DA. Lately, some social clubs in the northern part of the county had been pulling in customers and cash by featuring slot machines. Not pinball machines, like Little Joe had going in businesses all over town, which became an indirect means of gambling when a customer traded in games won for cash, but actual lemons-and-cherries slot machines, which spat out coins when you won. Social clubs were a Pennsylvania thing—essentially they were honky-tonk bars, but you had to be a member to get in. Membership usually involved nothing more than paying a nominal fee, but the fact that they were not open to the public meant they had fewer restrictions—they could stay open later, for example. They were also less likely to be raided by the police.

Little Joe didn't like this development. It was a threat to his pinball business. Russ told Sam they wanted him to raid the clubs and shut them down. It shouldn't have been hard. After all, slot machines were illegal. But remarkably, Sam refused. To understand why, I sat down with his son, Sam Junior. I knew him already. He was part of the posse of old guys who followed Frank Filia around town, meeting at Panera Bread twice a week, each of them nursing a cup of coffee, not wanting to shell out for a whole lunch, then splurging on the Thursday lunchtime pasta buffet at the Holiday Inn for Frank's set with pianist John Pencola. Sam was a bit of a singer himself. At least once during every Holiday Inn set Frank would give him the mic for a song. He was in his eighties, a tiny man, twisted by arthritis and Parkinson's disease. I can't describe the waft of feeling that came over me the first time I saw him perform. Sam was bent at a right angle, actually singing to the floor as he rendered "On a Clear Day" in a weak but pleasant voice.

I imagine every group of retired old men sitting around in coffee shops has at least one designated joke-teller. Sam was that guy too. The first time I met him at the Holiday Inn, right after he sang his song and I told him how much I liked it, he said, "I wrote a song myself once. It's called 'I'll Always Remember What's-Her-Name.'" When I laughed, he informed me that if Ella Fitzgerald had married Darth Vader she would have been Ella Vader. Later, when somebody brought up the subject of wine, Sam asked if we knew how to make an Italian wine. (Squeeze his *coglioni*.)

For our chat about his father, I met up with Sam at his law office, where he still put in regular hours. "What can you tell me about the slot machines?" I asked.

"It was like this," he said. "Joe and Russ wanted my father to bust these clubs and take out the slots. My dad wouldn't go along with it because he knew the owners. He had been their solicitor, and he thought if they lost the slots it would be death for the clubs. He said no. Joe and Russ were mad as hell." According to Sam, in crossing Joe and Russ his father upended his own career. "In '52, when my dad was up for reelection, Joe and Russ decided to pull back a little on their support, just to put a scare into him. But he ended up losing. His time as DA turned out to be the high point of his career, and he lost it because he wouldn't close the slot clubs. Later he ran for judge, twice, but he lost. He lusted after the bench. He was very bitter until the day he died. I told him, 'God doesn't want you to be a judge.'"

ON MARCH 18, 1951, a tall, rather bland-looking, middle-aged man in a light-colored suit strode onto the set of the TV game show *What's My Line?*, wrote his name on a blackboard for the audience to see, and took his seat next to the host. The idea of the game was for the four blindfolded panelists to ask questions and guess his occupation. Despite the fact that the guest was a freshman U.S. senator from Tennessee—not typically a position that would accrue celebrity status—they needed only a few tries to get it. Over the past year Sen. Estes Kefauver had become one of the most recognizable people in the country. Because the subject matter of the recently formed Senate Special Committee to Investigate Crime in Interstate Commerce— aka the Kefauver Committee—was of enormous popular interest, its proceedings were broadcast on national television. The hearings were structured a bit like a reality show. Kefauver and his fellow senators traveled around the country, visiting fourteen cities, and interviewed hundreds of people from different walks of life, many of whom were suspected of being major figures in organized crime.

A goal of the committee was to answer the question of whether there was such a thing as an American mafia—that is, whether an organized crime syndicate with Italian roots was running gambling and other illegal activities in cities large and small. Ordinary people on the streets of Johnstown—or Yonkers, Lansing, Lubbock, or Dubuque—knew perfectly well that there was, yet it was still in some way an unsettled question. There was a lack of certainty at the official level, which was connected to what many people chose to believe. Millie, for example, Little Joe's wife, who would spend her entire life with what you might call a front-row seat to precisely this activity, would say, "Don't be crazy! There is no such thing" whenever someone suggested that what her husband was involved in was "the mafia."

It's possible she believed it. What was Freud's formulation? "Knowing and not-knowing." Knowing without wanting to know. Russ and Joe, typical for husbands of the era, never talked business with their wives, which in turn gave the women plausible deniability.

Tony remembered the effects of the Kefauver Committee's hearings in his family home on Rambo Street in Johnstown, starting with his dad murmuring, "Jesus!" as he stared at the TV. "All of a sudden what they were doing was right there, in everybody's living room. My dad was calling Kefauver a dirty bastard. I was a kid and I thought they were the tough guys, him and Uncle Joe. It felt weird to see them acting scared."

Tony described a lot of nervous rushing around in that period, including a number of guys from out of town coming to the house. One, he told me, was a fellow named Kelly Mannarino. He paused in his reflection. "Have you come across that name?" He'd become steadily more interested in my archival research; he was curious about areas where it overlapped with his memories, maybe wanting a check on his own veracity. The Mannarino brothers, I had learned, were to the town of New Kensington, sixty miles to the west on the outskirts of Pittsburgh, what Little Joe and Russ were to Johnstown. Both organizations had emerged at about the same time. Where the mob had been attracted to Johnstown by the presence of the steel mills, and the money they brought, in New Kensington it was the Alcoa aluminum plant that had drawn them. There was an overlap of interest between the outfits in the two towns, which from time to time turned into a rivalry. Somebody who booked numbers for Little Joe in Blairsville, midway between Johnstown and New Kensington, might get the shit beat out of him. Boundary dispute.

Not long after his appearance on *What's My Line?* Senator Kefauver entered the presidential race, running as a Democrat against the incumbent, President Harry Truman. Campaigning in a coonskin cap and with the mammoth publicity of the anti–organized crime hearings working for him, he stormed through the primaries, gathering enough momentum that Truman decided to retire rather than face a humiliating defeat in his own party. But the party bosses—some of whom had links to organized crime and didn't care for the spotlight Kefauver had been shining—pulled a convention surprise, preempting the popular will and selecting Illinois governor Adlai Stevenson as their nominee instead. Stevenson, of course, went on to lose the general election to Dwight David Eisenhower, the general who had won the Second World War.

When the Kefauver Committee wrapped up, its work was packaged into a series of recommendations for how to deal with organized crime. One in particular, the establishment of state crime commissions, would eventually have a big impact on Little Joe's operation, but that took a long time to get rolling. Once the hearings were off the TV screens things in town went back to normal.

And what was that, exactly?

Normal, through most of the '50s, was a hundred people on the payroll of the G.I. Bank—bookies like Pippy diFalco, runners, money guys. Normal was weekly gin-rummy games for the high rollers, in a private room at Capitol Bowling Lanes, where pots could reach $10,000. Normal was cash pouring into the operation from tip seals. People rolled into City Cigar, the Clinton Street Pool Room, or other designated spots at all hours to buy them, at a dime or a dollar apiece. You tore your ticket off the board, opened the seal, and if your number matched the last one on the board you won six times your bet; if you lost, you threw the paper on the floor. Tip seals were big. Tony remembers being very young—this would have been just after the war—and going into City Cigar with his dad one morning before it had been cleaned up from the previous night. "The tip seals," he said, "were up to my ankles."

Maybe the most lucrative revenue source through the '50s was pinball machines. Little Joe, together with John LaRocca, bought a company called P and C Amusements, which distributed jukeboxes, and used it to blanket the county with pinball games. Pinball was nominally for entertainment but everyone knew the machines were there for gambling. The beauty of pinball to the mob was that, since coins you put in didn't correspond with a quantifiable product like cigarettes or candy, it was impossible to track the machines' earnings. The high-tech fun of the game plus the possibility of beating it for cash made them addictive. The *Johnstown Observer* looked into it in 1954 and found ordinary workers were dumping their paychecks into the machines a nickel at a time. "A lady called us the other day and said her husband lost over $30.00 of his pay in playing a pinball machine. We couldn't believe it so we began to make some investigations and found it was entirely possible."

The machines were lucrative not just for the mob, which controlled their distribution, but for the many kinds of businesses that wanted them. Most bars had them, and so did restaurants, candy stores, five-and-dimes, gas stations, and hotels. "Practically every bar and restaurant in the city makes enough from the pin ball machines to pay the rent," the *Observer* found. P and C had a thousand machines in operation at any one time, each making around $50 a week, for a total of more than $2 million a year—$17 million in today's money.

Turning pinball machines into gambling devices required the involvement of the host establishment. When you reached a certain point total as a player, you were rewarded with a free game. Once you had racked up a number of free games you went to the bar or counter, where you got a cash payout. Once a week, a guy from P and C came around to service the machines and settle up with the management. He would split the take with the owner and write a receipt for one-quarter of the total: that is, by mutual agreement, the vending machine company and the bar or café that housed the machines underreported their earnings by half.

The machines had an additional value. Because of their popularity, Little Joe was able to use them as leverage. If a business that had his machines was having a hard time making ends meet, he might send an accountant to look over the owner's financial situation. Joe could loan him a couple thousand, enough to get back on his feet, and take the payments on the loan, plus interest, out of the owner's share of the pinball money. If he needed help again later, Joe might suggest a different arrangement: a piece of the business in exchange for a bailout. Steadily, he worked his way into all sorts of legitimate businesses in town. By 1960, Little Joe's holdings included stakes in bars and restaurants around town, as well as City Cigar, the Melodee Lounge, the Gautier Club, the bowling alley and boxing gym, and a farm where he raised racehorses, including one called Moon Over Miami that Russ told my aunt he would give to her but, she said ruefully, never did.

I hankered for something like an official overview of how Little Joe and Russ worked things with the authorities. Of course, that wasn't possible. Everything was off the books: nods, handshake deals. But Tony had an idea. He suggested we talk to an attorney named Caram Abood. Abood had spent his entire long career in the Cambria County justice system. He'd been DA in the early '70s and then a county judge from the mid-'70s into the '80s. He had as good a vantage on the situation two decades before his heyday as anyone living.

Abood met us in his law office. He was tall and Lincolnesque, both in build and in the cragginess of his features; in his eighties but still practicing a bit. He and my dad weren't close friends but they greeted each other with the kind of quiet warmth that comes from living in a small town, where paths cross and re-cross over decades. "How you doing, Tony?" "OK, Cal, how about you?" "So good to see you. How's Rita?" My dad told him about the book I was working on, how he and I were trying to get perspective on Russ and Little Joe and how they did what they did.

Cal Abood wanted to start with a Charles Bronson story. Lots of the old guys in town have a Charles Bronson story. One of the biggest

Hollywood stars of the '80s had grown up in a poor-as-dirt railroad village in the hills just to the east of Johnstown. Abood told me about two kids he'd been friends with who used to hang out at City Cigar, named Tom Burns and Charlie Buchinsky. "Tom and Charlie came out of the war together. They both got the 52–20: the government gave you twenty bucks a week for fifty-two weeks, to get you started. They bummed around the pool hall for a while wondering what they were going to do with their lives. Tommy was a boxer. He said to Charlie, 'Let's go to Philly and see if I can get some work as a fighter.' Tommy eventually moved back home to marry his high school sweetheart. Charlie stayed and enrolled in acting school. Eventually he changed his name to Charles Bronson. And as you know, he became a big movie star. But he started out hanging around your grandfather's place."

"What did Tom Burns end up doing?"

"Hah! He became sheriff! We worked together. And he had to deal with Russ and Joe all the time. One day, though, who shows up in town but Charlie. He's a big star now. He's got his wife, Jill Ireland, with him. He wanted Tommy to come with him, to be the head of his security. He had a farm in Vermont, a home in Los Angeles, he was traveling the world. He needed someone he could trust. But Tommy didn't want to. His roots were here."

I told Abood I was trying to get a sense of Russ and Little Joe at their height—what the operation was like, how they set things up with the county's elected officials so that they could go about their business. "It was a very straightforward payoff system," he said. "They paid five percent of their take to whichever party was in power in the county, and in exchange they were left alone. Whenever an election was coming up, the party would call and say, 'The DA is going to be sending some officers. You should have someone at each of your shops, and you should have a few dollars and a few numbers tickets around.' Somebody had to take the fall. Then once they were at the county courthouse they would be sure to get the guy in front of Judge

Nelson. Judge Nelson was the friendly judge. 'Well, nobody got hurt. How do you plead? Guilty? A hundred dollar fine.' And that would be it. What they didn't want, but it happened sometimes, was to get in front of Judge Griffin. His nickname was 'Chains.' Judge Griffin didn't take any offense as minor."*

After we left Abood's office, Tony took me to meet his cousin, Frank Trio (not to be confused with Frank Filia, my mom's cousin). Frank, he said, would have another perspective on the power their uncle had had. Frank had lived with Joe and Millie for years and did odd jobs for them. Even in his eighties Frank was a ruggedly good-looking guy, with a chiseled face and a full head of lustrous dark hair. When we met I was struck by the fact that despite his age he seemed charged with pent-up energy. My dad had told me Frank had been a lifelong bachelor and tireless ladies' man. But all things pass. "So how you doing, Frank?" Tony asked as we sat down in his living room. "Well, I can still piss out of it," Frank said.

"Tell me about Joe," I said.

"I started out working as Uncle Joe's gardener," he said. After a while, since Frank was on his own, Joe and Millie told him he could live in their attic, which they made into a little apartment. "A little

---

* One of the old guys, named Jack Heinlein, told me a story that illustrated how Torquato's Democratic Party machine and Little Joe's organization worked together, and how his father got caught up in it: "My dad was retired from the Johnstown police force. One day he had a meeting with John Torquato and Joe Regino. And lo and behold, my dad became a county detective. It was understood that he would look after their interests." Things went along just fine for a long while, until one day Jack's father messed up. He was involved in a raid on one of Little Joe's gambling outfits. The understanding was that you would give advance notice of a raid, so there would be a modest amount of cash and betting slips around—just enough to look good when the news story came out. Somebody screwed up this time. They found $50,000 in cash in the place. Detective Heinlein had no choice but to continue with the bust. To make matters worse, it was in the paper. "They got Little Joe for fifty thousand bucks, and they got a picture of my dad in the *Tribune-Democrat* looking at the money," Jack said. "They were very good friends, but they had a falling-out after that. I told my dad that wasn't the brightest thing to do. He said, no, it wasn't."

while later, I'm downtown, and all of a sudden a cop pulls me aside and searches me. He knew I lived with Little Joe—he said he figured I was his gun man. That's what he said: 'gun man.' This guy was new to the force, he didn't know how things worked. I told Uncle Joe what happened. Next time I'm downtown, the same cop sees me, he says, 'Hi, Mr. Trio.' He always treated me with respect after that."

This prompted my dad to offer up another small example of the extent to which his father and uncle got their way. Russ, he said, would routinely pull up on Main Street in front of City Cigar, which was one building away from city hall, and leave his car there. There was no parking allowed on Main Street: the only cars would be his and Joe's. "They never got tickets!"

I wondered whether maybe he was exaggerating, building a stray childhood memory into a regular pattern, but then I came across a note on this very topic in the February 2, 1956, edition of the *Observer*, which reported more ground-level gossip than the *Tribune* did. Its publisher, Larry Martin, had begun a crusade against Joe and Russ, and over time he became snidely vocal toward Mayor Ned Rose, who had begun his term with some vigor but had steadily ceded power to Joe and Russ:

> And by the way, Ned, known racketeers, petty gamblers and pol-
> iticians make a habit of parking on Main Street directly opposite
> your office window during the late afternoon . . . while they lei-
> surely ignore the no stopping signs.

IT WAS ABOUT this time, when the organization was at its swagger-ing height, that Russ faced the biggest crisis of his career, if you don't count the self-generated ones. His boss and brother-in-law, Joe, had a falling-out with *his* boss, LaRocca. I got two different accounts of what caused the rift. One story was that Shangri-La was losing money; LaRocca blamed Joe and told him he wanted his investment back. Joe paid him, but considered himself mistreated—they had been business partners in the venture, which meant both ought to rise or fall on the investment. The other story I was told was that LaRocca had said something disparaging about Joe having adopted children. Which doesn't make sense on the face of it because apparently LaRocca himself had an adopted son.

The two men had been close since their days in post-Prohibition Philly. They had houses practically next to each other in Pompano Beach. Their wives were good friends. But now the rift between them threatened the operation in Johnstown. There was always pressure from guys in Pittsburgh trying to take over the local rackets: it was LaRocca who kept them in check. And the boys in New Kensington and Greensburg, who also turned in to LaRocca, would try muscling in on Johnstown as well whenever anyone's guard was down. Pippy diFalco, for one, seems to have caved in to their pressure, sometimes working with New Kensington and turning in to them rather than to Joe.

Suddenly everything was on the line. LaRocca sent a man to Johnstown and told Joe to make a place for him. Sam Fashion was from Altoona; his arrival in town meant that LaRocca didn't trust Joe anymore. "He was sent here to keep an eye on Little Joe," Mike Gulino told me. Joe was in a quandary because LaRocca wanted him to give Sam the sports book, which was Russ's territory. It was a bad time for Joe to stand up to the Pittsburgh boss. LaRocca was at this moment increasing his own power. He was pushing westward, moving to take over Youngstown, Ohio. And he'd become close with the Gambinos in New York.

Mike told me Russ was the one who saved Joe. "Russ found out," Mike said, "and he said, 'Joe, don't worry, I'll make it work.'" He gave Sam the sports book, but kept a watch on things. After a while, Russ saw they were actually losing money on sports. "Russ says to Joe,

'Sam Fashion don't know shit from Shinola,'" Mike said. "But Russ come up with another idea. He knew Sam was a real good cook. 'Why don't we put him in charge of Shangri-La?'"

So that's what they did, and Sam Fashion went for it. Maybe he was relieved. Joe had bought out LaRocca's share of the supper club; he now offered it to Sam. Sam was indeed a very good cook.* Business picked up after he became the chef.

Most of the old boys I talked to seemed to have liked Sam Fashion well enough, but those who had worked directly with him were of a different opinion. "He was so full of shit," Mike said. "He used to go to craps games. He thought he could skeech dice, but he couldn't make a seven with a pencil. I had to work with him for a while. Never trusted him."

My dad's cousin Frank Trio made the same point a little more forcefully. "I was a cook at Shangri-La. Sam Fashion was a no-good fuckin' bastard. A thief. He stole from the place for years, until Uncle Joe finally fired him. Then he asks me, 'Why didn't you tell me he was stealing?' I said, 'Uncle Joe, you always say you hate squealers!'"

The consensus of the old boys was that in negotiating a way through the split between his two superiors Russ saved the organization. Sam Fashion was accommodated, which mollified LaRocca, so that he didn't take any further steps that would threaten Johnstown. At least, not for the time being. Some of the guys likened Russ to an executive steering a company through difficult circumstances. "There were jobs at stake," one guy actually said. Several told me stories about how much Russ cared about the town and its people, that he felt something like responsibility. You needed money—he gave it to you, no questions asked. Mike in particular wanted to make sure I understood this side of Russ. "More than once I was with him," he

---

* To this day I make a cauliflower-and-anchovy pasta sauce that I learned from my mother, the recipe for which, she recently told me, originated with Sam Fashion.

said, "we'd get something to eat at a lunch counter, and when he got up to pay he bought lunch for the whole place, without telling a soul. He'd do things like that."

MY FATHER AND I had been trying to discover who his father was for three years now. After this much exploration, stitching together his memories and insights with all our other sources, we had a general sense of Russ in the mid-'50s as a man in charge. He had to have figured that he had well and truly arrived, that he had not merely beaten the system but changed it. He was basically part of the establishment. The payoffs formed a protective barrier. Behind it, he was flourishing in a way he could never have imagined even a few years before. Of course, he was also falling apart.

10

The Music

It was an Indian-summer morning in 1951, and Frank Filia was sixteen, walking down Main Street, aglow and alive and surging with all the possibility that this precise sunny moment held for him. The night before, he'd summoned his courage, walked into the Clinton Street Pool Room, and asked the boss, Yank Croco, for a job. Yank stared at the kid for a minute—he knew him; he came in sometimes and shot pool—and said OK. He could help out in the place, maybe run some numbers. A hundred a week. Come back in the morning.

And here he was, on his first assignment: go down to the newsstand and pick up the *Racing Form*. Even the price of it set this work apart: 35 cents! The regular newspaper cost a nickel. Then he heads back, opens the place up, takes the covers off the tables, cleans the felt, makes sure the chalk is stocked and the cue sticks are on their racks. He opens the paper, reads through the day's races, and calls the office, above City Cigar, to get the scratches from Johnny Oswald, one of Russ's main guys. Johnny's been at it for hours already. By now he knows which horses aren't running. Frank has to get the numbers of those horses so he can inform the bettors. First time Frank calls Johnny for scratches, Johnny corrects him on how to do it.

"First number: 23."

"Number 23."

"Wait a minute. Don't repeat after me. Just write 'em down."

"OK, but I was told to repeat . . ."

"You repeat when a guy's placing a bet. Guy says, 'Give me San Francisco minus three for twenty dollars.' You say, 'San Francisco minus three for twenty.' But when I'm giving you the scratches, you just listen and write."

But this moment, even before he starts, when he's strutting down the street about to start his first day on the job, is the one that stands out. "I honestly think that was the happiest day of my life," says Frank, a man in his eighties, who has lived a life of considerable hardship shot through with thin veins of sweetness, a life grounded on the philosophy of the gambler. "I was sixteen, walking down the street, the sun is shining, and I'm thinking, 'I'm in the *mob!*" He quit school on the spot. A hundred a week: that was what a middle-aged journeyman millwright at Bethlehem Steel earned, a union guy, with a wife and family. Frank said that that morning was the first time he understood what a city was. He saw the town as a machine made of many parts that fit perfectly together. An organism. You had the mills powering it all. The workers streaming into the gates with their hardhats and lunch buckets. Over there was the Woolworth lunch counter, where all the teenagers took their dates. Next to it the jewelry store where, a few years later, those same guys, now working in the mill, bought rings for the girls they'd made up their mind to propose to. And the realtor, where you went when you were ready to buy a house. The furniture store, to fill it. The place you bought clothes and things for babies. The schools. Even the store that sold you your gravestone. Every damn thing fit together.

And he was a part of it now, because the mob was a part of it. Everyone knew that. Everyone played the numbers, the pinball machines, the tip seals. They provided hope, exhilaration, energy. They were the juice.

Frank told me this was why he'd pressed me to write this book. He didn't want it to die and be gone forever. That moment, his realization, the beauty of the Clinton Street Pool Room, of the sweating and swearing men, the throaty laughter laced with menace on a hot summer afternoon, the lumbering bodies that suddenly became artful in bending over a table, the cue sticks angling like swords, of Red Picklo declaring he'd get a machine gun and wipe out all the motherfuckers, three-hundred-pound Joe Bruno who would make the guys guffaw when he'd take a couple of hot dogs with him to the toilet, the guy who thought he was a wolf-man, the drunk who would stagger into the poolroom and declare that he was going to invent perpetual motion. "I didn't know what the hell that meant. But I just loved it. The human thing. One time somebody took me to the ballet. I said, 'What the hell is this?' Then all of a sudden it hit me. They're speaking with their bodies! It was a wonderful world back then. It still is."

Frank was still a kid when he started at the poolroom. "We had our heroes. And you know who we admired most. Russ and Joe. But you didn't talk to them, not really. They were way up here. Intimidating." Frank would see Russ walking down the sidewalk, stopping a guy, engaging him in quiet, serious conversation, cigarette dangling, eyes narrow against the smoke. He sees Joe sitting on the bench in the park where he liked to muse on things. If you were a kid like Frank, you might get up your nerve, walk by and say, "Hiya, Joe," and he'd nod. Nice guy, helluva guy. But you didn't want to bother him. Everyone knew he liked this spot. (But how many of them knew why? How many knew that this was the very spot where, twenty years earlier, as a skinny kid, he'd drunk soda after soda, going in and out of the Dew Drop Inn to court Millie?) Russ and Little Joe, always in suits and fedoras, the big men at the top of the heap. "They ran the town. The mayor didn't. The mills didn't. They did. Everybody knew that."

———

BUMP AHEAD TO 1954. Tony Shorto is hanging out on Wolves' Corner, Main and Market, where guys congregate and wait for something to turn up. He's only fifteen but dressed like a twenty-year-old sharpy, in a tailored suit with pegged pants, baggy up top and tapered tight at the ankle. Suede shoes. Hair slicked back in a ducktail. Smoking a cigarette. Feeling pretty good but a little rootless—he'd cut school today. Not only that, he's decided he's not going back. He's free. But he doesn't know what to do with himself. Usually there's a crowd, but it's the middle of the day, not much going on. He decides to cross Main Street and go into City Cigar.

As he passes the bench in front of the place, he's aware of something moving. It's a man, a drunk who's stirring awake.

"Hey, kid!"

"Oh. Hiya, Chumsy."

"Hey, kid. Come here. This thing. I think I've got one in my ear. He went in my ear. It's crawlin' up around in my head."

"Oh, yeah? What can I do about it?"

"Can you look in there?"

He bends down.

"I don't see nothing, Chumsy. Maybe if you go back to sleep . . ."

As soon as Tony steps inside the poolroom Mike Gulino spots him, raises his eyebrows as if to say, *You know you're not supposed to be here.* Tony smiles: *It's OK.*

People are gathered around a table in back. Fat Pete is putting on a little show. He used to hustle on a national level—Indianapolis, St. Louis, Chattanooga, Winston-Salem—but as his condition deteriorated his game dropped. He has some kind of eye problem; he's now half-blind, and so fat he has to squeeze past the lunch counter in front. He can still beat most guys around here though.

Tony spots his friend Bob Meagher. "I saw Chumsy out front. Told me he had a worm crawling around in his head."

" 'Peachy, Peachy!' " Meagher says. "He calls me Peachy. I think he's a queer."

Sappy comes in, looking mean as usual. George Sapolich. He's a local boxing champ, runs craps games and is trying to start a poker game; turns in a percentage to Little Joe. He's tall and restless; his nose is bent. He's always pissed off at somebody. One time he clocked a guy in front of the movie theater and sent him to the pavement, out cold, a perfect stranger, just because he was in a bad mood. *You seen Pippy?* Nobody's seen Pippy yet today. *Owes me money. Someday I'm gonna kill that son of a bitch.* Sappy goes over to Meagher.

"Meagher, why don't you come down to my poker game?"

"Sorry, George, I don't play poker."

"Well, fuck you! Don't come to my poker game! Don't come anywhere near me, you shit!"

Meagher shakes his head. "Hey, George, do you punch yourself in the face at night to go to sleep?"

Sixty-two years later, Tony and Bob Meagher are sitting in Bob's backyard, laughing as they swap these stories about back in the day. Meagher segues to the present for a minute—he's got a sizable polyp in his colon but his prostate is surprisingly trim—then tells me how he walked into City Cigar one day and Buster Tenase, who was managing the place then, called him over. " 'Hey, kid, you wanna make fifty bucks?' 'Doing what?' I says. 'Take the pinch,' he says. Jesus Christ! I was never so mad. You know how when an election was coming city hall would call the place and tell them to get ready for a raid? Your grandfather would round up one of the old drunks, like Chumsy, to take the pinch. Guy like that already has an arrest record, getting busted doesn't mean anything to him. But I'm nineteen years old, I considered myself very sharp, full of promise. I was offended. I says to Buster, 'You must think I'm a real fucking loser.' I was so fucking mad, I walked out of the back door of the poolroom, which happened to lead right into the office of the draft board. I walked in there. I said, 'Take me.' And that's how I ended up in the army."

THEN THEY START talking about music—about the time, the precise moment, when music suddenly changed. "It was 1954," Meagher said. "You gotta understand we came from a great era. Tony Bennett was in his prime. Sinatra was in his prime. Such a great mixture of music, a soundtrack playing in the background of your life, wherever you went."

My dad interrupts: "The thing about it was, it was accessible to the general public, but it was intricate as hell. Complicated arrangements. Beautiful. Art—it was art!"

"That's it," says Meagher. "And then one day this guy comes along. And he goes: 'One . . . Two . . . Three o'clock. Four o'clock rock.' Huh? Then this prick goes, he goes, 'Five . . . Six . . . Seven o'clock. Eight o'clock rock.' And I'm thinking, What the *fuck* is *that*?"

"I hated it," Tony says.

"We all hated it," Meagher says. "It didn't suit our life."

Music guided Tony's development. He was precocious, dying to grow up, ready to be a man, if not exactly to act the part then at least to look it. ("Whoever heard of an eighth grader wearing tailored suits to school?" his cousin Marcia said. "That's what he did. Till he dropped out.") He glommed onto jazz early on—it had an arcane logic, a mystery you could ponder, almost like the mysteries of religion. That was partly why rock-'n'-roll never worked for him. Too direct. Woody Herman. Roy Eldridge. Gene Krupa. Eddie Shu. Jabbo Smith. As he got older he went deeper into it. Jon Eardley, a trumpeter who was from Altoona and whom Tony got to know personally before he made a name for himself in Europe. The guitarist Joe Pass was from Johnstown, had grown up in the same neighborhood as Russ. Mariano Passalaqua was his dad; Frank Filia's father had given Joe his first guitar. Jazz was a language. The human screaming of the horns, the syncopation, the narrow spaces of the jazz clubs, with their shifting clouds of cigarette smoke and the opaque, blue-black lighting, the mixing of races, the sweat on the face of a musician at work—all of it spoke to him, hinting at something.

Then Sinatra hit him. Right across Main Street from City Cigar was the Embassy Theatre. Tony walked out of it one night in October 1953. *From Here to Eternity* was the film. Burt Lancaster was the star, but Sinatra, in a supporting role, was the revelation. He'd been the big craze in the postwar years, fronting Tommy Dorsey's band, roomfuls of kids screaming at him doing his romantic cooing. Then, as with dozens of other pop stars, his career was over. He'd been exactly right for the time, the war and just after, and that was it. He faded away like the others.

But here he was, back, and in the most remarkable way. There had never been anything like it in American culture, an artist stopping his own free fall, taking his career by the horns, reinventing himself in front of the whole world. Landing a serious role in the year's biggest movie and playing the hell out of it.

One day in the car my dad started talking about all of this. He wasn't normally given to psychosocial analysis. I was intrigued by the amount of thought he had put into the subject, how he must have combed through it over the years. He talked about how the movie role served as Sinatra's pivot point, how he used the energy to recharge his music and his persona. Then he was suddenly changing music itself, leading his new label, Capitol Records, into uncharted terrain. The voice coming through the record player was pitched so personally, the vulnerability in the phrasing so raw. It had a new richness, a layer that wasn't there when he was with Dorsey, which hinted at life experience—dames, whiskey, wounds of the heart, being pushed around and learning to push back.

There was something else, which Tony didn't mention, maybe because it was too obvious. Sinatra was Italian. He was the signal that things had changed. You didn't have to live in some netherworld that existed alongside American society. You could be part of it; you could own it.

And I think there was one other thing as well, something in that voice, something very particular that registered in Tony's ear. The small-town element. Hoboken, where Sinatra had grown up, was another Johnstown, a little powerhouse of a factory town, narrow rectilinear streets forming a patchwork of ethnic ghettos. The money and power and muscle were there, just like in the big cities, but it was closer, more comprehensible. Growing up in a town like that gave you perspective. Frank Filia had discovered that too. The whole chain of being, from the bums on the sidewalk to the mayor puffing on a cigar in his office window, was right in front of you. You knew what it was all about. You felt, as you were coming of age, that you could take it on. You had the world on a string.

Tony jumped from that realization, that glorious burst of energy, right into the poolroom. He had to be there. He started showing up at all hours. The fact that his father didn't want him there made it tricky. The two of them were playing a game. Tony didn't quite get its rules, or why they had to play it. Because the poolroom was the center of things; it was where his future lay. But he had to calculate when Russ would be away. Then he could hang out, shoot pool, sharpen his game, chat up the bookies, watch the tip seals being delivered by the barrelful, listen to the clatter of the ticker machine, watch how bets were placed, see who the big players were, how they acted. All of this mattered. By now his parents knew he'd dropped out of school. His mother threw a fit. Russ and Little Joe dragged him to the principal's office, had a conference there. A skinny, handsome kid in a tailored suit, hanging his head but looking defiant as the adults had their adult conversation. You'll go back. No, I won't. The defiance was a cry for parental attention. And it worked. Not only his dad but his uncle took notice. The two biggest guys in town, making a fuss over him.

Tony didn't go back to school. The next day he was at City Cigar again, amid the cigarette smoke and the clack of balls. His game was getting pretty good. He'd never be a hustler, but that wasn't his path. He was supposed to be here. He was made for this. He knew everybody, from the bums to the lawyers shooting a game on their lunch break to the office workers and hustlers. People told him stories, bragged to him about his father; he listened with complicated pleasure as somebody described how Russ had beaten a guy out of $20,000 in a single card game. Tony knew his tactics. He'd watched as his dad practiced false dealing on the dining-room table. He was thrilled to hear the tales of his father's cheats, but as he described them to me I felt that something about these stories hurt too. Still, he talked to everybody, and he listened. He had a gift for chatter, a bright energy. He made friends easily. He may not have been good at cards, but he was a natural when it came to people, which his morose father was not.

Then one day a silence falls as Tony is bending over a shot. He turns around and there's Russ. Tony starts to bolt, but Russ has him by the collar. He lands a hard punch to the head, then another. He's a pretty meaty guy, and his kid's a skinny thing. Mike makes a move to step in but thinks better of it.

The beating itself wasn't the thing. What hurt, made this different from before, was the public humiliation. The businessmen, the off-duty cops. Sappy and Rip and Pippy. And Mike. In front of everyone, Russ told him, "I ever catch you here again, I will break your leg." And booted him out of the place like a bum. Rejection. Why? There was no answer. His father didn't explain with words. He spoke in gestures. You had to decipher them.

11

The Contradiction

THREE YEARS WENT by after Mike fractured the notion I had from childhood—that Russ had tried to pull Tony into the business but Tony had resisted—before I said anything to my father. Three years since Mike had told me it was the other way around, that Tony had wanted in but Russ beat him up in order to keep him out.

I'm not sure what held me back. Maybe wrestling with this topic threatened to breach a boundary I had established between my dad and me. Since his near-death experience we had become closer as we worked together on the mystery of who his father had been, but there was still a barrier of some sort. It had moved, softened, but it was there. And what was the purpose of this barrier? Maybe there was something beyond it that I would rather not know. Maybe there was a kid inside me who needed that original image intact.

Then he fell, right in front of me. We were leaving his house; I was going to take him to an appointment and then we were going to visit one of the old neighborhoods. He was supposed to use a cane or a walker when he went out, but he almost never did. There's a little stoop at my parents' house. I was standing on it, he was at the door.

His condition affected the leg muscles in particular—my parents had had to get one of those stair lifts installed in their home—so I held out a hand to help him step down. He reached for me, and as he stepped down he just collapsed. It was like his leg was made of twigs. Suddenly he was a pile of clothing on the stoop.

"He pushed me," he said later, when the doctor asked him what happened. Tony chuckled and I rolled my eyes. Next thing we knew, he was in the rehab unit of a nursing home. We were told the stay might be only for a couple of weeks, to monitor him and get him some physical therapy. But I knew better. These places didn't have revolving doors on them. We had reached a milestone in our journey.

The first time I visited him in the nursing home confirmed this. He was asleep. He slept the whole time. I watched him. I wasn't in a hurry. I thought about this, this project, and how we—him, me, his father, his grandfather—were beads on a string. The second time I visited, we chatted for a minute, then he fell asleep. For years now his sleep has been painful to watch: laborious, an enormous expenditure of effort to pull oxygen into those abused lungs. His mouth was open, his chest muscles snatching and straining. His stomach—which had still been quite large a year or so ago—was flattened and flubbery now; it contorted violently with every breath. He wasn't so much snoring as snorting, almost angrily, it seemed. A wave of anger shot through me. For a second I was just as mad as I was when I was a kid in the car and he insisted on smoking cigarette after cigarette, poisoning our air, clouding our childhood. He'd give a harsh chuckle at our pleas that he open his window, make a little joke out of our quibbling. Expertly unwrapping the cellophane top of the next pack, tossing it out the window ("Daaad . . . litter!"). Filling the dashboard ashtray with butts. Pushing in the dashboard lighter; when it popped he'd reach for it and bring its orange tip to the end of the next cigarette. Squinting through the piercing knife of smoke as he peered into oncoming traffic. The strained contortion on his face as he continued sleeping reminded me of the faces of some corpses you see, with the skin stretched taut, frozen in a final rictus. I sat there staring at the black-and-blue back of his hand as it clenched, and wanted more than anything to will him back into that thin, young father of four, that jazz-loving practical joker, bartender–cum–encyclopedia salesman, high school dropout in love with the idea of knowledge. One of his regular refrains was a statistic: that 90 percent of all scientists who ever lived were alive *right now*. He liked to sling brash insights, that guy, insights to shake your world, and he expected a "wow" to follow, and would look a little wounded if it didn't. He got his ideas from odd little magazines, the size of *TV Guide*, that blended business and marketing tips—"selling the sizzle"—sometimes with vaguely Christian messages. That '60s dad had broken free of the old world, the smalltime, small-town Italian American stuff, and was swimming in modern America. Mod furniture in the living room, Latin jazz on the console, fond of showing his exuberant love of life by giving his pretty wife a sharp slap on the ass, which embarrassed and thrilled us.

His phone starts ringing. It lurches him awake. "Oh, Russ." Rheumy eyes take me in. Then he completely surprises me by dropping his legs over the side of the bed and pulling himself up to sit. Hands on his knees, and we start talking. His voice is hoarse but he is here, with me, my dad.

There's a rustle from the bed on the other side of the room. "Did you meet Frank?" my dad asks. His roommate, it turns out, is Frank Pagano. I'm taken aback. "You mean from the Pagano brothers?"

"Sure!" Frank says.

I stumble into the mode of researcher, go over and shake hands, turn on the recorder on my phone. The Paganos ran a book back in the day. They had their territory. I had it on my list to track down and talk to someone who could tell me about it. I had a theory, or an idea anyway, which related to the murder of Pippy diFalco. It seemed too farfetched to think Little Joe would have had Pippy killed for skipping on his payments, but it was possible that Joe or Russ had told someone—maybe Rip—to put pressure on Pippy, and that things had gone too far. It was possible, in other words, that my grandfather had had a hand in the murder that sat near the center of this story. (My feelings on this question seemed to teeter both ways. On the one hand, I wanted to exonerate my namesake. On the other, were he involved in the deed, even indirectly and inadvertently, it would be pretty badass, and there was something thrilling in that, as if I might be able to convince myself that some of that had transferred to me.) But over time, as I talked to more and more people about how things worked, I formed the idea that the Paganos and their operation made that theory unlikely. From what everyone said, the Paganos didn't turn in a portion of their proceeds to Little Joe. And if they were able to be independent, I told myself it didn't make sense that another, even smaller-scale, bookie would be killed for exercising the same kind of independence.

I sat down beside Frank. He told me he was eighty-nine and that his wife was in here too. They could have put them in a room together, but she wanted her peace. So instead, as a consolation prize, he was rooming with Tony Shorto, whom he'd known since childhood. His arms were bone-thin, with silvery skin hanging off them.

I started asking questions, and a funny kind of triangle ensued. There was a divider in the middle of the room between the two men to give them privacy, but there was a mirror on the opposite wall, so they could look at each other that way. Both of them sat up in bed and we were all able to see each other in the mirror as we talked. I would ask Frank a question, he'd answer, then my dad would chip in some commentary.

RUSSELL: So, Sam was your brother, is that right?

FRANK: Sure. He owned Melodee Lounge—my brothers

bought it from Russ and Joe. What an entertainment spot. They had all the big names there. Tony, you remember Jon Eardley? Sensational trumpet player.

TONY*: Melodee Lounge is where Jon Eardley wrote "A Russ for Rita."†

FRANK: He played with Gerry Mulligan.

TONY: And Chet Baker.

FRANK: His wife was a wacko. The type of person who would have her Christmas tree up in July.

TONY: Frank worked at City Cigar.

RUSSELL: Really?

FRANK: Sure. I did everything. Racked balls. Took care of the place. I worked there when Buster managed it.

TONY: He means Buster Tanase.

FRANK: He was married to my sister Kate. God, what a death he had.

TONY: I told you about that.‡

RUSSELL: What was Russ like?

FRANK: Good guy, but he ran a strict ship. Pretty quiet. He had so much going on. They were good dressers, him and Joe. Hottest day of the year, white shirt and tie. Nice people to deal with.

RUSSELL: And what was Little Joe like?

FRANK: The mildest guy you'd ever meet in your life. He couldn't say the F-word for a mouthful.

RUSSELL: And he controlled everything?

* Looking at me in the mirror.
† I had heard all my life the story of how, right after I was born, my dad was at the Melodee Lounge to hear Jon Eardley and told him his wife had just given birth, and on the spot Eardley wrote and played a song for the occasion. Alas, it was never recorded.
‡ Buster Tanase was decapitated in a car accident.

FRANK: *Everything.* All the gambling.

RUSSELL: But your brothers had a separate bank, right? That's what everybody says.

FRANK: Nah! They liked to act like they were on their own. But at the end of the month every penny went to Russ and Joe.

This stopped me. There went my theory. I had it in my mind that the independence of the Pagano bank was exculpatory for Russ and Joe. It wasn't, really, but that's what I had decided. I had created a circumstantial out for my grandfather. And Frank had just destroyed it.

I asked Frank who he thought killed Pippy. "Rip was a shady guy," he said. "Rumor was he's the guy that killed Pippy. There was a lot of desperados in those days. But he was badder than most. You didn't want to get too involved with him."

Same story I'd heard from most of the others.

Frank then asked me to help him pee, which was a little forward, I thought, but I did it. Then he went to sleep. I went back over and sat beside my dad again. I told him I had made an appointment to talk to someone else I'd heard about from the old days, a guy named Tony Trigona, who had apparently been a bookie both in Johnstown and in New York City.

"Tony Trigona, sure!" Of course he knew him. This started a reflection. Tony Trigona was a cabinetmaker. My dad told me he had hired him to design the bar at the Factory, the disco he owned in the '70s, when he was at the height of his career as a small-town entrepreneur. "The whole time I was a bar owner I hated the look of bars," he said. "They're designed for losers. You all sit in a row and stare at bottles of alcohol. Even when I was a drinker I didn't like that. I asked Tony Trigona to make me a bar with curves, so people could naturally mingle. And it worked! It was the longest, curviest bar in western Pennsylvania. A lot of people met there and later got married."

Which brought me back to thinking about my dad in his prime. He'd been such a social animal. Again I thought about the contrast with his father.

I gave him a hug as I got up to go, feeling pretty sure this room was going to be his last home.

BUT DAMNED IF he didn't come back again. He hated doing physical therapy, but he knew they wouldn't release him unless he could walk twenty paces up and back on his own. He'd visited enough friends who had never gotten out of these rehab centers that he called them morgues. So he worked at it—not too hard, but hard enough—and in about three weeks he got himself sprung.

On my next trip to Johnstown we were sitting at my parents' dining-room table, Tony and me. His skin was saggier than ever—he'd once been overweight by a hundred pounds or more—but he was feeling pretty chipper. My mom was in the kitchen, which was about two steps away. It was afternoon, a milky light out the windows reflecting on the little windowpanes in their 1970s-era china cabinet. And now I was ready to talk, or rather to listen. Before coming I'd prepared myself by listening to the recording of my conversation with Mike of three years earlier, when he had corrected the story I'd grown up with. "I'm sorry, Russell . . . it wasn't like that . . . Your dad wanted to be a mobster in the worst way." I started by asking my parents how it was that I even knew, as a child, what my grandfather's business was. They didn't have an answer to that. We eventually agreed that kids just intuit things.

Eventually, in a sauntering way, I got around to wondering aloud when in my childhood I would have been told the story of Russ wanting Tony in the business but Tony refusing him. Here is what my dad replied:

"One of the things that came to light for me recently was I used to think that the horses that my uncle Joe and my dad had were at a farm right across from Pantana's farm. But that's not where it was. They kept them somewhere else. And I remember that now, but for years I thought that."

This was such a thorough non sequitur I could only see it as a dodge. He didn't want to go where I was going, so he just started talking about whatever. But I persisted. I said I grew up with the firm idea that he had rejected the mob career that his father had planned for him.

"No," my dad said then. "No."

My mom was suddenly right there with us. "No, it was the opposite," she said. "His dad didn't want him in the rackets."

"I know that now," I said, "because Mike Gulino told me."

"Yeah," my dad said. "Mike would have known that."

"But then why did I grow up thinking the opposite?"

Tony shook his head and gave a chuckle, as if he'd never heard such a silly thing. "I don't know," he said. "In fact, I'll tell you, my dad really beat me up when he caught me in the poolroom."

This was strange—sort of dismaying. I had expected, dreaded, and maybe also hoped for, a tussle when I finally confronted my parents with this contradiction. Or else there would be an apology. *I lied to you, made up a story. I wanted you to think I was a good guy.* I didn't expect total negation of the memory.

"So why did I think that was the way it happened?" I asked again.

"Maybe you just . . ."

My mother stopped. Maybe I just . . . made it up? That's what she was going to say. And why would I do that? To put a rosier gloss on things? But I didn't even know what those things were. I let the matter drop. But later, in the hour's drive home, I kept thinking about it. Was it possible? I'm traversing the terrain of memory, working with the reflections of the elderly, trying to tease things out of them that happened sixty, seventy, eighty years earlier. Memory, as we all know, is hardly an exact record. The mind fuses together events that happened years apart. People get added to a scene who weren't there at all. A red shirt becomes a yellow dress. And memories form and reshape over time, as if made of wax. They say that each time you recall a memory the physical act of recalling changes it a bit. The unconscious mind might need to soothe a raging conscience, or to ease the pain of a hurt that's too great. In the interest of self-preservation, *that* past will now be *this* past. In the case of my father, I'm trying to chip away at walls he may have built to protect himself from childhood pain. As a general procedure, I'd been doing what I could to check memories that all of my interview subjects were unearthing for me against hard documentation: police records, FBI files, news accounts. As well as against other people's stories. Trying to anchor the slippery stuff of human memory.

But what about my own memory? When had I been told this story about Tony and Russ? Who had told me? If I were being honest I needed to consider the possibility that this was some kind of childish invention.

I hit on an idea. I sent a text to my siblings. I kept it general. What did anybody remember from childhood about our dad and our grandfather and the mob?

Eva, the youngest of us, wrote right back. She had no childhood memory of any of it. Nobody ever talked to her about the mob or gambling or anything; most of what she had heard was recent, basically since I had begun working on this book. This made sense. I had a strong feeling that I had taken this information in quite early. At six years younger than me, she wouldn't have been aware of it.

Scott, who was next youngest, didn't reply to my text, which was typical—he doesn't like to get involved in family dramas, which he seemed to suspect this could become.

Then Gina texted. She is closest to me in age. And she remembered it pretty much the way I did, and recounted it in a way that suggested she still felt proud that our dad had stood up to the mob for us. I called her and we talked about it. She didn't remember how far back she had heard it, but she too thought it was quite early.

OK, that righted me. I could go on with my work. I hadn't invented the story. Somebody else had done it for me.

FRANK FILIA CALLED me. "I thought you'd want to know. Mike had a stroke." I hadn't been in touch with Mike Gulino for a year or more. I was involved in another book project, and had set the Johnstown interviews aside, except for these conversations with my parents. I'd meant to keep in touch with Mike, though, and instantly regretted not doing so. I called his house. Eleanor answered. She said Mike had actually had two strokes, and was now blind and had dementia. "He's in a nursing home. I couldn't handle it anymore." I asked if I could go see him. She said I could, but that he might not remember me or much of anything.

I went, expecting simply to sit with him, to be a friend, which I considered I was by this point. He was dressed, sitting up in a chair, staring straight ahead. The TV was on, on the opposite side of his room, but it was clear he couldn't see it. He was clutching a plastic Tupperware container with a lid on it. He could tell someone had come in, and turned toward me. I told him who I was.

"Russ Shorto! Goddamn son of a bitch, sit down and let's talk!" So that was a relief. I asked him what he was holding. "These are called hemp hearts. Nothing to do with marijuana. These are gonna save my life. If I'd run across hemp hearts sixty years ago, I wouldn't be in here. I'd be out walking around and enjoying life. I bought four cases. I eat them with my cottage cheese."

He ran down the list of his physical problems and how they had worsened dramatically since I'd last seen him. Before, when I was meeting with him regularly, his wife took him every day to the YMCA to go swimming. But that was over. "I just sit here all fuckin' day." He was indeed blind. And probably his ability to recall the recent past had suffered, but he was still tuned in to the era of zoot suits and Studebakers. I lobbed a question and he started talking. One thing led to another and soon he was going on about being in the army in Italy in 1952, running cons and making deals as he traveled. He said he made $50,000 selling flint in Sicily, and that he brought a trick top with him that he carried around to army bases. He'd sit down at a bar and challenge soldiers to spin it and bet on the number that came up: "The worst I could do was a tie." He went into some stream-of-consciousness name-dropping about those days. "I'm driving from Palermo to Messina on the intercoastal road, and who do I see but Tallulah Bankhead. She had a wine bath. We became friends. I knew Mario Puzo, knew him pretty well. His secretary had a deep voice, like a man's. I talked to her on the phone one time and thought it was him. She laughed. Only true thing in *The Godfather* was when he said the higher up you go, no matter what the business, the bigger the thieves. Even in the Catholic Church. *Especially* in the Catholic Church. I met Charlie Luciano in Naples. He started the mafia. He says what's your name. I says Michael Gulino, Johnstown, Pennsylvania. He had a place called the Snake Pit. He had guy whores in the place. That's the first time I ever heard of a guy whore. All these women came from the Netherlands to be with them. I stayed at the Excelsior Hotel in Naples. Twenty bucks a night, best hotel in Italy. They had a barber would come up to your room and shave you. I met Luciano through a friend, who said if you ever go to Naples look him up. So I go to his club. He had a great big pit there with nothing but snakes in it. I asked the waiter: Is Mr. Luciano in? I gave him my friend's name, a friend from Detroit. Charlie comes down. He says, 'Anything you want, any broad you want.' And every time I got to Naples I'd go see him. Jesus, it's good to talk about this stuff."

He was silent for a while. Then he looked at me. His eyes were different than before, seeming desperate to find something to grab on to. "How many people did you have to talk to until you started to realize that your grandfather wasn't such a bad guy?" he asked.

I stopped myself from saying that that was a leading question, the premise of which I didn't necessarily agree with. "You were the first," I said. Then, nudging him in another direction, I added, "Back then, men didn't explore their feelings. Maybe that's the essence of the relationship he had with his son—my dad."

He talked a little bit about his later career. In the '70s and '80s he built a huge sports book, which spanned the eastern part of the continent, from Toronto to Miami. That crashed and burned in 1985, when the FBI collared him. He was convicted, and served eighteen months in prison. What annoyed him about it, he said, was the way events had overtaken him. Here he was, running a gambling operation and getting busted for it while state lotteries—legalized gambling—had become the norm. "What a sap I was."

As I got ready to go, he tossed out one more memory of my grandfather, in which, again, he had an active role and Tony had a passive one.

"You know, a lotta times I brought Russ home," he said, "and we were arm in arm, because he was dead drunk. I'd bring him into the living room. Mary would be there, and your dad too. I'd lay Russ down on the couch. I knew it was hard on all of them. Russ used to lecture me, tell me to keep away from the whiskey. 'This stuff ain't holy water.' "

I told Mike I'd come back soon to see him.

IN OUR MOST recent conversation, my dad had applied a phrase to his teenage years, one that he'd used in the past: *misspent youth*. A wistful and a poetic phrase. And a vague one. It stuck with me over the next week or so. I went back through my interview notes. There was something Frank Filia had mentioned in one of our early sessions. Something about cats? I found it: *cat gang*. Only a mention, with a knowing smile. "Ask your dad about it." I didn't want to. Instead, I went to the Cambria County Library and the Johnstown Area Heritage Association and began paging through newspapers from the '50s.

Even without an index, it wasn't hard to find the cache of stories on the topic. "We read where some juveniles robbed a number of local business places and broke open safes . . ." "The Cats are again at work." "The Cats are breaking open safes, and entering locked doors . . ." "All the members of the cat gang from our district, and the other hoodlums who have been arrested many times, are back in school and are posing as heroes . . ." "Some boys boast that they are the kings of the Cats."

In the mid-'50s, the town was plagued by a gang of marauding teenagers wielding guns and knives. One account called it "a real reign of terror." The next time I was at my parents' house I prepped myself to ask my dad about it. But I didn't have to. The subject just came up. Tony was slightly different in this conversation than he'd ever been. Things were changing in some way. I guess the stint in the nursing home had done it. We had arrived at new territory, which apparently could be explored without drama. He was open, which was not in itself unusual—he took pride in following his "you're only as sick as your secrets" mantra. But now he was not just answering questions but reaching, offering connections. As we started talking, for example, he volunteered that his father had openly favored his brother over him.

"So when you were in your teens, you were never close to your father?"

"Never. I don't remember hugging him ever. I remember him showing my brother more affection than he did me. He would come home and give him baseballs and stuff."

"Why the difference?"

"I was older and I understood what was happening with him and my mother."

"Did you ever stand up for her?"

"Yeah. But it wasn't really necessary. He ran. He would never stick around and fight. She never let up on him."

"As a teenager, you were being a badass around town."

"Exactly. That pissed him off."

Then he told me about a couple of times, with his parents fighting and his father rejecting him, when he had bolted. "At fourteen years old I ran away to Florida. Me and Moose Eliot. And I ran away to Ohio, me and Joe Esposito and George Lopez. We went to Cleveland. Later when I was back home the FBI came to the house looking for Tony Morello!" His mood had lightened suddenly; he was laughing at his young self as he said this.

I was confused. "What? The FBI? Who was Tony Morello?"

"Me. That was the alias I made up when we ran off. I was traveling under an assumed name! I don't know how they connected it with me. Man, did my dad get pissed off at that!"

This was when my mother, who I think was thinking of the names of the kids he had run away with and their association with him, suddenly volunteered the information. "He was in a gang called the cat gang."

"That's where I met Rip," Tony said. "We were in jail together."

"For what?"

"Armed robbery. And five or six burglaries."

"What, you had a gun?"

"Yeah. In one of the first burglaries, we took about twenty guns from a sports store on Washington Street. We used them in the other ones. I did three months up in Ebensburg Juvenile Detention. I was fifteen."

What I didn't say, but might have, was something like *I know why you did it*. But I didn't know then. I was just trying to absorb this new information, which suddenly both of my parents were offering matter-of-factly. I hadn't yet put any puzzle pieces together. And while it was a surprise to hear of my dad as a teenage gun wielder, a prisoner because he couldn't become a mobster, at the same time it wasn't a surprise. Somehow, I had known this. I just hadn't heard it until now.

12

The Haven

SOMETIME IN 1956, Little Joe decided he'd had enough of Russ's drunken binges. He showed up at Russ's house, and he brought John Strank, their partner in City Cigar, with him. Russ was coming off a bender. He had failed in some decisive way, one of a string of failures to show up or otherwise to do his job. Joe and Russ had remained close through everything, but Joe believed in discipline. "Uncle Joe didn't want to do it, but he had to," my dad told me. I hadn't heard about this before. Mike Gulino was the one who had told me, and now when I brought it up Tony suddenly remembered the scene like he was watching it on TV. He had been there, listening from the top of the stairs. He remembered that John Strank was in the room, but that John didn't say much. He was there as kind of a mediator, a mutual friend, who solemnized and formalized the occasion with his presence. Tony heard his uncle tell his dad that he was letting him go, he had no choice, and he knew that Russ knew that was true. Russ didn't try to argue his way out of it. He just started crying. "I cried too," my dad said.

Shortly afterward, Russ bought a bar of his own. He called it the

Haven. Maybe he chose the name with his own needs in mind, though you would think if he was seeking refuge from drink he might have chosen another channel for his activities. Then Joe decided to give him a second chance. Russ jumped at it, vowed to reform, and soon went back to making his usual rounds on behalf of the organization: his morning shave and nails done at Pantana's barbershop on Washington Street, then stopping in at City Cigar, the bowling alley, the Melodee Lounge, and Shangri-La. The banks, the bookies, the takes, the percentages.

He remained in his brother-in-law's good graces enough that, in September 1956, he was given honored treatment. Russ's mother, Annamaria Previte, died then, seventy years after her birth in San Pier Niceto. Her last years had been spent mostly in bed, her white hair foaming around her head, making her a figure of wonder and terror to her younger grandchildren. She had lived more than half a century in Pennsylvania but never learned more than a few English phrases. Everyone I talked to remembered the funeral. Some said there were a hundred cars in the procession, that the funeral home was so stuffed with flowers they trailed all the way down the sidewalk. People had come from as far away as Pittsburgh to pay their respects. Little Joe and John LaRocca had conspired to make her sendoff a grand affair, a show of respect. Word was that Kelly Mannarino had contributed an entire truckload of flowers. Despite his lapses, Russ still rated.

But while he was back in the organization, from now on he had a new base. The Haven was something that was just his. Or rather, it was theirs: Mary was listed as the actual owner of the bar, and she worked there too sometimes. So they had a little bit of a partnership going. They were trying to start over. "I still love Chinky," Russ told Minnie. He gave his brother Tony a job at the Haven. It was a nice little bar too, on a lively corner, not downtown but at a crossroads where several neighborhoods came together. It's still there today.

The Haven was the kind of place where friends would meet for a drink and a few laughs. Russ and Mary were close with a couple named Alex and Vicky Yuhas. They would drive down to the bar from their house, just up the road in Southmont, and the four of them would have cocktails at a table near the front window. Alex was a supervisor at Bethlehem Steel; Vicky worked for a fur company.

Then Alex got sick, and Russ began to help Vicky out. Vicky was fourteen years younger than Russ—he was forty-three, she twenty-nine. She had been a beauty queen, Miss Cambria County. My way of gauging the start of their affair comes from Frank Filia. Frank had been building a name as a singer with the George Arcurio Orchestra throughout the 1950s. One night in late 1957 he was playing at the Forest Park Club and saw Russ in the audience. "It was such a big deal to me, because Russ never gave me the time of day. And here he'd come to see me. And he actually requested a song. 'All the Way.'"* The other thing Frank remembered about that night was that Russ had Vicky with him. It was Vicky who liked the club and pressed him to take her there.

This time, when Mary found out she took some pills. Actually, it was her second suicide attempt. The first time wasn't so scary; she went to the hospital and came back soon after. She had done so much for him, been the dutiful wife. Russ would bring business associates home at three in the morning; without complaining she would wake up, fly into the kitchen, and cook them a full meal: spaghetti and filet mignon.

But this was a particularly sharp betrayal. Something very heavy descended on Mary after she found out about Vicky. She slid into a studied listlessness. After sending the kids off to school, she would draw the curtains and sit alone in the dark house, letting morning

---

* The song had come out in October of that year. It was featured in the film *The Joker Is Wild*, in which Frank Sinatra plays a singer in the Prohibition era who is pressured by mobsters to work for them. He becomes an alcoholic. I have to think Russ saw it, and can't help but wonder if he felt echoes of his own life in it.

give way to afternoon. One day she went up to the bathroom and began swallowing pills. Apparently deciding that moving her body would hasten the effect, she proceeded down to the basement and started washing clothes. Tony wasn't at home, but he had been sensing the gathering darkness. Miraculously, an ambulance showed up at the house. The doctor came out of the emergency room wearing a serious look and said, "I don't know if we can save her."

Mary lived. When she came home from the hospital she was puffed up. Minnie told me that after that, when she would go to their house in the middle of the day she could often tell that Mary had been drinking, and the place would be messy and kind of odd. "There would be, you know, a hammer or something on the coffee table."

Life on Rambo Street lurched on. Tensions between Russ and Tony didn't lessen, but his mother's brush was death brought about a change in Tony. He was seventeen, filled with hurt, but now feeling the need to grow up. He suddenly regretted dropping out of school, and signed up for classes that would get him a diploma. He only went a few times, but he was trying. He had outgrown the cat gang. He still hung out with some tough guys. Rip, for one. Like everybody else, he was freaked out by the guy. Neither his father nor his uncle liked him to associate with Rip, for the same reasons they called on Rip to do ugly jobs. Around this time, Tony and Rip took a trip to Atlantic City. They swam around the steel pier together. The pier was a quarter mile out to sea. They were both in shape, both excellent swimmers. When I asked him why Rip of all people attracted him, he shrugged and said, "I was nuts!"

Smarting from his father's rejection, Tony started veering away from City Cigar when he was downtown and instead headed across Main Street to Weiser's Music Center. Kids his age were always inside checking out what was new, standing around with headphones on, bobbing their heads. Music had settled into a firm groove: "All Shook Up," "That'll Be the Day," "Little Darlin'," "Wake Up, Little Susie."

None of that existed for him. He'd slip into one of the listening booths, put a different platter on the turntable—"A foggy day . . . in London town. . . ."—and start snapping his fingers. He absorbed each of Sinatra's albums from those years—*Songs for Young Lovers, Swing Easy!, In the Wee Small Hours, A Swingin' Affair!*—and decades later could recite the song order on each and tell you who did the arrangement. Others his age were going to sock hops. Still kids and acting like it. Sinatra was a generation older, and most of the songs he sang were older still, but, for Tony, Sinatra was pointing the way. This was how a man behaved. This was how you showed toughness—with an open cut of vulnerability. This was how you held a cigarette, your whiskey, how you squinted to express world-weary resignation, how you treated a woman. This was how you invented yourself.

RUSS WASN'T THERE. Little Joe might have been there, in which case he was one of the middle-aged men running awkwardly across open fields in suits and ties and patent-leather shoes, fleeing the cops. John LaRocca was one of the runners—he got away. Kelly Mannarino from New Kensington got nabbed and was subjected to the indignity of being arrested and jailed like a common criminal.

It was a defining event in the history of organized crime in the United States, and the beginning of the end for the outfit in Johnstown. History books call it the Apalachin meeting. On November 14, 1957, somewhere around a hundred mob guys from all across the nation gathered at the country home of Joseph Barbara—the Little Joe of Scranton, Pennsylvania—in the rural town of Apalachin, New York. A state trooper noticed a large number of cars with out-of-state license plates in the area. The cops established a perimeter around the estate and moved in. The boys ran for it. About fifty-eight of them were collared.

What made the bust significant was J. Edgar Hoover, the all-powerful head of the FBI. Even after the Kefauver Committee had issued its findings on illegal gambling operations and their spread around the country, Hoover insisted that these were independent units and therefore not of major importance. There was no interconnected network; there was no American mafia that held councils and issued rulings over governance. One theory holds that Hoover maintained this position because he was a zealous protector of the bureau's image and he knew that hunting and prosecuting the mob would be a long and messy business that would likely tarnish it. Another is that Hoover was unable to take his eyes off what he felt was the real threat to the country: communism.

The Apalachin meeting made it impossible for Hoover to deny that there was a nationwide mafia. The men captured at the farmhouse included bosses from Utica; Rochester; Cleveland; Dallas; Pittsburgh; Philadelphia; Kansas City; Tampa; Providence; Springfield, Illinois; Springfield, Massachusetts; Elizabeth, New Jersey; and Los Angeles, as well as representatives of all of the five families that ran New York. The federal government was forced to recognize the mafia as a criminal organization that operated across state lines. Hoover immediately instituted what he called the Top Hoodlum Program to track mob activity.

Nearly five years after filing a Freedom of Information Act request, I received two CDs from the FBI filled with documents that detailed the movements of the federal agents who implemented that program in western Pennsylvania—who, sixty-odd years earlier, were doing what I had been doing recently: chasing after Russ and Little Joe and their colleagues. The first item was the memo from Hoover, dated ten days after the Apalachin meeting, ordering every FBI office to "open an active investigation on each top hoodlum." It listed fifty-one cities where "personal attention" was required, from Knoxville to Honolulu. LaRocca was identified as the "top hoodlum" in western

Pennsylvania. The directive made clear he wasn't the only target of investigation in the area: "Since each top hoodlum undoubtedly has subordinates carrying on legal and illegal operations under his direction, it will be necessary to fully identify and describe the activities of these persons." Agents were also instructed to break down their reports into categories. Suggested categories included "prostitution; narcotics; gambling (subdivided as to bookmaking, lotteries, basketball and football pools, coin operated gambling devices, dice games, card games, roulette, horse racing, etc.); illegal union activities; illicit alcohol; fencing of merchandise, including that moving in interstate commerce; hi-jacking; interstate transportation of stolen property violations; fraud against the government violations, etc."

Agents fanned out. In Johnstown, they managed to locate informants who worked for Russ and Joe at City Cigar and Capital Bowling. They began filing their reports, which included lists of cities to which telephone calls were made from their subjects' residences (Little Rock, Newark, New York, Philadelphia, Wilkes-Barre) and accounts of interviews, the copies of which I received were heavily redacted:

On 1/2/58 [_____] was interviewed at [_____] where he is employed in a junk business owned by [_____]. It is to be noted that [_____] are presently on parole and that [_____] parole will expire on 5/18/58.

The agents zeroed in on Little Joe:

The gist of the information furnished by these informants is that Regino is the head of the 'syndicate' in Johnstown, Pa., and as such is responsible to men more highly placed in the syndicate, allegedly to individuals in the Pittsburgh area. His responsibility in the Johnstown area is to see that protection is arranged for the various gambling activities—i.e., slot machines, tipseals, numbers and some card games, and to generally control gambling because of this protection issued to him. Openly he is the owner of the Capitol Bowling Alleys located at the corner of Franklin and Vine Sts . . . On 1/14/58 [_____], Johnstown Credit Bureau, advised that Regino . . . was listed as the co-owner of the City Cigar Store . . . She noted that the City Cigar Store has always been notorious as a hangout for gamblers of all types.

The FBI files mostly corroborated what I had learned from the Panera sessions and other sources. I allowed myself a flicker of smugness over the fact that my information was considerably richer than what the bureau had obtained, though there were a few interesting new details in the CDs. I learned, for one, that LaRocca had given money "to Samuel R. Di Francesco to aid him in his campaign for district attorney of Cambria County." That put the Pittsburgh boss directly in the midst of the activities of Joe, Russ, and the others in town as they became part of the establishment. "After his election," the report noted, "this group had control of Cambria County."

THE LURKING PRESENCE of FBI agents adds a wash of mystery to my mental image of the scene at the corner of Main and Market on an evening that has personal significance for me. It was December 1957, and the liveliest intersection of downtown Johnstown was crawling with holiday shoppers. City Cigar was doing a robust business, and people were streaming in and out of the Mission Inn next door. Tony happened to be on the corner, in front of city hall, hanging out with a guy named Louie Alvarez, when a woman stepped off a bus and met her friend. He knew one of them: Joyce Fratterole's family used to live next to his uncle. He introduced himself to the other girl, who fourteen months later would become my mother, and asked what they were doing. They were headed to the movies. When they came out of the theater, he was there, under the marquee, waiting. It was raining. He asked if he could give them a ride. Smooth fellow, he dropped Joyce off first, even though it would probably have been more logical to go to Prospect and then to Hornerstown. As he pulled up in front of Rita's house, he asked her out.

My mom, at nineteen, was sweet, shy, petite, pretty. She could have played a naïve bombshell in a Fellini film from the period, with her close-cropped black hair, bangs, and searching eyes. They were a match of personalities: Tony the oldest in a family of three children, who was used to doing things his way, Rita the youngest of five, the baby of her family, who didn't mind playing follow the leader. But there was a hidden inversion. If you encountered them at a party back then you would assume that the gregarious, self-assured, practical-joke-loving fellow was the stronger of the two and the somewhat hesitant date he was introducing everyone to would over time freely bend herself to his will. You would be right in that she followed him in many things, but as the decades unfurled she turned out to be the one with the grit and resolve to hold both her family and her husband together.

Both families' American identities were inflected by their southern Italian origins, but hers were more immediate. Her father had emigrated as a teenager, along with his brother. Dominico—who became Dominic—threw himself into America, and insisted that English be the language at home. But when his friends came over they roared at each other in Italian, and in many other ways, especially food, it was an Italian household. Dominic worked at the mill until one day his car was hit from behind by a bus; he used the money from the settlement to quit his job and open a corner grocery store. That's where Rita was working in the months between graduating high school and meeting Tony.

She knew who Tony was from the start; everyone knew City Cigar and the people connected to it. Her parents, when she introduced

Tony and Rita at Russ and Mary's house the day after their marriage.

him to them, seemed, she says, to act as though Russ's was a respectable career path, as if their daughter was dating the son of a prominent local accountant.

But a theoretical racketeer is different from a flesh-and-blood one. A photograph I have of my two grandfathers on the night they met, in August of 1958, taken the evening my parents returned from their hasty elopement to a spaghetti dinner Mary hosted for both families, shows Rita's timid shopkeeper father looking terrified as Russ sits beside him, smug and drunk, one arm proprietarily flung over the shoulder of his new relation.

———

AND HERE WE are, suddenly, at the moment—the murder that marked the beginning of the end for Russ. Pippy diFalco's death doesn't connect in any obviously direct way to my parents coming together, but in a small town and a small story all the threads pull on one another. There is, for one thing, the possibility that their best man was the murderer.

My parents met in December; in May, Rita was pregnant. In August, unable to hide it much longer but also unable to face their parents, they decided to run off to Virginia Beach, where they heard they could find a justice of the peace who would marry them. Tony was selling used cars; he borrowed one for the weekend. They packed a few things.

But wait. They wanted a witness. Someone to act as best man. "No, not a best man," Tony insisted when I suggested this. "He just came to drive the car." But why him, of all people? Tony shrugged. Rita offered that maybe he was the only person free at the time. I asked my mom if she liked Rip. "No! I was scared of him. He had a thing where he would date women and take all their money. He'd con them. He married this woman who was so nice, she was real straitlaced, and he was miserable to her. After they divorced he ran off with this other man's daughter, who was underage." Tony added: "That guy was so beside himself that Rip took his daughter away that he went after him. He thought he was going to kick the shit out of him. Rip broke his leg."

"So this is the guy you chose to take with you when you eloped," I observed. "The guy who had formerly been the head of a street gang. Who you met in prison."

They both fell silent. "I never liked him," Rita said. "I heard he died recently," Tony said. "He was living in Florida for a long time."

13

The Murder

IN FEBRUARY OF 1960, Pippy diFalco was a forty-five-year-old bookie well known around town. He worked for himself but turned in a percentage of his take to Little Joe's organization. Or was supposed to. He had a wife named Barbara who was twelve years younger than him, and a two-year-old boy. Just about all my sources knew him. My dad knew him. So did Minnie. Frank Filia crossed paths with him on a daily basis: "A funny guy. You never knew what he was thinking." Mike Gulino probably knew him better than anyone still living. They were partners for several years, working a book as a team. "I met him right when he came out of the service, right after the war. We trusted each other. Kinda. The thing about Pippy, he was the type of guy, if somebody was making money, he felt he was supposed to get some of it. Greedy. We had a nice little business together. Then, next thing you know, he's working for Little Joe and Russ, and our thing is over. Then he quits that and goes out on his own."

Pippy worked his own circuit, had about fifty regular customers. He'd meet them at City Cigar, the Mission Inn, the Show Boat, moving around town. Most paid cash—he'd add it to that big bank roll of his; for some he'd take their bets on credit.

He went missing sometime after two in the morning on February 7. The next day he wasn't at the Embassy Theatre to sit through viewing after viewing of the day's feature. The ticket takers at the Majestic and the State didn't see him either. He didn't show up at the Acme supermarket for bologna and sliced bread. Nobody at City Cigar or the Clinton Street Pool Room would likely have registered surprise at his absence. He could have been on an out-of-town run; otherwise, he often had good reason to lay low for a spell.

Barbara knew something was wrong right away. She was aware of his tendency to chase around after other women, but she also knew he was fussy about keeping in touch with her. Even when he went to Pittsburgh, three hours away, he would call—long-distance, collect—to let her know he'd arrived safe.

By mid-February, with Pippy's car still parked on Vine Street where he he'd left it, people began talking. Larry Martin, the editor of the *Johnstown Observer*, picked up the chatter. He and his wife, Peg, had taken over the weekly newspaper a few years earlier and given it new life. They were a good team: he editor in chief, she "office manager" and dogged reporter. They featured a gossip column on the front page and both worked hard to fill it with things that people were really talking about, things the daily, the *Tribune-Democrat*, didn't devote stories to until they had fully blossomed. "A well known 'man about town,' known as a 'bookie' to his friends, has been reported missing from his usual haunts for about two weeks," Martin wrote on February 18. The Martins had been hearing gossip about growing tensions between factions in the western Pennsylvania mob: "In fact, the New Kensington crowd is ready to move into the city lock-stock-and-barrel, if they haven't already. A conference is now being held in Florida to decide who is to take over what part." According to their information, within LaRocca's realm the New Kensington faction was ascendant, and Little Joe's Johnstown organization was slipping. The Martins wondered whether the bookie's disappearance was connected to this change in fortunes.

Little Joe was suddenly feeling pressure from within the city government as well. Ned Rose, who had come in as mayor in 1948 and had been a good friend to the organization, who seemed to be as much a presence at City Cigar as he was at city hall, was out. The man who had been elected to replace him, George Walter, was a newcomer who had run on a commitment to reform local politics. Walter was a young man with a PhD in sociology and a clean image that belied a tenacity. He had a freshness that reminded people of Sen. John F. Kennedy, whose face was everywhere these days and who later that year would be elected president.

Walter took over the mayor's office in city hall just weeks before Pippy went missing. Given the way he'd campaigned, there was little likelihood of him stopping in at City Cigar for a collegial game of pool, but Joe and Russ tried to get him on their side anyway. A decade later, when the Pennsylvania Crime Commission held public hearings on mob activity in the state, Walter testified that on four separate occasions representatives from vending-machine companies in Johnstown, which were owned by Little Joe, had offered to make contributions to his political campaign; that five times during his term he found an envelope containing $400 cash on his desk; and that a prominent Johnstown businessman had offered to make him vice president of a new corporate franchise in exchange for him agreeing to a "controlled gambling" arrangement like the one that attorney Caram Abood had told me was in effect in the '50s. "We would arrange for each one of the numbers banks to contribute one victim for each term of court," Walter told the Crime Commission in describing the plan put before him, with the idea that these regular scapegoats would make him "respectable with the *Tribune-Democrat*." Walter said he refused.

The boys supposedly tried something similar with the new district attorney. Ferdinand Bionaz had likewise entered office on the winds of change. He told the Crime Commission in 1971 that two men had approached him when he ran for office saying they wanted to contribute money to his campaign. One was Little Joe. The other was George Bondy, who had accompanied Russ when he took Tony for his memorable trip to Atlantic City to introduce him to the gambling world. "Mr. Regino said that he felt I was a great guy because I had adopted two children, he had adopted a child, and that we should have something in common," Bionaz told the Commission. He went on to say that Little Joe had told him "he had friends who needed encouragement from time to time. And that he wanted to have a district attorney that wasn't going to go out and cut throats." Bionaz said he told Little Joe he didn't need his help. Nevertheless, after he won election he said he found an envelope containing $1,000 in cash on his desk.*

In January, then, District Attorney Bionaz and Mayor Walter became allies. Before Pippy diFalco's disappearance had even become public knowledge, Bionaz announced an assault on the local rackets. Then in late February, the city police started looking into the Pippy diFalco situation. A detective named Milan Habala became the point man, trudging through the snow, darkening the doorway at City Cigar and other places Pippy was known to frequent.

In early March, with no news on Pippy's whereabouts, the Martins pushed further in their gossip column, and seemed to be taunting those in power: "It's been over a month since 'Pippy' was reported missing. What's the mystery? Is it getting too hot for certain people? The big time rackets are really tough." They added a dig at Little Joe, suggesting that his throne had been usurped—"There's a new czar in the gambling game in Johnstown and anything can happen"—then

---

* I should note that Mike told me that Joe had told him the meeting didn't happen this way. According to his account, Bionaz was the one trying to use the fact that both men had adopted children as a way to cozy up to Joe.

wondered aloud about Pippy: "If he was taken for a ride will his body ever be found? He's not the type to disappear without letting his family know where he is going."

It was a confusing time for everybody. The Apalachin meeting of a bit more than two years earlier had roiled the organization, in western Pennsylvania and elsewhere, with federal agents sweeping into pool halls and nightclubs, giving bookies and other lower-level operators a scare. Local police departments and politicians, some of whom had been party to mob activity if not actual partners, were likewise in a state of turmoil. With the waters so cloudy and unsettled, it is just possible to see the outlines of what was happening in Johnstown. Someone outside the local organization was trying to take advantage of the confusion, making a play for the town's rackets, even as some within law enforcement were trying to crush the rackets altogether. Meanwhile, Little Joe was determined to steady the ship and ride out the storm.

In the midst of all this, a melodramatic little subplot played out, something that people at first got a kick out of as it unfolded in the newspapers. A couple of ordinary gamblers called Perry Holloway and John Lee played the numbers with the Pagano brothers and claimed they hit big but the brothers refused to pay up. That wasn't supposed to happen. If you had a bank and one of your players won a hefty payout, requiring you to come up with more money than you had at the time, you were supposed to go up one rung—in this case, to ask Little Joe to cover the winnings, or even LaRocca. You didn't welch. Holloway said he went to Pete Pagano and complained, and in response Pagano slugged him and told him to forget about it or he'd wind up dead. Holloway didn't forget about it but instead took the unusual step of hiring an attorney. Donald Perry filed charges, the case went to court, and Pagano was found guilty of threatening Holloway's life. Pagano, the *Tribune-Democrat* reported, "was ordered to post a $2500 peace bond for one year."

At the *Observer*, Larry Martin folded this story into his coverage of the missing bookie: "Within the past week there have been several instances of threatened violence over the numbers racket. Some of the operators are not paying off on big hits. In fact they are even claiming that the police are in cahoots with the gamblers—even after they are arrested and taken to jail."

Some readers found it funny that the rackets were now so wide open that you could hire a lawyer to represent your gambling interests. For Little Joe, though, this was ugly as hell. He prided himself on running a tight ship. And the only thing worse than publicity was bad publicity. If people started thinking that a gambler might not get his winnings, his business was over. He was operating a bank, after all, and banks were built on trust.

Spring arrived. The trees on Main Street and in Central Park came into bud. As the buds opened into pale green leaves, Larry Martin got some new info—not what had happened to Pippy, but that he had known he was getting himself mixed up in something. He published another column. "Again we ask: 'What happened to Pippy?' He's been mysteriously missing since February 14th. Who is he? He's 'Pippy' De Falco [*sic*] and was known for years as a small timer in the local gambling fraternity. He sold tickets on baseball, football and basketball games and made a few dollars but nothing in the big time. He never seemed to step on anyone's toes until early this year, when he was warned he might run into trouble."

District Attorney Bionaz and Charles Griffith, the Johnstown police chief, meanwhile, assured people that they were working doggedly to uncover clues. But so far there weren't many. Pippy just seemed to have vanished.

Larry Martin continued his coverage. He and Peg were getting tips suggesting that powerful people were involved in the bookie's disappearance. It was, he wrote, "no secret among the 'syndicate boys' and some politicians and 'respectable businessmen' with close connections with the 'syndicate' that Pippy was becoming a nuisance . . ." I infer from this that the Martins were hearing that Pippy had shifted his allegiance back and forth from Little Joe's organization to another one, making him an annoyance not just to Little Joe and those local politicians and businessmen who allied themselves with him, but to those in the rival organization as well. Martin also said his newspaper was now being threatened, and not by mobsters but by Johnstown businessmen: "This paper was warned that if we didn't 'lay off' the Pippy case and forget it we would lose some advertising business."

The Martins didn't lay off. As more days went by Larry Martin became more strident, needling the police, wondering why they didn't look for answers—as well as evidence of a corrupt partnership between city hall and the mob—in "the City Cigar store." He taunted the police for not investigating City Cigar "even though the place was almost next door to the mayor's office."

Then, in May, Donald Perry, the attorney who had represented gamblers Holloway and Lee against the Pagano brothers, went to the police with a letter he had just received. "Leave the numbers racket alone," it said, then added, "You don't think P. defalco was swimming in February, do you?" In place of a signature, the letter contained a drawing of a black hand.

The letter—along with an anonymous phone call to Perry's office, telling him, as Perry reported, that "if I didn't keep my nose out of the numbers racket, I would have my head blown off"—changed everything. The long, sleepy period in which the city tolerated the rackets as a supplement to people's lives, a provider of harmless amusement, was suddenly over. The media had been feeding people a stream of stories about mob activity at the national level. Right at the time Pippy went missing, Robert F. Kennedy's book *The Enemy Within*, detailing the mob's infiltration of labor unions and telling a story of extortion, theft, bribery, and lies on a massive scale, was published and became a bestseller. Suddenly it seemed that this same malevolent force had arrived in Johnstown. Death threats, the overt connection of the city's quaint smalltime gambling culture to the mob, the real Italian mafia, even connecting it to the Mano Nera of the old days, the increasing likelihood that Pippy had been murdered, and the suggestion that the writer of the letter had not only been involved in the murder but was hinting at how it was done, associating it with water and drowning: it felt like the town was waking up from a long dream of innocence into dark reality.

Mayor Walter ordered twenty-four-hour police protection for Perry. On May 8, the raids started. The police had long kept an eye on George Sapolich, who had a reputation for violence and was known to have mixed it up with Pippy in the past. When he wasn't boxing, Sappy ran craps and card games for Russ and Joe out of a place in the Cambria City section of town called the Recreation Center. Chief Griffith authorized the raid; Detectives Philip Vickroy, Ray Bender, and Mel Causer went in via the front door, while two uniformed officers entered from the rear. They found Sappy, "with an apron on dealing cards," and a small group of gamblers. "Some money was on the counter but George scooped it into his trouser pocket," the report noted. The detectives arrested Sappy and booked him on a "156-4-25 charge," running an illegal gambling establishment.

They also arrested another man they found on the scene, who was named John Kon but whom people called Horsey. They took a statement from him, which I want to quote at length because of the level of detail it contains about the satellite operations that Russ and Joe oversaw—because this book is called *Smalltime* and Horsey evokes meaning of the term better than I can:

I, John M. Kon, have been informed that I do not have to make a statement if I do not wish to and that anything I do say may be used against me in court.

Pretty close to a month ago, George Sapolich asked me if I would paint his place at 604 Broad St. So I painted the place and he give me two dollars and a fifth of wine. A couple days later he called me back again to put some second hand linoleum down and he gave me a bottle of wine. I drank about half of it and then he got mad because I wasn't doing it right so he spilled the wine down the sink and I walked out.

Then later on he got a couple pool tables in the place and then one day he came to me when I was sittin on the steps by the Roosevelt Club and he asked me to get in the car and when I got in the car I thought I was going to get something to drink. I asked him for a drink and he said to me Horsey, I'll get you a drink but I want you to do me one favor. So he asked me if I would sign the lease to take over the poolroom and he would pay the rent and everything and pay me $14.00 a week and let me sleep there because I had no place to stay. We left there in his car and went up to Roxbury somewhere and went to a house. Then the man that George took me to give me two pieces of paper to sign. He told me it was a lease and to sign it and I did. I didn't have my glasses on and I didn't feel to good because I was drinking so I don't know what was on the paper and I couldn't read what was on it. Then he brought me down to the Gay Inn and gave me seventy-five cents for a drink.

Since that time I stayed in the place and cleaned it up and fixed the lights and everything. Every night he would give me enough for a drink to keep my nerves steady.

The God's truth, about two weeks ago about 4:30 in the afternoon George told me to keep the front door locked so that the law don't come in on them and they went in the back room and was gambling. There was four guys back there.

About a week or a week and a half before Palm Sunday, they were playing cards in the back room. And I remember one night after midnight there was a card game.

I seen them rolling dice on a table in the back room one time.

And today when the Detectives came in I was standing by the

counter and George and this kid was playing cards for a quarter a game. Kliney was there too but he didn't play. He just stood and watched.

The organization that Joe and Russ had built into a multimillion-dollar enterprise had grown and prospered in part on revenues from slick nightclubs and card games where the pots got into the thousands of dollars. But mostly the world that my grandfather lorded over from the end of World War II to the start of the Kennedy administration—which was now facing an existential threat—was Horsey's world.

Two days after this bust, the police picked up a bookie named Lucille Savering and got her to detail the work she did for Little Joe. Her statement pointed to where the police were heading with their newfound zeal: "The money is picked up by Frank Torchia who is the pick up man for the GI Bank."

Two days after that, at four in the afternoon, six policemen staked out a room upstairs from the Clinton Street Pool Room. Above the poolroom was the Gautier Club, and above that was a little attic office. For years the city ignored the fact that the boys took bets here—it was one of the places that fed bets and cash into the office above City Cigar—but the official policy had just changed. They waited for about fifteen minutes downstairs, then the door opened and out came Frank Filia. They marched him back upstairs, searched him, searched the place, found betting slips everywhere, and asked him to sign a statement that detailed the work he did here and the activity that went on. "I go to work everyday at 10:00 AM," it began. After getting things ready, his statement said, "I just lay around and draw to pass the time away waiting for the phone to ring in order to take bets on the horses." He outlined the procedure for taking bets. Milan Habala, the detective who typed up the statement, tried to get him to say that Yank Croco, who ran the poolroom, also took bets, but Frank scratched that line out. Normally, Frank said, he left at six, but "I knew something was wrong today and that the town was hot so I decided to leave early." Habala, clearly trying to make a sharper connection between the gambling and the murder, added the line "I figured it was the police because I heard diFalco was picked up." But Frank scratched that out too.

Habala told Frank he was under arrest for running an illegal gambling operation. But there was something else. Habala was looking at the drawings Frank did to pass the time. Nice drawings. The kid had talent. He mentioned the drawing on the death-threat letter that was sent to Donald Perry. Everyone knew of that letter by now.

"I swear to God, my knees started shaking right then. The only time in my life my knees were actually shaking with fright." I was back at Panera Bread with Frank, just the two of us, and we were going over that day. I showed him the statement they made him sign. "Jesus, this takes me back," he said. "I didn't say these things. He wrote them down and I signed it."

"Who did?"

"Milan Habala, that cocksucker. See, there's a guy that's no good."

"I was kind of under the impression, because he was so determined, he was working the gambling beat for years, that he was basically just trying to be a good cop."

Frank looked at me through his glasses and squinted, scrunching up his nose. "I'll tell you something I learned in life. The guys like me, the guys who hung out in poolrooms and ran some numbers, that type, they're maybe good, maybe bad, but mostly they're not bad. The legitimate guys are worse."

"Including Habala."

"Habala's mother wrote numbers. He used that. He became a cop because he knew where everything was, how it worked. He was promoting himself. We all knew that. I got so pissed off I told him one time, 'I'll beat your fucking brains in.'"

"What did he look like?"

"Chubby little guy, liked to wear a big hat."

"So they tried to connect you to the writer of the letter."

"They thought they were on to something about Pippy. They knew Pippy had worked at the same place. He would come in every day. I was just a kid—I only took bets. But Habala looks at my drawings and figures, 'Look at this, we have a connection to that business.' He was ready to connect me to a murder! I was on TV that night."

"What? How?"

"They had a guy with a camera. He's chasing me down the street when they're taking me to the jail. I said, 'Get the fuck outta here!' So there I was on TV, tied to all this shit. I thought my career was over. It was the worst possible timing."

"Why?"

That weekend, it turned out, he was due to get his big break. The band was playing at the War Memorial Arena, which had four thousand seats. "'The George Arcurio Orchestra, Featuring Frank Filia,'" Frank said, reading it off the marquee he could still see in his mind's eye. "I got arrested four days before the show. I figured that was it, I was done-for. People said to Junior,* 'You better not use Frank.' But Junior was good, he told me to play—the show must go on. And guess what? I walk into the arena . . . and everybody is shaking my hand! Guys are saying, 'You look good on TV, Frank!'"

THEN THEY FOUND the body.

In late May, something peculiar was spotted in a flood-control dam on the Conemaugh River thirty-five miles west of Johnstown, hauled ashore, and carted to the morgue in nearby Greensburg. After more than three months in the water, there wasn't much for a wife to identify, but Barbara diFalco drove to the morgue along with Pippy's

* George Arcurio was known as Junior.

two brothers. The remains had been stripped of all clothes, presumably by the waters, but a shoe was still attached. It was a corrective shoe, used to help someone with a misshapen foot to walk. "That's my Pippy!" Barbara cried. "That's him. That's his shoe. Oh my God!"

The coroner issued his report: "Death was not due to drowning. The examination of the body showed the most likely cause of death was a puncture or stab wound of the right side of the chest, which caused a collapse of the right lung." It was the coroner's professional judgment that the wound would likely have been made by an ice pick or a thin-bladed knife.

DIFALCO FIRST SLAIN, THEN TOSSED IN RIVER went the *Tribune-Democrat*'s banner headline on May 27.

The next day, just as people were digesting this news, yet another body was pulled from the Conemaugh River. A man named Walter Cook had gone missing the day after Pippy. When the second body turned out to be Cook's, the city went into a whirl of speculation. Was the mob on a killing spree? "According to one source," the *Tribune-Democrat* declared, "Cook and diFalco reportedly were seen together at a suburban tavern the night of Feb. 6. The same source claims the two men were on such friendly terms that Cook called Pippy 'son.'"

Chief Griffith and District Attorney Bionaz announced the intensification of their efforts. "I am asking anyone who has information on this case to call me," the police chief told the *Tribune-Democrat*. "We are investigating dozens of leads." Mayor Walter assured people that "The investigation is continuing—both on the diFalco case and on gambling." The state police were now involved as well. "From now on," Bionaz announced, "when we pick up anyone we think is involved in the rackets we will be asking questions about murder—not about the numbers."

Overnight, business at City Cigar slowed to near nothing. The ticker machine was taken off the counter. A few guys wandered in and shot desultory games of pool. Nobody asked for tip seals.

*The Tribune-Democrat of May 27, 1960, reporting
the discovery of Pippy diFalco's body.*

A week later, the police announced progress, of a sort. They had thoroughly investigated Walter Cook, the man who had disappeared around the time Pippy had and whose body had turned up just days after Pippy's. They had determined that there was no connection between the men. The person who had originally said Cook knew Pippy had corrected himself—Cook actually knew someone named Pepper. Cook wasn't a gambler. There were no linkages between him and the rackets. While diFalco had been murdered, Cook had apparently fallen into the river and drowned. The timing of the deaths was a coincidence.

Over the next several weeks Detective Habala led his squadron of officers on raids all over the city. In Prospect, they approached "Calvin C. Sanders, colored, aged 33," outside the home of a known gambler and tried to apprehend him, but he ran. They chased him all the way down William Penn Boulevard, fired warning shots, and eventually nabbed him. They found on his person an envelope "with 11 slips amounting to $11.77." In Minersville they picked up "Albert Fisher Jr., aged 22," whom they suspected of being a numbers writer; he confessed, but asked them not to force him to plead guilty "due to his chances being ruined in going to further his education." They made other arrests: on Central Avenue, in a barbershop on Chandler Avenue, and, together with the state police, in Somerset County.

On August 9, Little Joe made an attempt to stop the raids. His associate, Russ's pal George Bondy, asked Detective Habala to meet him at Bondy's place, the Mission Inn, next door to City Cigar. Habala entered and took a seat at a table. Bondy came in, sat right beside him rather than opposite him, and tried to hand him a piece of folded paper with money inside. "This writer refused the offering and Mr. Bondy placed it on the writer's lap," Habala wrote in his report. Bondy got up and sat across from Habala and tried to level with him. All the banks in town were suffering. He made a point of noting the G.I. Bank in particular. He "told this writer that if he plays ball he could go far especially if any promotions are to be made," Habala wrote. "He further stated that he and his organization are consulted on said promotions." Habala said when he stood up the money fell on the floor. He didn't pick it up.

Sometime in the next couple of weeks, Little Joe closed down City Cigar. It never reopened.

The searches and busts continued through the fall and into the New Year. In January, the police raided the Gautier Club and arrested four women and three men. "At the time of entry into the club,' Det. Sgt. Philip Vickroy noted, "the last girl on the 'bill' was performing in the nude on the stage." The club shut down after that.

By May of 1961, however, a year after Pippy's body had turned up, the authorities were no closer to solving the murder. "Who killed

'Pippy' DiFalco?" the *Tribune-Democrat* asked. "A full year has passed since the body of the West End man—known to police as a small-time gambler—was found floating in the Conemaugh Flood Control Reservoir, near Saltsburg. But, despite a far-ranging investigation, the identity of his slayer has never been established." The odds of finding the killer weren't looking good. Mayor Walter told the paper that "city police have gone as far as they can go." He believed a wider net had to be cast, but he complained that the state police "have shown no inclination to actively pursue the investigation."

BUT THE CASE didn't die. At almost that same moment, at the national level, Robert F. Kennedy, the new attorney general, launched a campaign to raise awareness of the extent of mob activities not only in major cities but in small ones as well. One of the places he highlighted was Newport, Kentucky, a city about half the size of Johnstown, which, as Kennedy told a Senate subcommittee, "was long known nationally for wide-open gambling and prostitution." Law enforcement became crooked in cities of this size, Kennedy said, because it was easy for the mob to corrupt the authorities with money. His strategy was to bring in the IRS and the FBI, assist community crusaders, and get voters to throw out corrupt local officials.

On September 15, President Kennedy signed into law three bills targeting organized crime, which called for cooperation with local authorities. Two days later, the Johnstown police department suddenly renewed its investigation into the local rackets. Of particular interest to the authorities now, Detective Habala indicated in his reports, were eight men, including "Russell 'Russ' Shorto," George Bondy, and "Joseph 'Little Joe' Regino (who is the supposed head of the organization)." The Johnstown Police Department sent a letter to Robert Kennedy detailing their findings. Habala learned from an informant that, with City Cigar out of business, the organization in Johnstown was now headquartered "at the Shangri-La Lodge." He typed up a memo to the chief of police telling him he had made a decision "to contact Superior Judges in Pittsburgh and some members of the Internal Revenue to anticipate the latest move by your office (concerning the letter sent to Att. Gen. Kennedy) . . ."

My assumption is that Russ, Joe, George Bondy, and the others on the list were interrogated at the time, though I couldn't find records of those encounters. Shortly afterward, however, the city's official attention seemed to zero in on one person. When they learned that that person was about to flee, they took action. On September 26, the police received a call from an informant: the suspect had contacted a waitress at the Seafood Restaurant downtown, saying he was leaving town but would stop in to pick up his football betting sheets. The cops conducted a "stake-out for apprehension of Erwin 'Rip' Slomanson" at the restaurant. They watched the place from 5:30 in the afternoon until 10:30 that night, then they gave up and went home.

The next day Detective Habala spotted Slomanson farther down Main Street, in front of Lee Hospital, "alone and driving his 1961 Chevrolet, color black." Habala opened the passenger door and jumped in. Slomanson asked if he had a search warrant. Habala did, and showed it to him. The detective and two officers searched the car and found "1372 football sheets for this Saturday." Slomanson was arrested on gambling charges as well as for carrying a concealed weapon.

At the police department, a high-level group—three detectives, the chief of police, and Mayor Walter—convened to interview the prisoner. The man who was suddenly the subject of the city's official attention, however, "refused to give a statement of his activity." The only thing Rip offered was when Habala asked him why there was a heavy hank of electric cable under his car seat. "I use that to defend myself with in case someone would get after me," he said.

They kept on him, pestering and questioning and needling, until, in December, they gave up. He pled guilty to violating the gambling laws and paid a $400 fine. They had nothing else: no witness, no evidence, no confession, no way to tie him to the murder. They let him go.

14

The Fallout

PIPPY DIFALCO'S MURDER is a fault line in this story because it changed everything for my grandfather. The Johnstown mob was a source of stability in Russ's otherwise very unstable life. It gave him purpose. It served as the foundation of his world, a foundation that he himself had helped build. The pressure from the authorities following the bookie's death fractured the mob in town. Trying to follow Russ thus becomes even more complicated in the 1960s. He had already been on a downward course emotionally, even when he was rising professionally, but from now on he seemed to break up into pieces. His path became more erratic, his "choices" even harder to fathom. Where I can make him out most clearly is in negative: in the fallout, the imprint he made on other lives.

I did, however, stumble onto one excellent source, who gave me, among other insights, my only window onto Russ's activities during the period around Pippy's death. Alexis Kozak was Alex and Vicky's daughter. It was Russ's affair with Vicky that pushed my grandmother to try to kill herself. I hadn't even known that Vicky had had a daughter. It was my aunt Sis who suggested one day, out of the blue, that maybe I would want to talk to her. I phoned Alexis and was instantly intrigued. Not only was she willing to talk, she seemed eager. Plus, she lived in town.

To put us in the mood for chatting about back in the day, we agreed to meet for lunch at the Holiday Inn during one of Frank Filia's Thursday-afternoon sets. We took our seats as Frank was crooning in his velvety tones about being blue every Monday and looking forward to Sunday.

Alexis was a lively, chatty woman in her sixties. And she knew a lot. Russ and Vicky somehow kept their convulsive affair going throughout Alexis's childhood and early adulthood, which meant Alexis had a perspective on Russ that no one in my family did: an intimate view of him in the period of his life after City Cigar. She told me right away that she had liked him. He was kind to her, and he would take her and her mother and various friends out for extravagant dinners: "Nobody else was ever allowed to pick up the check."

Russ brought a whole new energy into her household, which Alexis found fascinating. "I was always watching what he did," she said, "the way he acted." She found it thrilling, for example, that Russ never left the house without a .32 revolver. She said that as part of his entourage she spent a lot of time at Shangri-La (which did indeed become the hangout after City Cigar closed down), eating pasta with her mother upstairs while in a room downstairs Russ, Joe, Sam Fashion, and other guys would hold a weekly meeting. A couple of times she and her mother were with Russ at Shangri-La and he got so drunk her mother made the decision to take him to the hospital. She remembered one time a pal of his suggesting as they rushed off, "Make sure you tell them he has chest pains. That way they'll take him right away."

Then Alexis asked me if I'd heard about the murder of Pippy diFalco. She said she had a memory of the night his body was found, something she had never told the police—because no one knew to ask her. "How interesting," I said.

Around two o'clock in the morning on May 26, 1960, the day the discovery of the body was made public, while newspapers carrying the story were still in the process of being printed, her parents' dining room was suddenly full of men. It was the middle of the night, but the men were loud—pumped up on the news that the whole town would soon be discussing. First reports—which would soon be corrected—were that there were no signs of injury, no "visible evidence of foul play."

"I remember waking up and hearing all the noise," Alexis said. "It was crazy down there." She was eleven at the time, peering downstairs. "The room was full of these guys. The only two I knew were Johnny diFalco and Russ. And my mother and father were there. They were talking about Pippy and everyone was all worked up. You have to remember that my mother and dad were best friends with your grandparents. That gang never came to our house. But I think they wanted to meet somewhere neutral. The police wouldn't have connected my dad with them at all. And the next day I saw in the paper that they had found Pippy in the river."

Alexis didn't remember any particular things that were said, only that the body had been found. At first her memory of that night—the fact that Russ and some of his colleagues had gotten advance notice of the discovery of the body—seemed to me vaguely incriminating; Alexis had always thought so too. Then I realized the story could have been broadcast on the late news, and in fact later found that WARD radio had reported it sometime after midnight. Besides, even if they had gotten word from someone on the police force, that didn't necessarily mean anything other than that they knew the cops had linked Pippy to the rackets, and that they had to be prepared for a new level of scrutiny.

Thinking more about Alexis's memory, and whether it offered any evidence for or against Russ's involvement in the murder, it seemed noteworthy that Pippy's brother had been with the guys. Johnny diFalco had been part of the organization since its earliest days. The fact that he was there as the boys discussed this news struck me as potentially exculpatory. If their group had caused Pippy's murder, it seemed unlikely that they would have plotted what to do about the body's discovery in front of the dead man's brother.

On the other hand, Russ's behavior throughout this period was distinctly odd. I had given my daughter Eva the box my aunt had kept in her attic that contained all the personal documents Russ had left behind when he died. She pored through it and came up with some anomalies for this period:

1. Russ had an appraisal done on the building that the Haven was in, presumably meaning that he was thinking about buying it. The striking thing about it was the date: February 5, 1960. Two days before Pippy went missing.
2. Russ took out five life-insurance policies in 1960, with the Lincoln National Life Insurance Company, John Hancock Mutual Life Insurance, New York Life, the Knights Life Insurance Company of America, and Metropolitan Life.
3. The police subpoenaed Russ's personal bank account in 1960, looking at his transactions from February to May, precisely the period of Pippy's disappearance.
4. Where he seems to have been an indifferent record keeper throughout his life, Russ saved very detailed financial information—down to every canceled check—from 1960.

Eva and I discussed all of this. I ran it by some people who are savvier in financial matters than I am. On the first point, the appraisal on the building that the Haven occupied, it was dated *before* Pippy went missing. Even if I were playing devil's advocate and assuming that Russ had a hand in the bookie's death, it surely could not have been the case that he and his associates were *anticipating* it. And if they somehow had been, I couldn't see a connection between it and Russ considering a real-estate purchase.

On the second point, I mentioned the insurance policies to Tony and he had an instant response. "My dad was obsessed with life insurance. He was convinced it was a racket. He thought he could outsmart the insurance companies. He was always buying policies, taking out loans on them, cashing them in."

The audit of Russ's finances for the period of Pippy's disappearance clearly meant he was under suspicion of being involved in some way, which stands to reason. But it doesn't mean anything else. And the records that were audited showed mundane transactions, mostly related to his bar.

I finally concluded that the fourth point, the level of detail of Russ's recordkeeping in this year, was the key to his odd behavior at the time. City Cigar closed its doors in the aftermath of Pippy's murder. Capitol Bowling, of which Russ was a partner, was sold. Bookies were being busted all over town. The G.I. Bank went dormant. The cops were presumably monitoring his every move. What Russ's unusual activity tells me is not that he was potentially involved in murder but that in 1960 he was a very scared man. The box of records provides a financial snapshot of someone whose life had cracked open. The Johnstown mob, after all, was his life's work. The enterprise that he had built from scratch and to which he had devoted himself for fifteen years was being raided, invaded, dismantled. The insurance policies, the liquidation of companies, the audit—all of this did relate to Pippy's murder, but to its aftermath rather than the act. It showed the effects of the government crackdown—from the federal level to city hall in Johnstown—on one life.

By the latter part of 1960 the only thing Russ had left, in terms of financial resources, was his bar, the Haven. That's where he seems to have retreated for a time. And, funnily enough, that's where I was.

Tony and Rita's first child, the reason for their elopement, had been born the previous February. Tony had followed Sicilian tradition and named his firstborn son after his father, but he and Russ were "estranged" around this time, as my mother put it. But while they may not have spoken much, the new family needed a home, and Mary went to work on Russ, cajoling, reminding him that the apartment next to the bar was going to be available soon. My mother told me that despite the tensions between them she knew Russ cared about his son. "All of our parents were concerned—there we were, teenagers with a baby. Everybody wanted to help. He let us move in there. And he never charged us rent." Mary rounded up some furniture, her sister contributed a bed, and Tony and Rita set up home.

I have exactly one memory of that apartment, which must be from when I was about three and a half because that was how old I was when we moved out. There was a white wall, and a door in that wall. My memory is of one time when the door opened, and suddenly you were in the bar. I know that's why it stuck with me: the shocking incongruity, the dizzy feeling of unsettledness, that you were in your home but suddenly you were in a dark world of adults being adults, the sort of place from which a small child instinctively recoils. And that, of course, was Russ's world.

Not long after the little family moved into the apartment beside the Haven, Mary put a crib up at her house. She and Russ would drive down to the apartment, pick up the baby, and bring him to their place. This was when Russ told Tony that they would keep me. I guess Russ liked having the baby around. With his world falling apart, it was soothingly normal. He saw that Mary liked it. Maybe he figured it would be good for the two of them. The kids—meaning Tony and Rita—were too young to be parents anyway. He and Chinky could raise the baby. It would settle him, help give him a new focus, now that he had to rebuild his life. On the other hand, his relationship with Vicky would have been hot and heavy at this time—maybe he figured that raising her grandson would distract Mary, give her something to focus on so that she would stop nagging him.

I imagine that when I heard this story as a child—that my grandfather had tried to take me but my dad had pushed back, *Like hell you will*—my reaction was giddy relief, a feeling of narrowly missing falling into a chasm. Maybe what I thought of was that door in our first apartment opening up and me being swallowed by the blackness.

Tony knew his father was serious in wanting to take his baby: "They did that kind of thing in the old country," he told me. "They did it here too." He didn't yet know about the con with Isabel's son, but others of his father's generation had swapped kids around—because somebody was too young, or deemed to be mentally deficient, or didn't have room or resources for one more, and somebody else had had a baby die recently and had all the clothes and things ready. You made decisions like that in a family, divided things up depending on who needed what. The paterfamilias issued the pronouncement. A Sicilian thing. Tony knew all that. But he had a right to his family and his future. "I got mad as hell," he told me. "The fact that he would even think that." He didn't remember the scene, what the words were that passed between them.

But he had an ally. "Mary wasn't going to let it happen," my mother told me. Mary could be withering with Russ, and not just about his other women. *Don't be ridiculous. Don't you see this is how kids become adults? Your son is a man now. You wanted him away from your affairs. Well, now he's away.*

Rita and Mary conferred on such things. Rita was still a teenager when she became part of the family, and Mary welcomed her. While Rita changed diapers and such, Mary confided in her new daughter-in-law in a way she never felt able to share with her sisters. Russ's infidelities: she tolled them, the women's names, the lipstick traces, every little painful thing.

Rita's own mother was not well and never had been—had never

truly been a mother. She had a mental illness that grew steadily worse once her children were born and growing; she lived mostly at a state mental hospital now. Mary was another mother, who opened up to her at once, which was warm and lovely. In opening herself, she revealed mostly pain. Rita accepted that, and empathized. "I loved her dearly," she told me. She said Mary talked to her about her childhood, being the oldest and the only one of her siblings with a different father, the hard life on the farm. She never seemed to have had close friends. She talked about how she would go off on her own as a girl and spend a day at a swimming hole. She glowed when she talked about her time in New York: Fifth Avenue, Central Park, Childs Restaurant, the Staten Island Ferry. "She was an independent woman by nature," Rita said, "and I feel like she really was able to be herself in New York."

THE RACKETS DIDN'T completely die out following the 1960 crackdown. There was a lull for a year or two, then Little Joe's organization slowly reemerged, albeit in a more muted form. A police report in May 1963—written by Detective Habala—indicated that Russ was back in charge of sports betting, along with Sam Fashion, and he was now, as well, "one of the Heads of the G.I. Bank." Habala listed forty-eight people working for Russ, either in the numbers or "the Fashion-Shorto organization" that ran a sports book.

But it wasn't the same. The level of authority that Little Joe had exercised in the postwar years was gone. The fear and respect weren't there, not like before. As a result, there were lots of independent operators around now. Dean Dallas had a separate bank. So did Al Fisher, John Mihalick, and a guy named Mickey Yon. Nick Sikirica ran a sports book. George Bondy, too, seemed to have gone out on his own, specializing in Empire treasury tickets, which were essentially illegal lottery tickets. And Rip Slomanson was back in town as well, running his own sports book, and had several guys working for him.

I have only a few scant pieces of information concerning Russ's professional life in the '60s. He continued as Little Joe's lieutenant for a time, but in a reduced capacity. In addition to his work for his brother-in-law, Russ sold the Haven in 1965 and started another bar in Richland, a suburb to the east of town, called the Jockey Club. He ran card games out of there.

Russ's personal life, meanwhile, became ever more complicated. If I am searching for a personality in researching this book, and feel continually thwarted at trying to locate it, in this period it is particularly frustrating. It feels as though Russ tried to hide by dividing himself up among different women—as though he'd hit on the brilliant idea that creating enough chaos would keep him distracted from looking at what was at its center. I had the feeling he was hiding from himself.

His affair with Vicky was fiery; maybe it was exciting to carry it on behind their spouses' backs, but it had to have been utterly exhausting. Meanwhile, Isabel never went away. She was still cleaning for Joe and Millie, from which position she was able to oversee her little boy's childhood. And now she had gotten Russ to let her do the cleaning at the Haven. For more than a decade she had persisted in believing that Russ would leave Mary for her. Certainly he knew that was her hope; maybe he led her along. I suspect he was too weak to stand up to her force of personality, too weak to sever ties with her, and rationalized that keeping her in his employ was a workable compromise, just as he had thought that giving their child to Joe and Millie was a solution.

But naturally Isabel found out about Vicky. Vicky thus replaced Mary as the object of her ire. One night Vicky and Alex were at the Haven. They had brought Alexis with them. It was getting late; Alex left because he had to work in the morning. Vicky and her daughter stayed until closing time—in other words, just when Isabel showed up to start cleaning. ("My mother thought nothing of keeping me out till two in the morning," Alexis said.) As Russ locked up, he told Vicky he would take her and Alexis downtown to Coney Island Hot Dogs for a late-night snack. "So we waited and we followed him in our car," Alexis told me. "And all of a sudden here comes Isabel following everybody. We were driving up Roxbury Avenue and she sideswipes my mother's car. Your grandfather got out of his car and started screaming at her. He didn't see it but she had a hatchet. She hit him right in the top of the head with it. All I could see was blood coming down. I was sure he was dead. Isabel took off and my mother and I took him to the ER. My mother called your grandmother and told her what happened. And she said, 'Let the bastard die.' "

Russ lived. Mary's suffering continued. While I was interviewing various women in my family, I asked for their thoughts about my grandmother's situation. She was married to a man who was a pathological cheat not only at dice and cards but in life, in his marriage. His behavior bred psychological chaos, drove her to the depths of depression and maybe to the brink of madness. Why didn't she leave him?

Everyone had the same answer. "Women didn't leave their husbands," Minnie told me. "A lot of times they had good reason to, but they didn't do it." As long as Russ kept returning home at night, Mary was trapped.

Finally, in 1964, he moved out. The last straw was when Vicky showed up at the family home to confront him and Mary—and she was clearly pregnant. My guess is that Russ had made an effort to deny that he was the baby's father, and that set her off. My aunt says a loud shouting match ensued, with Vicky doing most of the shouting. That was too much for Mary; and at last it was too much even for Russ.

Mary was relieved once Russ was gone. Years of black, corrosive tension drained away from the household. "I don't know why he didn't do that years earlier," my mother said. "They were torturing each other." I think the answer must have been Russ's weakness. As much as he needed the affairs, he also needed the relative stability of a home life.

My sharpest and warmest memories of my grandmother are from precisely this time—after Russ left home, beginning in the summer when I was five years old. My mother had her hands full with my younger siblings; I liked being with my grandmother, so for a time I spent mornings and afternoons at her house. She doted on me, fried me steaks for lunch, set up a tray in front of the TV for me to watch daytime reruns of *I Love Lucy* and *The Honeymooners*, smiled at me with her watery eyes. I didn't mind her steadily pouring herself little glassfuls of beer throughout the day from the quart bottles she had delivered by the case. I knew they were meant to help her. At times she could be almost light. She had a dog named Bee-Bee. I loved it when she fried four eggs: two for me and two for the dog. She spent the whole day with Bee-Bee, talking to her. I listened resolutely as she told me that Bee-Bee standing beside the front door and growling in a rolling "ow—OWWW" sound meant that the dog was attempting to speak English: "I wanna go OUT." I knew she believed that.

She was also perfectly capable of enveloping me in her painful reveries. I don't remember her railing against her husband, but I knew that ache was there. She would at times go off on jags against "the Serbians." I didn't know who the Serbians were, but they were clearly awful people. I had no idea that she'd had an abusive stepfather, let alone that he had been a Serb.

I suppose I understood that my grandfather had recently moved out. I have dim memories of just before—him sitting at the kitchen table, a napkin tucked into his shirt top, her waiting on him—and I guess I understood that an event like the husband leaving the home only happened following great turmoil. Strange to say, but I found the house, on those languorous afternoons when it was just my grandmother and me, to be simultaneously a place of comfort and mystery. I loved exploring it, and it occurs to me that I was trying then to do what I am doing right now. I knew that things had happened in this house. There was a story, and I was trying to report it. I felt that my exploration needed to be carried out with some stealth. I had to assume an air of nonchalance. I studied the objects as if they held clues.

On the mantel sat a bust of two lovers twisted into a kiss. I recognize it now, looking at it in my mind's eye, as Art Deco in style. The man and woman were so molded to each other, the lips so fused, they suggested a union of utter completeness. In the basement was some leftover paraphernalia from Russ's days as an operator of illegal casinos: dice in a cage that had a handle you could turn; a bright-green board playfully divided up into circles and squares. Toys that weren't toys.

On the banquette in the dining room there was what appeared to be a set of books, but if you opened the top you saw they weren't books at all but a kind of box. Inside was a kit for making drinks: tumblers, shaker, strainer, shot glasses. This object seemed particularly significant. Why would you need to hide this activity behind a literary facade? Who was it being hidden from? I seem to have known both to associate my grandfather with alcohol and that he hid things from people. I opened this little chest only when I was alone, and only once or twice.

In spite of the heaviness of the atmosphere, I felt content being with my grandmother in her home. I loved my own house, but it was a chaotic place of babies and toddlers. Here it was quiet, and I had my grandmother to myself. She and I valued each other. Of course, I didn't appreciate the timing. It didn't occur to me that my grandmother had replaced one Russell Shorto with another.

WHEN VICKY'S BABY was born, in 1964, her husband, Alex, accepted him as his own son. They named him Sandor, after Alex's father. The boy had a fraught life. Alexis remembered a time when Sandor was two years old and Isabel showed up at their house and picked him up off the front porch. She started to take him, Alexis screamed, Vicky came out. Isabel put the baby down and ran. "She resented Sandor," Alexis said. "She was going to kidnap him."

I don't know how to characterize what supposedly happened next, so I'll just quote what Alexis told me: "A man went to Isabel's apartment soon after that and threw acid on her face. Apparently it was a message—to tell her that enough was enough." Alexis wasn't sure the man succeeded—nobody mentioned to me that Isabel's face was disfigured after that. I asked her how she knew this, and she said she remembered Russ telling her mother about it. I asked if he said it with surprise or concern. "No, I think he was sort of chuckling," she said. In other words, she said, Russ was telling Vicky that she wouldn't have to worry about her son's safety anymore, because Isabel had been scared off.

This story shocked me more than all the stories surrounding Pippy's murder. I didn't know what to do with it. I still don't.

Alex died in 1972, of lung cancer. After that, Russ moved into Vicky's house. He and Sandor were then much like father and son, after a fashion. Russ would get the boy out of school early so he could take him to the racetrack. "Sandor loved the track," Alexis said. "He loved gambling. He idolized Russ." Russ took Vicky, Alexis, and Sandor to the Shangri-La, or some other fancy supper club, three times a week. "Sandor and I grew up with that kind of lifestyle. Russ and his friends lived for the present. We loved being with him." Sandor accompanied Russ on trips around town, to meet bookies and gamblers. Sometimes the boy would whisper to Alexis, in a thrilled voice, "This is the mafia!"

But here's a strange thing. Vicky would not admit that Sandor was Russ's son. She made Sandor call him Uncle Russ. Sandor knew better; he longed to have the relationship clarified. As a defiant teenager, he would yell at his mother, "I'm a Shorto—I know it!"

And here's a stranger thing. The way people in my family under-

stood the breakup of my grandparents' marriage was that when Sandor was born, Russ left Mary for Vicky, and later, when Alex died,
he and Vicky lived together as a couple, even though he remained
married to Mary. But Alexis told me it was more complicated than
that. When Russ moved into Vicky's house, he slept not in Vicky's
bedroom but in Sandor's. He and Sandor shared a set of twin beds.
Alexis never once saw her mother and Russ being affectionate with
each other.

Alexis and I put our heads together. What we concluded was that
Russ and Vicky had a child together during their affair, which forced
Russ out of his married home. He lived after that in the apartment
above the Jockey Club. But by the time Vicky's husband died—
when Sandor was eight years old—Russ and Vicky's relationship had
become something else. They were no longer lovers but rather two
people disillusioned with each other—Vicky had originally thought
of him as a mobster with lots of money, and it was looking increasingly
like he was more of a broke old drunk—who were now connected by
a child and nothing else. Russ couldn't go back to Mary, and Vicky
wanted a father figure for Sandor, even if she refused to have the relationship acknowledged. So Russ moved into her house, as something
between a tenant and an uncle.

But even that was fraught. About the only thing they did that
reminded Alexis of some couples was fight. "They fought all the
time," she said. "I remember one time my mother threw a sweeper at
him." Where my family believed that Russ was off enjoying himself in
another relationship, he seems instead to have exchanged one domes-
tic hell of his own creation for another.

I met Sandor twice when I was in my late teens. He struck me as
painfully earnest and desperately longing for something. Because of
the tension between Vicky and my grandmother, there was very little
contact between him and my family. Sandor wanted nothing more
than to have that very contact. Some in my family actively shunned

him, preferring to pretend he didn't exist. My father, however, as if he felt an obligation to make amends for his father's moral failings, went out of his way to embrace Sandor. He would meet with him, the way he did with the AA people he counseled, and commiserate, talk, even pray with him.

Sandor died of a brain tumor in 2007, at the age of forty-two. Tony visited him in the hospital, and referred to those visits many times. "He just wanted to be loved," he would say, getting almost angry, as if one of us were arguing the point with him. "I told him he was my brother and that I loved him. He just wanted to belong."

AS FOR RUSS's other out-of-wedlock son, the one raised by Joe and Millie, I don't recall ever meeting Joey before I started on this project. Once, right after my first Panera Bread session with Frank and the guys and just as I began doing research, he came to my parents' house at my dad's request, along with some other relatives, to share stories about the very old days of Antonino and Annamaria. When I had tried to bring up more recent matters, Joey balked. He didn't want to go there. I understood. His situation was different from Sandor's because he had grown up as part of our extended family—as Russ's nephew. But learning later in life that he wasn't who he thought he was could not have been easy. A few years later, however, when I was near the end of my research, and realized that I couldn't write about Russ without some involvement on Joey's part—Joey was, in a way, as central to the story of Russ and Joe as the mob was—I asked my aunt to contact him again.

This time he agreed to sit down and talk about himself. I didn't know how he felt as he approached our meeting, but I was nervous. Would he throw up a wall of outrage when I brought up his parentage? Did he openly acknowledge it? How awkward was this going to be? I brought my aunt along, telling her it would make Joey more comfortable, but I was also thinking of myself.

His emotions weren't apparent. At seventy, he was gruff, grizzled, manly. He had an interesting way of dealing with sensitive material. I would ask a question, and his first answer would be dismissive. Then he'd circle back around and give a blunt, forthright reply. When I steeled myself and asked how he had found out that he was actually Russ's son, he was vague, meandered off onto another topic, so I thought that was in essence his answer. Then about five minutes later he said, "I found the adoption papers." I respected this approach. It seemed to me he was saying, *Look, I'll help you, but this is hard stuff. Give me a minute.*

After a bit he became more direct in his answers, or as direct as he could be.

RUSSELL: Did you ever confront your parents about the fact that they weren't your parents?

JOEY: I said something to my mother. I never said anything to my dad about it.

RUSSELL: What did Millie say when you told her you knew she wasn't your mother?

JOEY: She started crying.

RUSSELL: Did you ever tell Russ you knew he was your dad?

JOEY: I think I probably did, but I don't recall.

This seemed both extraordinary and totally believable.

RUSSELL: Did he treat you as special in any way?

JOEY: Not that I can remember.

Joey talked about his life growing up: how his mother was "the sweetest of them all," who had only one rule: you had to be at the dinner table at the stroke of six. As for his father: "Him and I didn't really get along." Little Joe, he said, was never happy with him, was always berating him. "You never heard him raise his voice to anyone," he said, reflecting what others had told me. "Except he raised his voice at me all the time. My sister got good grades, she could do no wrong. Her wedding was huge."

I had heard from many people about this wedding. It was held at the Shangri-La and was just about the most lavish affair the town had ever seen. There were eight hundred guests, tents, flowers, lines of limos. Some people told me they believe the wedding actually contributed to Little Joe's downfall—that the spectacle of it caught the attention of state investigators who were just then looking to crack down. My dad told me that when he saw *The Godfather* several years later its famous mob wedding scene brought him back to the wedding of Little Joe's daughter, and suddenly his whole background came into focus.

I asked Joey why he thought his dad was so hard on him. My aunt sharpened the question: "Do you think that he resented that you were my dad's son?"

"I think he resented that I wouldn't do what he wanted me to do," Joey replied. "He wanted me to be an attorney. I wasn't going to do that. I hated school. When I went to college I thought it was all about how much you could drink."

I asked Joey about Isabel's involvement in his childhood. He said she was always around the house in his early years, caring for him and his sister. Then, suddenly, Little Joe got fed up with the situation. Isabel had become progressively more involved—more of a mother, which was increasingly awkward for Millie. "He told her to get out of town," Joey said. So after Russ had forced Isabel to give up her child, and Russ and Joe together had demoted her from mother to servant, Little Joe chased her away. Isabel spent the next several years in California.

Then she came back and somehow picked up where she had left off, working for Joe and Millie and doting on Joey and his sister. "She was always buying us presents," Joey said. When he turned sixteen, she bought him a ring with a diamond chip in it. That was the closest she came, during his childhood, to acknowledging their relationship.

Then, several years later, Joey was a young man sitting at the bar at El Rancho Steak House getting drunk with some friends. Isabel happened to come in. "She came up and gave me hell for wasting my time," he said. "I gave her hell back. She said, 'How can you talk to me that way?' And then she said . . . 'I'm your mother.' And I said, 'I know.'"

Isabel died in 1999. Joey said he was pretty close to her at the end.

Joey told me that when Sandor was in the hospital dying he went to visit him. Joey felt an urge to connect. They were linked by this odd bond—they were Russ's unacknowledged sons. But Sandor wasn't having any of it. He said Sandor was bitter and angry at his fate, and lashing out. Joey left feeling angry.

In all of these stories and events—involving Joey, Isabel, Sandor, Alexis, Mary, Vicky, Alex—Russ was present in his usual way. He was the offscreen actor, the boundaryless protagonist whose morals were relaxed enough, whose hold on himself was tenuous enough, that he let other lives play out across the decades, simply backed away, and left people to puzzle out their places and their identities.

SOMETIME BETWEEN 1965 and 1970 Russ stepped out of the organization for good. This time, according to Mike, he went to Joe rather than wait for Joe to come to him. "Russ says to Joe, 'I just can't quit the booze. I'm no good to you anymore.'"

Russ's world had shrunk drastically, thanks to the combination of federal, state, and local authorities and his own life choices. Once, he had practically run the town. What he had from now on was a small sports book of his own and the Jockey Club, which catered mostly to his aging friends.

As it turned out, he got out at a good time. The Kefauver Committee's recommendations from the early 1950s took more than a decade to come to fruition, but in time they led to President Lyndon Johnson's creating a President's Commission on Law Enforcement and the Administration of Justice, which in turn led to the formation of the Pennsylvania Crime Commission. In 1970 the Crime Commission made a study of organized crime in cities around the state. "During the course of that survey, Commission investigators received allegations that a serious condition existed in the Johnstown area with regard to large-scale illegal gambling operations and their relationship to local government and law enforcement," its 1971–72 report read.

The commission held hearings in Ebensburg, the county seat, at which it heard testimony from dozens of people who were involved in the rackets, both on the law enforcement side as well as those who were "managers of and participants in illegal enterprises." They interviewed Mayor Walter, District Attorney Bionaz, and Detective Habala. Among the higher-ups on the other side of the equation they subpoenaed John LaRocca, Joe Regino, George Bondy, and others, most of whom invoked the Fifth Amendment. There is no indication in the published records that Russ was subpoenaed.

The commission's report was published—in book form running to 185 pages—and on October 30, 1971, the *Tribune-Democrat* took the extraordinary step of printing it in its entirety, making for a bombshell of an issue. Little Joe had gone to enormous lengths over the decades to keep his profile so low as to be almost nonexistent. He had carefully burnished the persona of a quiet, respectable businessman. Now he was openly identified to the people of Johnstown—friends and neighbors, people who had admired him as part of the fabric of society—as an "underworld figure," as "Cosa Nostra captain Joseph Regino." The city was informed that "Regino has a criminal record of arrests for assault and battery, highway robbery, gambling and sale of narcotics." The report stated that "underworld 'summit' meetings were held at the Shangri-La lodge." It outlined the scope of Little Joe's operation and how it functioned.

Little Joe seems to have been mortified by this public outing. He was probably especially enraged at the inclusion of the narcotics charge. That had been when he was very young, and he was never convicted on it. It may have been trumped up. People insisted that he and Russ had always been adamantly opposed to drugs as part of their operation.

I was told that Joe arranged to have every copy of that day's edition of the newspaper destroyed. I don't know how he would have accomplished this feat, but the issue is missing from every library that carries the paper on microfilm, and it's even absent from the *Tribune-Democrat*'s own archives.

15

The Salesman

SOMEWHERE ALONG THE way, without our quite realizing it, my father and I had shifted our focus in our search for his father. Where for three years or more we had been chipping away at Russ like archaeologists working a dig, excavating his life from the Prohibition era to the Kennedy administration, we were now talking mostly about Tony: *his* past, *his* path. We seemed to have tacitly agreed that the eldest son was an extension of the father, that even though my dad had not followed Russ in the rackets his course had nevertheless continued from his father's.

Our study of Russ in 1960, then, when he was running scared in the aftermath of Pippy diFalco's murder, segued into reconstructing what Tony was doing at that time. We chuckled a little when I pointed out a funny dynamic in Tony's life as he set off into adulthood, with a wife and a young child to support. Before, he had desperately wanted to be part of the local mob but his father wouldn't let him in; now he was trying to establish himself apart from his father's world, to separate from it, but his social circle was still comprised of guys from the rackets. Rip, when he wasn't under threat of a murder charge or running his own book, would stop by the apartment from time to time. One of the first businesses Tony started was a spaghetti takeout service, and his partner was Nino Bongiovanni, the guy who had run the lunch counter at City Cigar, who was arrested in the raids following the murder of Pippy diFalco and later would be busted for taking part in one of Mike Gulino's scams.

And when it came time to baptize Tony and Rita's baby, Sappy Sapolich, the disgruntled prizefighter turned game runner, ended up being the guy who stood in the nave of the Church of the Visitation of the Blessed Virgin Mary, on McKinley Avenue, broken-nosed and hunkering, as my godfather, alongside Rita's sister Jean as godmother, reciting the rote answers to the questions that were intended to guarantee the moral rectitude of the sponsors prior to an infant's baptism:

Do you believe in God, the Father almighty, creator of heaven and earth?	*I do believe.*
Do you renounce Satan?	*I do renouce him.*
And all his works?	*I do renounce them.*
And all his allurements?	*I do renounce them.*

In later years, on the rare occasions when our family would run into Sappy—I remember a church barbecue of some sort, a group of guys huddled around a picnic table, a pile of wrinkled dollar bills in the middle, him with a visor on his head and a cigarette hanging from his mouth, pausing in the dealing of cards to engage me in a solemn handshake—I found it disorienting to think that this man was to oversee my spiritual development.

Eventually I learned why Sappy was nominated for the role. One of Tony's runaway episodes during his cat-gang days in his early teens had ended with the police finding him and calling Russ. Russ looked around for someone who would go to Ohio to fetch him. Sappy said he'd get the kid. From the moment Tony saw his lumbering form coming to retrieve him he had looked at the boxer as a protector. Five years later, as a young father, he turned to Sappy much as his father had.

Tony's feelings, too, were still firmly stuck in the detritus of his father's world as he moved into his own orbit. Anger was hardening him; he was in the process of walling his father off from his family. Five decades later, in my parents' living room, with him lying back in his easy chair, the oxygen tube clipped insouciantly to his nose as he worked his chewing gum and stared meditatively at the ceiling, we talked a little about this, but only a little. It was a hard place to go. I asked my dad what he thought the root of the anger he held back then had been. He didn't mention what now seemed to me palpable, that his rejection of his father was related to what he incorrectly perceived to be his father's rejection of him. And I couldn't bring myself to suggest it to him, to say that his father's use of fists rather than words to protect his son had been understandably misinterpreted; that Russ had wanted to keep Tony out of the rackets for his own good, but Tony had viewed it as his father not thinking as highly of him as he did of others—of Mike Gulino, for one; that, maybe, he'd decided his father didn't love him.

There were plenty of other reasons for him to be angry. There was the pain his father had caused his mother, and the outrage at Russ trying to take his child.

In my dad's mind, though, the thing that grew as he and my mother built their family was hurt on behalf of his own children: "The years went by, and he never lifted a finger to be a grandfather. He never came by. He wouldn't have known you kids if he fell over you on the sidewalk. I was so mad at him for a lot of years."

———

TONY'S CAREER PATH had basically been set when he was fourteen and somehow got a job selling pots and pans door to door, and realized that he was good at it. Not long after, he went to the library and checked out the Dale Carnegie book *How to Win Friends and Influence People*, devoured it, and committed himself to, as that forerunner of all self-help manuals put it, "develop a deep, driving desire to master the principles of human relations." "It was the first book I ever read that I wanted to read," he said. It clicked with what he knew in his bones, that sales was nothing more or less than making a connection with people. Instead of getting his high school diploma he took a fourteen-week sales course, in which all the other students were middle-aged men. "Act enthusiastic AND YOU'LL BE ENTHUSIASTIC!" he exclaimed, characterizing for me its essence. He got a job working alongside two veteran salesmen, selling siding door to door. One of them had a lisp and a schtick of earnestness: "He'd say to the customer, 'My mouth ith moving but my heart ith talking.' I almost fell on the floor laughing. But the thing was, he meant it. I learned a lot from those guys."

Over the next few years Tony pulled himself out of the crisis that was his early life, and supported a wife and children, by embracing sales as if it were a religion. He might at one time have imagined he would be selling numbers or tip seals, but as it turned out it didn't matter to him what the product was. He sold cars, pasta, and encyclopedias with equal vim. One time he bought a hillside that was covered with evergreen trees, hired some guys to cut down all the trees, sold them at Christmastime, then sold the hillside. He steeled himself against the waves of rejection that come a salesman's way by devouring a syllabus of his own selection, working toward a self-bestowed degree in self-help. *Think and Grow Rich. The Power of Positive Thinking. Selling the Sizzle. Psycho Cybernetics.* Paperbacks of those books—dog-eared, splay-backed, with whole paragraphs viciously underlined, the margins stuffed with his slanted all-caps printing—littered the landscape of my childhood. He had his philosophy reduced to a motto: "A Winner Never Quits and a Quitter Never Wins." He tried to drill it into me. Even as a child I demurred—something in me warned that it was too pat, too cheesy.

His attempts to imbue his eldest son with his hard-earned wisdom reached a climax when I was in fifth grade. He marched me into the dining room of our home, where a bookcase lined one wall, then commanded me to pull out the dictionary and look up the word "impossible." Even though I didn't know exactly where this was going, I could sense that it was one of his gimmicks. He handed me a pair of scissors and instructed me to cut the word out of the dictionary. *Why?* I had a love for books (which he had instilled); it seemed sacrilegious.

"Because it doesn't exist."

"Yes, it does. It's right here. I-M-P-O-S . . ."

And there was that beam of his, his face lighting up because he had you right where he wanted you.

"Nope. Doesn't exist."

Despite my resistance, the image of that page of the dictionary, with the little rectangle neatly sliced out of it, remains in my memory. A winner never quits. Tony never did. Tony. How could you not fall in love with such a father? People said he looked like Robert Vaughn in *The Man from U.N.C.L.E.* He was a secret-agent body double, a jazz aficionado, an up-and-comer, a fashion plate and man about town; a winner not despite but because of the many failures. *You know who struck out more times than anybody in the history of baseball? Babe Ruth!* I had no idea whether that was true, but he forced me to grin at the wisdom. He told me about his own failures in sales, making them seem the saddest stories, then turned them inside out with the kicker that each failure fired him up for the next round. And the next time, he'd win: sell a Pontiac off the lot, or whatever else was put before him. He loved the game, he was good at it. It wasn't about the stuff; it was about attitude. Your attitude about yourself and the world and how, dammit, the two were meant for each other.

It dawned on me, as we sat in his living room reliving the first stage of his career, that this mindset, this dynamo, came right out of the clashes with Russ. It wasn't just, as I had always thought, a freakish contrast of personalities between father and son. There was a direct line between what Russ had been and what Tony was becoming. Surely without intending any such thing, Russ, in shutting his son out of his life and the rackets, in fomenting a hurt, put this spin on him, set him on his razzle-dazzle trajectory.

THEY BASICALLY DIDN'T speak for ten years. In that time—the mid-'60s to the mid-'70s—Tony rose as a small-town entrepreneur. He graduated from selling cars and books to buying and selling houses, becoming a player on the local real-estate scene. Along the way, he started a bar, which he slyly called the Office Lounge ("Where were you, honey?" "At the Office . . ."). Small towns being what they are, the Office happened to be located a block away from the Haven. Russ had sold the Haven a few years before, but it was still in business, and the contrast between the two was generationally striking. The Haven's crowd was comprised of people who, like Russ, had had their heyday in the Eisenhower administration. Thanks to Tony's personality, the Office took off right from the start, and it filled with relatively hip young adults clutching glasses of "Chablis," "Burgundy," and Mateus Rosé—people who'd come of age amid Watergate and were trying to shake off the gloom of that era and suss out a brighter future for themselves.

Eventually, Tony was able to fulfill a dream and buy a house for his family in Westmont, the upscale suburb with the best school district. But he needed $5,000 for the down payment.

"Where did you get it?"

"Borrowed from my uncle Joe."

Beat.

"You took money from a mob boss?"

"He was my uncle! I paid him back right away."

Then one day at the Office—it was the afternoon; no customers, Tony was alone behind the bar getting the cash drawer ready for the evening—the door opened and there stood Russ. Russ tended to mumble; he said something about how he liked the place—it had class. The back wall was deep-blue wallpaper with the Manhattan skyline outlined in silver. They talked about little things. And Tony felt his heart softening. Russ was a little over sixty but looked older: ravaged and sad-eyed. Wasn't it better to reconcile before it was too late? Tony asked him what he was up to. Russ mentioned a deal he was working on, an investment. A book. Tony knew perfectly well he didn't mean the kind you read. Russ was wondering: maybe Tony would like to get in on it. Tony said it was nice of him to offer, but he'd have to pass. Russ said he understood. But if his son could see his way to giving him a loan—a couple thousand was all he needed—he would be able to get the money back to him, with interest, within a week or so.

Tony lent him the money. A week later, Russ came back. He almost had all the pieces in place. He just needed another two thousand bucks, then he'd pay the whole four thousand back plus another thousand.

"It went on like that," my dad said. "When I was down ten thousand, I knew I was being conned by my own father. He didn't see it as a con, I don't think. I said to myself, 'This is ridiculous.'"

"Did he ever pay you back?"

"No."

Jump ahead a couple of years, and Tony is now at his career peak. He has parleyed the success of the Office into another venture, opening a huge disco in the suburb of Richland. It was in a former factory; he called it the Factory. All of his people skills were paying off, and his promotions—Foxy Ladies Nite!—were right on target; the place was packed every weekend.

And once again there comes an evening when Tony looks up— this time across a sea of customers, over the long curved bar and toward the entrance—and sees his father standing there. An old man in a suit that harkened back to an impossibly bygone era, blinking, looking around at the roomful of young people, their faces patterned with dots of light from the disco ball, moving to the bass-heavy beat of Donna Summer. The next time Tony looks up, he is gone.

I wondered, while Tony was telling me this, what Russ was thinking. I wondered if he was thinking that, after all, his son had followed in his footsteps, replicated the kind of small-town entrepreneurial realm that Russ had created, but had done it differently—on the up-and-up. Or maybe he'd just wanted to hit his son up for money but saw that he was too busy.

RUSS'S LAST YEARS were hard. He had several heart attacks, which tore through him like hurricanes, leaving wreckage. A picture of him at sixty-five shows a man you'd swear was in his eighties. He was popping nitroglycerin pills like candy. He still lived at Vicky's house, but they couldn't stand each other. Each had tried at different times to break away, but they ended up sabotaging each other's attempts. Once, when he was still feeling vigorous enough to experience indignation, Vicky came home and mentioned warily that a man who worked at a clothing store in Westmont had asked her out. She was suggesting, sort of, that maybe they should give each other some room. She was still in her forties at the time; it wasn't too late for her. Alexis told me that shortly afterward the man called Vicky in a panicky voice, asking her to please stay out of his store. Russ had come in and threatened to kill him.

He was fading fast though. Sometime in late 1980 or early '81 Russ asked my aunt if she would let him move into her house. He said he couldn't take living with Vicky anymore. "Dad, Mom stays with me now every weekend," she told him. "I can't have you both here." Not long after, he made his final trip to the racetrack in West Virginia, where he had one more heart attack, while clutching 37 tickets—trifectas, exactas, quinellas—totaling $305 in bets. His last gamble. The hospital called my parents. My dad called my aunt. "I still feel bad that I told him he couldn't stay with me," Sis said. "He didn't have long to live."

Just before Russ's funeral, Sis told her mother about Joey, that he was Russ's son. She hadn't had the strength to tell her before, or maybe she didn't think her mother had the strength to hear it. "I would have raised Joey as my own" was Mary's comment. As it turned out, having the information helped her get through the funeral. For years, she'd felt a coldness from Russ's sisters and their children. It hurt her; she didn't understand the reason. Apparently there was awkwardness in their knowing Joey's parentage while she did not.

The awkwardness seemed to melt away with Russ's death. At the funeral, which was a large affair—hundreds of people trooping through Ozog's Funeral Home on Broad Street and filing into Saint Emerich's Church on Chestnut Avenue—Russ's family members came up to Mary, one by one, the Verones and Shortos and Basiles and Trios, kissed her, held her, treated her as the aunt, in-law, matriarch that she was. I was there, just graduated from college and now, with my brother and four of Russ and Mary's nephews, a pallbearer. I watched my grandmother playing the role of widow, assuming it like an actress. Her tears opened up as the relatives came to her, one after the other, and told her how sorry they were for her. She was weeping,

I suppose, over what one can't help but weep over at the funeral of a spouse: the inexorable linearity of life, the imponderability of what was and might have been, the massive ache of humanness. And I imagine she felt relief.

LITTLE JOE DIED four year later, in 1985. His funeral was even bigger than Russ's, with a parade of Lincolns and Cadillacs that made the evening news. The obituary in the *Tribune-Democrat* differed from what he might have hoped for before the Crime Commission hearings. He was acknowledged as president of Keystone Sales and owner of the former Shangri-La Lodge, but that information was buried. The newspaper led by calling him "a reputed local organized crime figure" who "was considered by the Federal Bureau of Investigation to be a lieutenant in the western Pennsylvania La Cosa Nostra."

Shortly after his death, a special agent for the Pennsylvania Crime Commission gave the *Pittsburgh Post-Gazette* a kind of epitaph for Joe, Russ, and others like them, the men who had built their smalltime fiefdoms in the postwar era: "They are growing old and dying off, and it does not seem that people are knocking down the doors to become members because there is a lot of independence. People figure, 'Why should I give this organized guy money when I can just keep it all for myself?'"

I VISITED MIKE one more time in the nursing home. He had deteriorated since I'd last seen him. He would die within a few months, at the age of eighty-seven. We talked about a lot of things, but he seemed to have something in particular on his mind concerning Russ and the influence he'd had on his life.

Before, I hadn't quite been able to fathom the gap between the way Mike thought of my grandfather and the way people in my family viewed Russ. But listening to him now I had a little epiphany. Maybe, to Russ, Mike had not just been—as Mike himself had told me—a kid who was already tainted by the rackets and therefore a kindred spirit. Maybe Russ could allow himself to get close to Mike—to view him almost like a son, to love him—because their relationship wasn't burdened by the harm that Russ was at that time doing to his wife. Several times my dad, in talking about his father, had used the word "shame." "He was filled with shame." I didn't get it, and when I asked him to explain what he meant, he couldn't. Now suddenly I did get it.

That behavior didn't cloud Russ's relationship with Mike. He didn't have to feel guilty. He could be himself. *He never broke character:* Tony saying that to me about his father meant that he knew there was a facade he would never get past. Whereas Russ could reveal himself to Mike. Mike felt the genuineness—it must have been a relief for both of them, in a world of hard guys, a transactional world, to allow yourself that kind of openness—and he never forgot it. I wondered if the chance to relive that special relationship, to feel it again, wasn't what motivated him to want to sit with me hour after hour over the years.

What Mike wanted to talk about in particular was his final con. He laid it out for me, describing it as a kind of homage to Russ. It was such a bold piece of work, and so clearly an extension of what he took to be Russ's teaching, that I later spent some effort in corroborating the details, unpacking how it all went. In executing it, Mike brought his mentor's philosophy, born of the post-Prohibition world, into the era of Bill Clinton and Madonna and Nintendo. And, like in a caper film, where the old crew gets back together for one more job, he reunited some of the guys from Russ's era.

He began to hatch the idea for his last con, which he called "The Box" and which federal prosecutors later dubbed the "Johnstown Sting," when he was doing time for bookmaking. As he'd told me before, he was pissed off with himself. He and Russ and all the guys had come of age at a time when gambling was supposedly immoral and therefore illegal; they'd devoted their lives to devising ways to feed the eternal hunger people had to bet, to try to beat the odds. Then, over the previous decade, he'd seen the government muscle in and take over that business, as if the state were just another mob outfit. All of a sudden state lotteries spanned the country. He'd been busted for running a book when states were basically doing the same thing. He wasn't going to make that mistake again. He'd go back to his roots. Run a con. But what?

One day after he got out of prison he was sitting in the steam room at the YMCA when another guy sat next to him. They got to talking. His companion was an older gentleman, a businessman, clearly very conservative. When Mike said his name, the man remembered reading about his arrest and his bookmaking empire. Mike was struck by how much this straitlaced fellow knew about bookmaking—and by how much he didn't know. "That's when it hit me—a little knowledge can be dangerous. I said to myself, 'I can beat this guy. And there are a million just like him.'"

The fellow from the steam room knew that even in an era of state lotteries illegal books remained popular. There were lots of guys who didn't want to give a share of their winnings to the IRS. The man knew some of the ins and outs of illegal bookmaking, including the fact that bookies "lay off" to other bookies: make bets with other bookmakers in order to cover potential losses. Mike began to envision a con that revolved around layoffs.

Of course, if you want to scam somebody who knows a thing or two about bookmaking, you have to go to great lengths to show that your operation is secure. That's why it's called a confidence game. You have to convince the guy you're scamming that he isn't being scammed. Mike started thinking about a box. Back in the days of the G.I. Bank, Russ and Joe had a contraption that looked like a toolbox, which had a lock and a timer fixed to it. The day's betting slips went into it. It was closed and locked to signal the end of the day's action. It stayed locked until a set time, when it sprung open. It was a security device to prevent past-posting: making bets after the number was known.

So one day, a guy named Rich Sapolich—who happened to be the son of Sappy, my godfather—got a call from Nino Bongiovanni, who had been a friend and associate of Mike's from back when Mike ran the Harrigan table at City Cigar and Nino ran the lunch counter. Rich was an electrical engineer who was good with his hands, good at making things. "Nino calls me up and says, 'Mike wants to talk to you,'" Rich told me. (I'd arranged to meet him at the Holiday Inn. Also on the scene for this particular lunchtime chat session were Frank Filia, Sam Di Francesco, my dad, and a talented pool player from the City Cigar days called Chooch Boscola.) "He wouldn't say what it was about. I go to Nino's place. He says we're going to take a ride with Frank." This was Frank Pagano—the guy who was my dad's nursing-home roommate. Frank and Mike also had a friendship that dated to City Cigar.

Frank showed Rich a box—one of the boxes Russ and Joe used for the G.I. Bank, which Mike had somehow gotten his hands on. "It was a sort of comical old-school technology, but it worked," Rich said. "Apparently it was made by a guy who was a bomb expert in World War II. Mike asked if I could make one, only better."

Rich made the box. He told me he spent ten months getting it right. (Mike complained about this: "Richie was a genius, but it took him a fuckin' lifetime to get anything done.") They tried out the box. Then he completely redesigned it. "It was really nice-looking," Rich said. "It looked like it could have been on the space shuttle. I like clean design."

Once the box was ready Mike's job was to find the mark—"the fish," the guy who was going to take the bait. Greedy guys, guys with lots of money who wanted more. Guys who were smart, but not as smart as they thought they were. He found them everywhere. Doctors, dentists, accountants, engineers, real-estate developers...

Mike's story was that he was a bookie's bookie, taking layoffs from bookmakers all over Pennsylvania and surrounding states. The fictional bookies were supposedly taking bets on the daily number from the Pennsylvania state lottery. What he needed, he told the fish, was an investor, someone who could cover him in the event that a number hit big. He didn't come off like he was selling himself; it was the investor who had to prove to him that he had the funds and the discretion. Mike was well known as a bookie. Guys heard about his new venture and lined up, asking to be let in. "What, my money's no good?" one of them complained when Mike declined to let him invest.

They lined up because it was such a sweet deal—there was no real risk involved. They weren't gambling but investing. The odds of the numbers game were such that the house was guaranteed to earn roughly 40 percent of the total amount bet. Mike would split that with the investor. The reason he needed an investor was because of the daily fluctuation: some days a number would hit big, and instead of profiting they would have to pay out. That was the investor's only job, to come up with half the winnings. Mike told the investor he prided himself on paying winners within twenty-four hours. So if a number hit, the investor had to be ready to make a payout on the spot. And he was careful to warn the fish about the size of the action: with bets ranging from $100 to $500, and 600-to-1 payoffs, the fish might have to come up with $40,000 or $50,000, or more. "And I told them this is all cash. When you win, you get cash. If you have to pay, you pay cash."

With the fish on the line, either Frank or Nino would show up at his house or hotel room just before 7 p.m., when the lottery number was drawn on TV. (Once the FBI was on to the sting, they set up a video recorder in a hotel room where Mike was meeting a prospective fish, who was actually a government agent. They captured him assuring the man of Nino's trustworthiness. "He's an extension of my right arm," Mike says on the tape. "The only thing about me he don't know is when I fuck my old lady.") They would then watch TV, see the day's number pulled, and at 7:01 the high-tech lock on Rich's box would pop open and together they would go through the bets in the box to tally things up.

The box contained ten slips, each of which listed about fifty numbers played, along with the amount bet on each. These bets had supposedly been called in to Mike's secretary throughout the day. The fish was told that the box was locked at 6 p.m., when betting closed. The trick of the whole scam—Rich's ingenious element—was a tiny printer concealed in the lid. The instant the winning number was announced on TV, Rich, who was sitting in a car nearby, radioed it to the printer, which printed out a slip with the number and dropped it in among the others, thus assuring that the fish would have to make a payout rather than receive one. The slip also showed the amount the fictitious winner had bet. "We were pretty conservative at first," Rich told me. "But we got bolder as we went. I started with winning bets of around $20,000. The highest was a quarter of a million."

"But I guess sometimes you let the fish win?" I asked Mike.

"No! Why let him win?" Their first fish was a doctor from Greensburg. After he had lost badly for several days in a row he told Mike he was going to quit at the end of the week if his luck didn't turn around. "I said to Nino and Frank, 'He's gonna go till Sunday then quit. We have to cripple him.' Frank said, 'No, let's let him win once. Then he'll stick around.' I said, 'Fuck you. I didn't put all this money into this thing to let some fucking doctor win. *We* are the guys who have to win.'" They took him for a total of $465,000 before he quit.

Mike was stunned by how well the con worked. And it kept working. Next they took a doctor from Pittsburgh for $430,000, a real-estate developer from Johnstown for $300,000, a dentist from State College for $280,000. The owner of a dog-kenneling business later admitted to the jury in federal court that he couldn't even remember how much he'd lost: "I was in such a state of panic, I didn't know." A retired urologist from Johnstown played along for three days, lost $157,000, then threw in the towel.

Mike prided himself on his ability to keep the fish on the line. The urologist told the court that Mike had gone so far as to advise him on what to do with all the cash once he started winning, giving him tips on how to avoid the notice of the IRS. After a few losses, Mike would tell the fish that he had hit an unlucky streak, with bettors winning several days in a row, but that that only meant the odds were now heavily in his favor, he just had to stay in the game—the only way he would lose was if he bailed out. Another physician in Johnstown kept listening, and kept paying up, until, after twenty-eight days, he'd given Mike $247,000 in cash. "After suffering a staggering loss, I had no interest in continuing this misadventure," he told the jury.

Some investors left in anger, some in confusion. Virtually none, it seems, realized at the time that they had been conned. One time Mike showed Rich a wedding invitation. Not long before, they had taken a doctor for close to $1 million before he bowed out. He sent Mike a little handwritten note, apologizing for not being able to keep up his side of what he still believed was a business arrangement. To show his regard for his former partner, he invited him to his daughter's wedding.

The Johnstown Sting ran for seven years before the feds caught up with Mike and his compatriots. By that time, it was all getting too much for them anyway. There was no goal, no endgame. They just kept taking money from rich guys who were greedy enough to give it to them. They were constantly looking over their shoulders. And they didn't know what to do with the money. They had it stuffed in their mattresses and attics. Frank Pagano had more than $50,000 in a coffee can in his garage. They were starting to get on one another's nerves, too. Rich was feeling weird about Mike. He slowly came to realize that Mike wasn't in it for the money: "He just loved to beat these guys. He wasn't going to stop until he was forced to."

In 1995 a fish in Ohio whom Mike was in the process of luring turned out to be an FBI informer. Rich and Frank both testified in exchange for leniency; Frank wore a wire to help build the case against

Mike. (I mentioned Mike to Frank in the nursing home. "There was nobody in the world closer than Mike and me, but we don't even talk now," he said with some sadness. "We parted ways over that box.") The feds found evidence that Mike had bilked people out of a total of $2 million. Mike chuckled and told me it was five times that amount.

The trial played out in the *Tribune-Democrat* over the course of 1996. Mike was tickled by the fact that right up to the trial itself federal agents believed that the fictitious book had been real; they kept pressing him to know where earnings from it were stashed. "That's when you know you pulled a hell of a con," he said.

Mike's lawyers argued that he deserved probation due to ill health. PRISON FOR SCAM ARTIST ran the ultimate headline: the judge ruled that his crimes demanded jail time. After his earlier imprisonment Mike had sworn off bookmaking and returned to the purer business of running a scam, but the end result was the same. He got eighteen months in a federal penitentiary.

MIKE SAID HE wanted to relate the details of his last con to me because Russ had been the guiding force behind it—because "I owe everything to Russ." Being a kid and watching Russ play gin rummy for big money in the room behind the bowling alley in the late '40s, cheating fearlessly, had been, for him, the equivalent of a college education. As he described those card games—the cigar smoke, the sweat and the booze, the guys in their suits with their ties shimmied loose, the heads of department stores and banks and factories drawn together by their common hankering for this ancient form of competition—I thought for the first time about the two sides to Russ's career, which I had lumped together but suddenly realized were quite different. He had started out as a cheat then altered his course once Joe came to town and brought the mob franchise with him. Joe had given him an unparalleled opportunity—

I'm tempted to say an offer he couldn't refuse—with the result that Russ became a kind of company man, a manager of an expanding enterprise. That came with all the pressures of any corporate position, in addition to those pressures that were unique to the rackets. I wondered if the shift into that line of work wasn't what drove him to drink. If I thought through everything people had told me, it seemed he had been most in his element when he was a cheat, pure and simple.

The package of skills that characterized a successful cheat—the poise, the coolness, the outrageous assumption of sincerity—was what had attracted and even moved Mike when, as an impressionable teen, he met Russ. And here was what seemed a true conundrum: These two men had become close because each had seen himself in the other. They forged a bond out of mutual respect and openness. They allowed themselves to be naked before the other, without artifice. And yet what led to that genuineness, what each saw inside the other and identified with, was an innate aptitude for deceit.

It was as a kind of gentleman con artist that Mike chose to remember Russ. He really wanted me to appreciate that, to see it as a virtue. "Everybody thought Russ was a sonofabitch, but when he was cheatin' he was slick as can be," he said. "Those card games were big. He was playing with guys who ran companies. Some of the players were in the rackets—murderers, guys from out of town, guys you didn't want to fuck with. It ain't easy to con guys like that. But when Russ would go to get his card, he'd take three—right in front of you. You didn't see it happen, and you didn't see them extra cards in his hand. Then, the hand before he was going to knock, he'd get rid of them. He could make a deck of cards talk. I saw him beat a guy for $20,000 in a single game and the guy never had a clue."

Mike's unseeing gaze slowly scanned the room as he came down from this heady memory, and finally settled on me. One of the last things he said to me was so disorienting, and I guess so sweet in its intent, that I laughed out loud: "You got good genes."

16

The Winner

My mother surprised everyone.

She was always the stronger of the two. As far back as I can remember, Tony seesawed, emotionally and, in later life, physically. Rita was the anchor, the steady force. Then—this was about a year after Mike Gulino died—she had a knee replacement and wound up with a staph infection in the joint. Suddenly we were caught up in a full-on life-threatening situation: infectious-disease specialists, lengthy hospital stays, cannonades of antibiotics.

It was while my family's attention was thus diverted that Tony decided that he, too, would sign up for elective surgery, on his prostate. My siblings and I were so focused on my mother's condition nobody paid much attention. Had we been aware of what was happening one of us would have put a stop to it—called the urologist and asked what the hell he was thinking by selling an elderly man in poor health a risky surgery whose sole purpose was to help him pee a little better. Tony's general practitioner had made clear a few years before that his health was so compromised that he should only undergo surgery as a last resort.

The antibiotics treatments eventually did what they were meant to do for my mother. Her health improved and she went home. But for Tony the unwarranted operation set off a chain of medical crises. To stop the incessant bleeding in his bladder they took him off blood thinners. A day later, he had a stroke. He couldn't open his eyes, couldn't do much of anything, but he could talk a little. We had our heads bent over his hospital bed.

"Dad, you had a stroke. Do you understand?"

"I had a stroke," he whispered.

His personality seemed intact. A male nurse came into the room and told him he was looking pretty good. "You're full of shit," he replied.

The neurologist told us the hopeful thing about a stroke was that all the damage happened at once. Over the coming days, we could reasonably expect to see some improvement.

But a day later he was worse. In the hours I spent in the waiting area outside the intensive care unit, I ruminated. Naturally I thought about Tony as a man, and about my dad as my dad. But I couldn't help but see what was happening in light of everything that he and I had been exploring these past four years. Even a week before I would not have thought of this as likely material for the last chapter of a book, but suddenly it was feeling like the end of a story, one that had begun in the hills of Sicily a century and a half earlier.

My mind went back to where it had been during my dad's sudden decline of four years earlier—that long, sleepless night of regret—and to the surprise that followed, when my father got a reprieve, a gift of a basketful of years and months and minutes in which to breathe the air and wince in pain and laugh sometimes, to watch his grandchildren's lives unfurl a bit further. I thought of how he and I had put that time to use—the flawed but earnest effort we had made to understand the enigmatic father who had come before both of us. And lately we had shifted to Tony, his own life, and how it had spun away from his father's. We had gone through his early years, the power-of-positive-thinking period, the young salesman on the rise. But his body had decided to give out just as we were reaching the next phase of his life, when his career came to a halt.

There was a central event to that period. He lost the family house. Tony was a hot local entrepreneur and this was supposed to be his biggest business deal yet. He had hooked up with a couple of out-of-town guys, go-getters like him, and they were going to build a shopping center in the suburbs. For some reason he was the one who had to put up the collateral for the loan: our house. But the going got tough, and the other partners skipped out. The bank took what it could.

And Tony proceeded to blame himself in the most ornate fashion. He became a superhero of self-blame. This all began as I was heading off to college, and I couldn't deal with the steaming pile of drama. I simply pushed it all away. I threw myself into the persona of a college freshman, which I felt almost totally justified in doing, scouring the readings for Poli-Sci 101 and Intro to English Lit as if the key to my future was to be found encoded in them. It took a few years for my parents' financial crisis to play out, during which time I did everything I could to wall myself off from Johnstown. As if physically ricocheting from the epicenter of family ruin, I decided, on graduation, that I had a longstanding desire, of which I was previously unaware, to live in Japan. My mother was quietly packing up the dishes and books and keepsakes; the moving truck was backing out of the driveway. I was on the other side of the world, learning the characters for the Tokyo subway stops and teaching English as a second language, doing a thorough job of not thinking about what was happening.

Losing the house proved to be a crisp dividing line. My parents' life ever after was shrunken and hollowed-out compared with the razzmatazz of the family Tony had led through my childhood.

Disappointment. That was what colored my adult relationship

with my father. Wicked, stinging disappointment. But not about him losing the house.

Or no. Something stronger. Betrayal. A feeling of having been strung along.

Because he quit. It was amazing to realize, as I paced the hospital halls, that he was only in his mid-forties when he lost the house and filed for bankruptcy. Still young, able to bounce back. But he collapsed inside himself, became lost in guilt and remorse and failure. When I went home over school breaks, to spend a few hasty days in their rental house, I couldn't look at him. My mother eventually found work—as a bank teller, then selling real estate—to make ends meet. Eventually he slipped into the guise of a semi-functioning adult, getting work flogging life insurance. But his heart wasn't in it. He wallowed for decades. Over time he became a font of a different kind of wisdom, which came from the AA meetings he now attended religiously. Humility and forgiveness. Those became his bywords. He was very big on forgiveness. I assumed it was meant reflexively: it was what he craved.

I never gave it to him. I couldn't have cared less about losing the house. As he himself had taught me, things like that might well happen when you took risks. It was the other thing I couldn't forgive him for: setting me up. Because, without my quite being conscious of it, I had drunk the Kool-Aid. A winner never quits. Except he quit and stayed quit. At the very moment I was heading out the door, ready to take the directive that had been hammered into me through my childhood and begin applying it in my own struggles with the world, he reversed course. He left me standing there. He conned me.

The balance of his life spooled slowly out. AA meetings, bowing out of visits with old friends. Altering his personality: becoming a bit of a clown, endlessly repeating the same silly jokes. Sitting at home with the television, the volume set to drown out conversation and reflection.

I wasn't conscious of the con at the time, let alone of how I had internalized it. I never had it out with him. Had I been able to do so, maybe I could have been close to him. Instead, in terms of our relationship throughout my adulthood, I opted for pleasantness, a lack of friction. I established my distance, set up the perimeters, and patrolled them. Sitting there, looking out from the fifth-floor hospital window onto the remains of the once-mighty little city where we were both born, I realized that this whole business between us—my feeling burned by my father's failure to live up to the "wisdom" he had instilled in me, my taking it out on him, on both of us—had been working its way into my consciousness over these last four years, when we spent so much time together, digging at the roots of our family tree. While we were looking for Russ, trying, as far as my dad's psyche would allow, to piece together his relationship with his father, I was engaged in the same thing, working at the knot that had lodged between the two of us. But I never brought that awareness to the surface. I didn't broach the subject with him.

HOSPITAL VIGILS HAVE their rhythms. There were times when we took turns at the bedside, my siblings and I, and times when we were all there together. My brother did a long day's stint on his own, then he went home and for a while my sisters and I happened to be at Tony's bedside together. He couldn't open his eyes or talk anymore, but he was aware. He knew who was there and what we were saying, and he could move his mouth in the shape of words. We rambled, saying whatever we could think of.

It occurred to me that my sisters might not have heard the elopement story. I started telling it—Tony and Rita dashing off down South in a loaner car, with Tony's infamous pal Rip as their wingman. I could tell he was following along so I kept going, adding whatever details I could think of: Virginia Beach, the sea air, getting hitched. The justice of the peace had been a man named Harry Umphlet. "You and mom laughed at that name, right?" Tony nodded. He was enjoying this, it seemed.

"And then you called your parents and told them you had gotten married."

Nod.

Something occurred to me, something I hadn't asked before. "Did you tell your parents that Mom was pregnant, that that was why you'd run off?"

He gave a very vigorous shake of the head. No way.

So there. Breaking news. We were still at it, still mining the past. Doing history.

A WHILE LATER, I was alone with him. He was quiet and so was I. I was thinking about how we were very different, he and I, but at the same time we had so much in common. Including the fact that we had each spent our adult lives blaming our fathers.

But even as I thought that—there, in that ugly room, with the soulless beeping of the machines and the fluorescently sad lighting—I realized it wasn't true. I suddenly found that I now believed something he had been telling me for years, which I had insisted on rejecting: that he *didn't* blame his father. He'd overcome that, long ago. Wasn't that part of the AA motto, which he quoted with regularity: . . . *grant me the serenity to accept the things I cannot change . . . ?*

We had spent more time together in these years than at any period since my childhood, but, as meaningful as it had been for both of us, I had continued to dismiss his pat philosophizing. I believed it to be a variety of laziness. The aphorisms, I felt, were a way of short-circuiting hard work, jumping right to the payoff. Whatever the situation, whatever stage I was at in life, he always had his selection of pablum on offer. My irritation was decades-old, knee-jerk.

And, suddenly, it didn't exist. Acceptance. Simply that. The serenity to accept. It spread through me as I watched him lying there, helplessly intubated—horrible word—as he alternated between periods of calm and wracking pain. Maybe it is so commonplace a thing as to be not worth noting: when you are losing someone, you are flooded with an appreciation of what you took for granted. But it didn't feel commonplace. It felt true and solid and important.

And just like that, over the course of a long second or two, like that footage on TV of an iceberg shelf that has been quietly melting for years suddenly collapsing into the sea, I felt the absurd mass of expectation and disappointment I had been holding on to for so long simply give way. I allowed him to be the person he had been all the time. I became quietly but intensely aware of what suddenly seemed a mind-numbingly obvious realization: that he had dealt with the seriously dysfunctional family of his childhood by injecting an effervescent energy into the family that he and my mother reared. We weren't the scarred victims of his troubled past but rather the beneficiaries of it. And not only that. Those things he said, the cheap paperback wisdom, all those trite sayings: they were true. I had clung to some petty wish that he would express himself more loftily, or with more nuance. It used to piss me off that he didn't have the patience for nuance. I thought that that meant he was wrong—that he had, I don't know, skipped over genuine understanding. What bullshit. This man had lived a real life. He had done precisely what he could with what he had been given. And he was entitled to derive the insight out of it that he had distilled.

I started jabbering. Holding his hand, I said every damn thing I could think of, the cheesier the better. I'm here with you. Thank you for your wisdom. Thank you for the bright and bold ride you took us on. Thank you for suddenly upping stakes when I was eight years old and moving us to California for a year, which happened to overlap with the Summer of Love. Thank you for making us eat pasta sauce with snails.

And, yes, OK: thank you for telling me that you forgave Russ, for saying that the poor guy (your expression) had a heavy bag of rocks to carry around (your expression) and that you forgave him for the pain he inflicted on seemingly a whole village worth of people. For concluding that the psychic wreckage he had dealt out had been coiled up in him by circumstances. And for apparently believing that this awareness on your part somehow absolved him. I don't agree with you on that, but thank you for believing it. Thank you for taking the work we did together to heart—not for your own sake, because it wasn't something you needed, but because you realized I did. Thank you for showing me how to do history, which, it suddenly occurs to me, is nothing if it doesn't involve a consideration of how human beings try to balance their inevitable failures and stay afloat amid currents that are destined to sink them.

THE TIMING MY dad selected for his death meant that his funeral ended up being a bit of a reunion of all the people I'd been spending time with these past few years—or those who were left, anyway. All the cousins and siblings and children were there at the funeral home, of course. The Panera Bread guys hung out together near the back, commenting on who came and went like a Greek chorus. As we filed up to the coffin, I held the hand of my nine-year-old son, Anthony, and heard him whisper a sobbing farewell to his namesake using his term for his grandfather: "I love you, Tap-tap." Maybe all Italian funeral homes end the viewing by pumping Sinatra's "My Way" through the sound system; maybe we should have expected it. But it hit us with the force of Grade-A schmaltz. The cheesy stuff is real.

Afterward, there was a luncheon at the country club. One by one, people stood up and told stories about Tony. Knowing chuckles skittered around the room, occasionally expanding into full laughter.

Suddenly I wanted something. I went over to Frank Filia and asked if maybe he would like to sing a song. "Ah, Russell, I'm sorry," he said. "I don't do a cappella."

I surprised myself: "Please, Frank."

"I'm sorry."

I sat down. Some more stories, more gentle laughs. Then Frank shuffled over, stood behind me, his hand on my shoulder. Everybody fell silent.

Sky, so vast is the sky, with faraway clouds just wandering by . . .

Almost in a whisper, he gave us the song he'd sung a while back at the Holiday Inn—Tony's favorite, the moody, brooding, impressionistic melody that my dad, channeling Sinatra, would intone for my mother in the car when they took their backseat full of small children for a Sunday drive. A song about wind and trees and sky and clouds. A meditation on being human, on having a heart that longs for individual meaning in the midst of nature's imponderable vastness. A song that ached of love and impermanence.

Frank looked around the room as he finished and saw what he had done. It was a love song, but everyone was in tears. And just like that he switched gears, broke into "C'è la Luna Mezz'o Mare," the song Italian Americans sing at weddings, with a bouncing beat that pretty much compels you to clap along idiotically, makes you feel like you're a peasant on some vine-covered hillside. Everyone knew it, everyone sang, though I don't think many knew the meaning of the words— which are about a girl who has to marry but isn't sure which suitor to take, so she asks her mother to choose for her. The chorus cycles between the different options, which all end up being the same: marry the shoemaker and he'll hammer you, marry the farmer and he'll plow you, marry the butcher and he'll "sausage" you.

Frank was a pro. At the end everyone was laughing, exhaling, letting go of something.

AFTER THE CARS had wound up the hill to the east of Johnstown and followed the hearse into St. Anthony's Cemetery, we stood under a tent to listen while the priest intoned a few words. Then the funeral director explained why we were not actually gathered at the gravesite but a hundred yards from it. It seemed that when they started to dig they encountered an enormous boulder, which would take considerable time to remove. People chuckled: Tony was known for his stubbornness. He would have enjoyed the metaphor.

The family members walked over to the burial spot. We stared into the pit the diggers had begun. We held hands. This was where he would be. I turned to my right, attracted by something. The anomaly that had caught my eye was an object that should have been a gravestone but instead was a metal spike sticking out of the ground. It was a placeholder. Apparently when someone dies and is buried, you have to let time go by, a year or two, to let the ground settle, before installing a permanent stone. There was a card attached to it. I read it.

Michael Gulino. That was the name on the card that marked the burial spot right beside my father. I looked at it again. There was a little picture of Mike on it, too, taken maybe ten years before I'd met him.

I looked up, let my eyes sweep over the rolling acreage that the cemetery occupied. The gravestones went on and on, a somber, tasteful, unmoving parade. It was beyond logic to think that the placement was coincidental. Yes, this was the Italian cemetery in town. But there were more than four thousand gravestones, well over ten thousand people buried here.

The answer to the riddle of the placement of the two graves, or part of the answer anyway, would seem to have been right in front of me. Carved into a charcoal-colored stone in the row behind Tony and Mike were the names of Russell and Mary. I had not been so thorough in my questioning of Mike as to ask whether his close relationship with my grandfather carried as far as his final resting place. I would never know the details of the arrangement Russ made with his protégé, whether he had given or sold Mike a portion of the burial plot that had come into his possession.

Later I called the church that runs the cemetery and learned that Russ had purchased his burial plots in October of 1960. That marked yet another out-of-the-ordinary move—along with selling his businesses and buying a handful of life-insurance policies—that he made in the year of his unraveling, the year Pippy diFalco was killed.

When we were back at my mother's house, something else popped into my mind that might have been another piece of this final puzzle in my search for my namesake. I suddenly recollected my dad saying something a long time ago—it might have been his own father's death and burial that prompted it. At that time I was more likely to be embarrassed by this sort of information than interested in it. Tony was going on about the legendary card games Russ would host, how he would cheat with skillful abandon. And how the guys he beat would settle up with him in all kinds of ways, depending on what their business was. Sometimes a priest was in on the game, gambling with money from the collection plate. And because of *that*, I seemed to remember Tony saying with a laugh, as if it were a punchline, as if somehow it just stood to reason in a crazy kind of way, his dad had wound up in possession of the real estate where, one day, they would all find themselves.

Epilogue

IT WAS A January afternoon, but I had the rental-car windows wide open because the whipping breeze, salted by the Atlantic Ocean shimmering on my right, was mild and humid. The towns rolling by coalesced into sprawl: Port St. Lucie, Vero Beach, Palm Bay, Titusville. Exiting Route 95 at Daytona, I made a couple of quick left turns and pulled into the nursing-home parking lot.

"I'm here to see Erwin Slomanson. I believe he's in Room 17C."

The attendant, a Black male nurse, led me down the hall and opened a door. "Slow Motion! You got a visitor!"

A while back, I had brought the Panera guys what I thought was some news, telling them that my dad had heard that Rip had died. They surprised me by reacting skeptically. I think it was Chooch Boscola who said, "Rip did that before—put out a rumor that he died." Toward what end, nobody knew. I decided I should devote some time to seeing if he was still around. None of the guys had been in contact with him for a long time. They agreed, though, that he had been in Florida for years.

Eventually I got the phone number of somebody named Debbie,

who was either a niece of Rip's or the daughter of an old friend of his. I called. She was happy to talk about Rip. Yes, as far as she knew he was alive. She gave me the name of the nursing home—and a heads-up. "I was down there in Florida with him a few years ago," she said. "We were in a bar. This guy was hitting on me. He kept at it, the way some guys do. All of a sudden Rip sticks a gun up to his head and says, 'She said no, OK?' That's Rip."

The door opened into a pleasant room with two beds, a table between them, and a TV. Both beds were neatly made. Rip was sitting on one of them, dressed in a blue-and-white checked shirt, jeans, and sneakers. He was thin and, for a man in his late eighties, looked quite fit. He had white hair and a frothy white mustache. When I came in he was playing solitaire on the bed. A cartoon was on the TV.

I had called in advance. He didn't seem to remember. He reacted to my introduction of myself as though he hadn't heard it before. "You're Tony Shorto's son? Holy shit! Russ's grandson! No kidding!"

He had a bright, friendly voice; he exuded cheery energy. I could see my dad, seventy years earlier, getting caught up in it. He had apparently been all over the country in his time, from Chicago to Miami, but Johnstown was his prime. He remembered. As I brought up names, he had stories. "George Sapolich was a boxer—I used to run around with him, but he had a different perspective on life than me. He just wanted to hold on to his territory. I wanted to expand, to get out of town. Mike Gulino! Mike was a flashy guy. He had control of certain areas. Russ Shorto . . . very quiet. Little Joe! Oh, man. Little Joe hired me to do jobs. He'd want me to go get money from whoever owed him."

"How did you do that?"

"I had a gun! A .48. I'd stick it in the guy's face. Go right up to him, in a bar or wherever, I didn't care. I'd beat the shit out of them. I was pretty well known. They didn't fuck with me. Jesus, you're bringing back memories! Hey, what was your last name?"

I had to pause a second. "Shorto."

"No shit! Are you related to Tony?"

"Yes. His son."

"So you must be related to Russ!"

It went on like that. He would burrow down into some little moment from deep in the '50s, recalling all the color and juice of it, then his brain would hit the Reset button.

"So my dad, Tony Shorto. You met in prison?"

"Yeah! I was the boss of the Cat Gang! We had DAs, twelve-inch pegs, three-inch rises. We were notorious! We robbed Penn Traffic! We'd go beat people up."

"Tony did that?"

"Oh, yeah. Well, Tony didn't like that much. He was a little different. Most of the guys in the gang, they were lonely, depressed, had nobody to talk to, so they hung out together. Tony wasn't like that. He was . . . personable."

"You went with my parents when they ran away to get married."

"Yeah! We went to South Carolina, I think. Somewhere down South. Your mother was a sweetheart."

"Tell me about Pippy."

"Pippy! He and I had a big disagreement about a bet. I had a fight with him. I was pretty bad in those days. Six-foot, one-eighty-five and all muscle. I was notorious!"

I took a breath. I had never asked this question before. I tried to say it in a relaxed manner. "Did you kill him?"

"Me? Nooooo! Pippy was all right. We tolerated each other."

"Did . . . do you have any ideas about what happened to him?"

"I remember exactly how it happened."

"What? You were there?"

"Sure. He came into the cigar store, flashing money—two pock-etfuls of hundreds. They had pool games for money. Christ, there was like two thousand bucks on the table. There was an after-hours club next door. Later I was up there and he was up there. I saw him being a big deal. He liked to be a big deal. There were these three guys up there. I don't know who they were but I know they were from Greensburg. There was a lot of trouble with guys from Greensburg trying to get into Johnstown. Little Joe had to keep them out. Pippy interfered—got into their territory. That's why he got killed."

"And you think the guys from Greensburg did it?"

"Or Little Joe."

"What?"

"Pippy went back and forth. He would work for Little Joe, but then go work for the guys in Pittsburgh. And that's against the rules. I don't know who killed him. But Little Joe could have had somebody come in and do it."

"Why wouldn't Little Joe get you to do it?"

"Me? I didn't want to get involved in killing. I was too good-natured! I was mean . . . but I was good-natured."

There was a little hiccup in his eyes. I thought a memory had surfaced, that the incongruity of "mean" and "good-natured" might have shaken something loose. He looked at me closely. I waited.

"What'd you say your name was?"

Acknowledgments

I WOULD NEVER have written this book without Frank Filia, who prodded me at just the right time and in just the right way. Then, once I was receptive to the idea, he took me by the hand and led me into a wondrous and alien world. A thousand thanks to you, Frank.

I also want to pay homage to Mike Gulino. Through years of interviews, Mike was vivacious, pugnacious, and gloriously open. He was a hell of a guy. I miss him.

Of course I have to acknowledge my parents, Tony and Rita Shorto. Over and over again they opened themselves up, explored hard places, willingly gave of themselves, knowing that it would be for public consumption but believing that that was right. As my dad said many times, "You're only as sick as your secrets." They have always been my touchstones.

Other members of my extended family also obliged me, in many cases sharing things that I know were difficult for them. I am very grateful, and I know this book is greatly improved by their willingness to mine the past. Thank you Minnie Bermosk, Anna Marie Bortoli, Marcia Guzzi, Mick Muto, Joseph Regino, Ron and Cindy

Shorto, Frank Trio, Eugene and Carol Trio, Guy Yasika, and everyone else who chimed in with recollections and perspectives.

Not surprisingly, some people in my family were not happy about this project. I understood their misgivings, and I only hope that they will find some good comes of it for them. And if not, well, I'm sorry.

I am also very grateful to all the other people who sat down for interviews, who searched their memories and shared their rich and full lives with me. Thank you to, among others, Caram Abood, Connie Bonk, Chooch Boscola, John Buser, Sam Di Francesco, Tony Gerglie, Bill Glosser, Barry Harrington, Jack Heinlein, Alexis Kozak, Debbie Levi, Bob Meagher, Don Mishler, Frank Pagano, George Raptosh, Joe Rovida, David Rudel, Joe Russell, Rich Sapolich, Rip Slomanson, Ron Stephenson, Tony Trigona, and Bill Wilson.

Many people helped me with information in one way or another. A special thank-you to Joe Ruggeri and Mario Italiano, my San Pier Niceto informants; Chip Minemyer, editor of the Johnstown *Tribune-Democrat*, and David Sutor, reporter at same; Craig Foust, former chief of police for the city of Johnstown; Sgt. Charles Jeffers of the Johnstown Police Department; and Richard Burkert, president of the Johnstown Area Heritage Association. Julie Pitrone Williamson gave me invaluable genealogical assistance. Jeanine Mazak-Kahne, associate professor of history at Indiana University of Pennsylvania, shared with me her deep knowledge of the western Pennsylvania mob. The late Randy Whittle, Johnstown's historian, shared insights as well as some of his collection. Barry Rudel and Donald Bonk helped arrange interviews and provided perspective. Sylvia Williams helped me to sort it all out.

Thank you to my readers, who improved the manuscript with their suggestions and corrections: Markus Alkire, Anna Marie Bortoli, Gina Dominique, Baird Hersey, Max Levinson, Dennis Maika, Michael Martin, Tim Paulson, Anna Shorto, Rita Shorto, David Strome, Eva and Scott Trout, and Pamela Twigg.

Anne Edelstein, my agent and friend, has been with me since the beginning and brought an entirely new level of empathy and care to this book, which was enlivened by her work on her own family story. My daughter Eva Shorto transcribed interviews, organized documents, and read and critiqued the manuscript. Her eye for story, structure, character, and language elevated the whole project. My other daughter, Anna Shorto, and my stepson, Reinier Koch, also transcribed interviews. Pamela, my wife, put up with all the usual stuff and helped me puzzle and think and feel my way through the material.

The people at W. W. Norton have been wonderful to work with. Julia Reidhead, my editor, was somehow able to detach herself from running the whole company whenever I asked for attention. She devoted herself to the manuscript with wit, style, compassion, and great insight. She truly helped make it what it is. Thanks also to Laura Goldin and Jessica Friedman, to Bee Holekamp and Don Rifkin, and to Rachelle Mandik for copyediting with grace and intelligence.

A final thank-you to Joe Barbera, George LiCastro, Joe LaRocca, Don Verbano, and Butch Verbano: the Panera guys, who lived the stuff of *Smalltime* and whose stories set my imagination afire.

A Note on Sources

This book tells a story that is rooted in the many smaller stories that its participants told me. Its core is a series of interviews—several hundred hours' worth, with dozens of people, conducted over a period of more than seven years. But what was I to do with this material, which often included rumor, secondhand reflection, and memories subject to the effects of time? I write both history and journalism; the two professions share a common approach to sources, whether the information comes from old pieces of paper in archives or elderly people in nursing homes. For items that are relatively small or noncontroversial—what color somebody's Cadillac was, say—a single source suffices. For anything more problematic, standard practice is to seek two independent sources. Regarding the notion that my grandfather regularly carried a gun, for example, while his children never witnessed him doing so, two people, both of whom knew him intimately at different times in his life, told me, independently of each other and without my prompting, that this was the case. That was good enough for me to state it as fact.

Naturally, in a book such as this, many assertions or claims fall into a grayer area. The whole matter of who killed Pippy diFalco came at me in a vast cloud of gossip, speculation, and hearsay, anchored by a certain amount of journalism and police work. Some people gave me details about the night Pippy went missing that were not included in the official record, but I could not corroborate their information. If I thought such single-sourced details were worth including—whether they concerned Pippy's murder or anything else—I made sure to indicate as well the less-than-certain foundation on which they rested.

As a writer of narrative history, I was determined both to weave the smaller family story I tell in these pages into a wider historical context and to double-check assertions that people made from recollection against the written record. In other words, if this book was to be largely a memoir, I nevertheless wanted it to fall as well into the category of history, and to be undergirded by a base of documentation. I obtained or corroborated many personal details by means of census records, birth and death certificates, funeral registers, family photos, ship manifests, naturalization papers, tax returns, gambling slips, IOU's, and the like. Here, arranged by subject matter, are other sources I consulted, both to corroborate (or question) stories and to provide context.

Italian History

Finley, M. I. *A History of Modern Sicily.* 3 volumes. London: Chatto & Windus, 1968.

Lewis, Norman. *The Honoured Society: The Sicilian Mafia Observed.* London: Eland, 1984.

Micale, Antonino. "San Pier Niceto: Avvenimenti e personaggi." Unpublished manuscript.

Moe, Nelson. *The View from Vesuvius: Italian Culture and the Southern Question.* Berkeley: University of California Press, 2006.

Ruggeri, G. *San Pier Niceto nel 1714*. Palermo: Associazione Mediterranea, 2015.

Washington, Booker T. *The Man Farthest Down: A Record of Observation and Study in Europe*. Garden City: Doubleday, 1912.

With the help of Joe Ruggeri and Mario Italiano, I also made use of records in the town hall of San Pier Niceto, Sicily.

Mafia, the Numbers, Prohibition, and Italian American History

Abadansky, Howard. *Organized Crime*, 9th edition. Belmont, CA: Wadsworth, Cengage, 2010.

Andrews, Kenneth, and Charles Sequin. "Group Threat and Policy Change: The Spatial Dynamics of Prohibition Politics, 1890–1919." *American Journal of Sociology* 121, no. 2, September 2015.

Boissoneault, Lorraine. "A 1957 Meeting Forced the FBI to Recognize the Mafia—and Changed the Justice System Forever." *Smithsonian*, November 14, 2017.

Bonano, Joseph. *A Man of Honor: The Autobiography of Joseph Bonano*. New York: Simon & Schuster, 1983.

Bologna Boneno, Roselyn. "From Migrant to Millionaire: The Story of the Italian-American in New Orleans, 1880–1910." Doctoral dissertation, Louisiana State University and Agricultural & Mechanical College, 1986.

Burbank, Jeff. "Robert F. Kennedy's Crusade Against the Mob." The Mob Museum. http://themobmuseum.org/blog/robert-f-kennedys-crusade-mob/.

Finkel, Ken. "John Avena and South Philadelphia's Bloody Angle." The Philly History Blog. https://www.phillyhistory.org/blog/index.php/2014/03/john-avena-and-south-philadelphias-bloody-angle/.

Kennedy, Robert F. "Statement by Attorney General Robert F. Kennedy to the Permanent Subcommittee on Investigations of the Senate Government Operations Committee." United States Department of Justice, September 25, 1963.

Laurino, Maria. *The Italian Americans: A History.* New York: W. W. Norton, 2014.

Luconi, Stefano. "Italian Americans and Machine Politics: A Case-Study Reassessment from the Bottom Up." *Italian Americana* 15, no. 2, Summer 1997.

———, "Machine Politics and the Consolidation of the Roosevelt Majority: The Case of Italian-Americans in Pittsburgh and Philadelphia." *Journal of American Ethnic History* 15, no. 2, Winter 1996.

Maurer, David W. *The Big Con: The Story of the Confidence Man.* New York: Anchor, 1940.

Pegram, Thomas. *One Hundred Percent American: The Rebirth and Decline of the Ku Klux Klan in the 1920s.* Lanham, MD: Rowman & Littlefield, 2011.

Pitkin, Thomas Monroe, and Francesco Cordasco. *The Black Hand: A Chapter in Ethnic Crime.* Totowa, NJ: Littlefield, Adams & Co., 1977.

Sanchez, Tanya Marie. "The Feminine Side of Bootlegging." *Louisiana History* 41, No. 4, Autumn, 2000.

Saverino, Joan L. " '*Domani Ci Zappa*': Italian Immigration and Ethnicity in Pennsylvania." *Pennsylvania Folklife* 45, Autumn 1995.

Schiess, Michael. "The Mob, the Mayor, and Pinball." What It Means to Be American (blog), October 4, 2016, https://www.whatitmeans tobeamerican.org/artifacts/the-mob-the-mayor-and-pinball/.

Turkus, Burton B., and Sid Feder. *Murder, Inc.: The Story of the Syndicate.* New York: Da Capo, 1951.

Veronesi, Gene P. *Italian-Americans & Their Communities of Cleveland.* Cleveland Memory, Cleveland State University Library, http://www .clevelandmemory.org/italians/index.html.

von Lampe, Klaus. *Organized Crime: Analyzing Illegal Activities, Criminal Structures, and Extra-Legal Governance.* Los Angeles: Sage Publications, 2016.

Wasserman, Ira M. "Prohibition and Ethnocultural Conflict: The Missouri Prohibition Referendum of 1918." *Social Science Quarterly* 70, no. 4, December 1989.

White, Shane, Stephen Garton, Stephen Robertson, and Graham White, *Playing the Numbers: Gambling in Harlem Between the Wars*. Cambridge: Harvard University Press, 2010.

Yeager, Daniel. *A First-Year Course in Criminal Law*. New York: Wolters-Kluwer, 2018.

Johnstown and Western Pennsylvania

I made extensive use of the archives of the Johnstown *Tribune-Democrat* and the *Johnstown Observer*; of records from the Johnstown Police Department, the Cambria County Courthouse, the library of the Johnstown Area Heritage Association, and the Cambria County Library in Johnstown; and of FBI files on Joseph Regino and John LaRocca obtained through Freedom of Information Act requests. In addition, the following sources were particularly valuable:

Arnold, Carrie. "A Scourge Returns: Black Lung in Appalachia." *Environmental Health Perspectives* 124, no. 1, January 2016.

Berger, Karl, ed., *Johnstown: The Story of a Unique Valley*. Johnstown: Johnstown Flood Museum, 1984.

Comte, Julien. "'Let the Federal Men Raid': Bootlegging and Prohibition Enforcement in Pittsburgh." *Pennsylvania History* 77, no. 2, 2010.

Johnstown City Directory, R–L. Pittsburgh: Polk & Co., 1910–1965.

Mazak-Kahne, Jeanine. "Small-Town Mafia: Organized Crime in New Kensington, Pennsylvania." *Pennsylvania History* 78, no. 4, 2011.

McCullough, David. *The Johnstown Flood*. New York: Simon & Schuster, 1968.

Pennsylvania Crime Commission. *1971–72 Report*. Lingletown, PA: Office of the Attorney General of the Commonwealth of Pennsylvania, 1972.

————. *Organized Crime in Pennsylvania: A Decade of Change, 1990 Report.* Lingletown, PA: Office of the Attorney General of the Commonwealth of Pennsylvania, 1991.

Pittsburgh Post-Gazette. "Mafia Vacuum." March 5, 1987.

Pizzola, Peter M. "The Significance of Unionization at Bethlehem Steel in 1910 and 1918–1919." Master of Arts Thesis, Lehigh University, 1996.

U.S. Department of Labor. "Coal Fatalities for 1900 Through 2019." Mine Safety and Health Administration (MSHA). https://arlweb.msha.gov/stats/centurystats/coalstats.asp.

U.S. War Production Board. *Report of War Plants and Services in Urgency Rating Bands III Thru VII, 1945.* U.S. National Security Resources Board,

Whittle, Randy. *Johnstown, Pennsylvania: A History, Part One: 1895–1936.* Charleston, SC: The History Press, 2015.

————. *Johnstown, Pennsylvania: A History, Part Two: 1937–1980.* Charleston, SC: The History Press, 2007.

Illustration Credits

Page 13:   Courtesy of the Johnstown Flood Museum Archives,
            Johnstown Area Heritage Association.
Page 15:   Boston Public Library.
Page 24:   Frank Filia.
Page 190:   Johnstown *Tribune-Democrat*.

SMALLTIME

Russell Shorto

SMALLTIME

Russell Shorto

DISCUSSION QUESTIONS

1. This book is both a memoir and a work of history. How does it fit or not fit those genres based on others you've read? How do the two perspectives (personal and historical) work together to enhance the story?

2. "In a small town and a small story all the threads pull on one another" (p. 175), Russell Shorto writes. What are the threads of this story, and how do they pull on one another?

3. Did you see yourself/your family in Shorto's story and his coming to terms with his family and his past? How so?

4. Describe the author's relationship with his father. How does it grow in importance over the course of the book? How do his opinions and feelings about his father change? What does this mean for the author in terms of his own personal growth?

5. How did *Smalltime* challenge or expand your understanding of the mob?

6. Shorto shows how immigrants like his ancestors, shut out of legitimate professions, pursued the American Dream by providing goods and services—alcohol, gambling—that were illegal but that most people used. Do you see this pattern today? What do you think it says about America and the idea of the American Dream?

7. Shorto writes that Prohibition, far from being a drive by church ladies to improve their menfolk, was really an effort to preserve "American values" by lashing out at immigrants and urban elites. How does this connect to present-day, polarized America?

8. What stood out to you in the section on Sicily and Shorto's great-grandfather, Antonino Sciotto, who came to America? What was most interesting or surprising?

9. Shorto writes that his grandfather Russ "learned [as a boy] what many never do their whole lives: that while the system appears rigid it is actually a highly fungible thing; that it's possible for a tough-enough guy to leverage guts and power and recast it according to his will" (p. 71). Do you believe this to be true? How did Russ and others do this, and what are other examples of this idea?

10. The lost world of the small-town mob that this book conjures has both darkness and charm: what are examples of each that stood out to you? How do they exist together?

11. Did the book make you smile or laugh? When and how? Did the book move you? Which parts or relationships or themes?

12. Why do you think the author dedicated the book as he did: "This is for all the Shortos"?

SELECTED NORTON BOOKS WITH
READING GROUP GUIDES AVAILABLE

For a complete list of Norton's works with reading group guides, please go to wwnorton.com/reading-guides.

Diana Abu-Jaber	*Life Without a Recipe*
Diane Ackerman	*The Zookeeper's Wife*
Michelle Adelman	*Piece of Mind*
Molly Antopol	*The UnAmericans*
Andrea Barrett	*Archangel*
Rowan Hisayo Buchanan	*Harmless Like You*
Ada Calhoun	*Wedding Toasts I'll Never Give*
Bonnie Jo Campbell	*Mothers, Tell Your Daughters*
	Once Upon a River
Lan Samantha Chang	*Inheritance*
Ann Cherian	*A Good Indian Wife*
Evgenia Citkowitz	*The Shades*
Amanda Coe	*The Love She Left Behind*
Michael Cox	*The Meaning of Night*
Jeremy Dauber	*Jewish Comedy*
Jared Diamond	*Guns, Germs, and Steel*
Caitlin Doughty	*From Here to Eternity*
Andre Dubus III	*House of Sand and Fog*
	Townie: A Memoir
Anne Enright	*The Forgotten Waltz*
	The Green Road
Amanda Filipacchi	*The Unfortunate Importance of Beauty*
Beth Ann Fennelly	*Heating & Cooling*
Betty Friedan	*The Feminine Mystique*
Maureen Gibbon	*Paris Red*
Stephen Greenblatt	*The Swerve*
Lawrence Hill	*The Illegal*
	Someone Knows My Name
Ann Hood	*The Book That Matters Most*
	The Obituary Writer
Dara Horn	*A Guide for the Perplexed*
Blair Hurley	*The Devoted*

Don't miss best-selling author Russell Shorto's

Revolution Song

RUSSELLSHORTO.COM

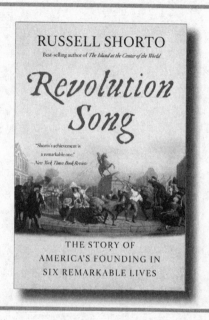

"A tour de force."

—Gordon S. Wood

"An engaging piece of historical detective work and narrative craft."

—*Chicago Tribune*

"The intertwined stories of *Revolution Song* give a sense of how far-reaching a phenomenon the War of Independence was."

—*New York Times Book Review*

W. W. NORTON & COMPANY
Independent Publishers Since 1923